ACKNOWLEDGMENTS

We would like to express our appreciation to those who contributed to this book.

Publisher and Editor: Cliff Stieglitz
Art Director: Guillermo Hernández
Production Designer: Brian J. Woodruff
Copy Editors: Stephen Goodrich, Cheryl Della Pietra
Technical Editor: Brian Lynch
Cover Design: Guillermo Hernández

Books are available for bulk purchases at special discounts. For information, contact Airbrush Action.

Published in the United States of America by:

Airbrush Action, Inc.
P.O. Box 438
Allenwood, NJ 08720
Tel: (732) 223-7878
Fax: (732) 223-2855
E-mail: ceo@airbrushaction.com
www.airbrushaction.com

survive the test of time

HOUSE OF KOLOR

CALIFORNIA COMPLIANT

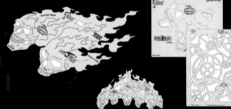

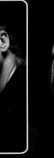

TABLE OF CONTENTS

A WHOLE NEW BAG OF TRICKS

This sequel to *Automotive Cheap Tricks & Special Effects* is not a revision but an expansion. It details additional new tricks and techniques for both the beginner and the artist of intermediate skills. Like the original, this book contains new step-by-steps and techniques used by today's top kustom painters to achieve award-winning paint jobs. Unlike the original, most of this book has never appeared before in *Airbrush Action* or any other publication. Some of the new chapters revitalize classic techniques from automotive kustom history; others respond to requests for specific effects the original book did not cover—additional instruction in muraling, guitar kustomizing, freehand airbrushing, and a variety of other goodies. Basically, there are more job chapters and fewer panel chapters than in the original text, though we do have a few good new panel chapters in here, too.

Showing actual techniques in workshop settings, the *Automotive Cheap Tricks* books and DVDs teach painters not to be clones, but to analyze the painting process. Through these demos the artist learns not only the promised effects, but also the techniques of reverse engineering and process painting. With this practical "process" method of learning, readers can readily modify the effects shown to suit their unique styles.

In the automotive kustom kulture, new styles appear every year, and innovative techniques are always on the horizon. This second book is proof of that. What's more, every technique displayed here is used on a regular basis at my shops, Air Syndicate Inc. and Kal Koncepts. To state it simply, these techniques work. I stake my reputation on them every day. Although materials and equipment change over the years, I still stand by every single chapter and technique in my first book, and the same goes for this one. Consider them additions to your growing arsenal of kustom painting tools and skills.

I hope you like this book as much as the first; and if you don't already own version one, may version two light a fire under your butt to go get it.

As always, "Paint to live, live to paint."

Craig Fraser
Air Syndicate Inc.
www.gotpaint.com

FOREWORD

"I first met Craig about 12 years ago when I bought some airbrushed art from him at a car show. I really dug the art, and at the time I thought no way this dude could have done this. I made a trip up to his shop in Bakersfield. It was true! He was actually the man cranking it out. This lead to a decade of Craig Fraser putting his thumbprint on West Coast Choppers.

Craig took our bikes and put them out of sight with his amazing artwork. Nobody could touch us! He also painted several of my cars, including my purple-pearl, candy-orange, and lime-green Buick Rivera. Once, while I was away in Europe, I let Craig stay at my loft for a couple weeks. I came back to find a huge 50-foot pirate mural painted on my wall. Sick! All of this and I still can't believe it comes out of the head of this red-haired white boy. Wierd?"
– Jesse James.

THE ZEN OF KUSTOM
PAINTING

"There is a lot more to it then just some tape, and a couple of colors..."

What can I say about kustom painting that hasn't already been said? Actually, quite a lot, since very few people talk about it. Sure, everyone has an opinion about what looks good; but try to nail down a philosophy of what top painters do, and you'll find most of us are in the dark. Painting something killer and describing how it's done are two very different things. Just because a kustom painter creates one amazing paint job does not necessarily mean that he or she can catch lightning in a bottle next time. Heck, even a broken clock is right twice a day. By that definition, even the worst kustom painter has two awesome paint jobs in him. According to some people, painting something killer is easy; you just copy. That's done every day out there. But becoming a trendsetter who originates outstanding paint jobs time after time—now, that's what kustom painting is all about!

"Nothing is original." How many times have you heard that excuse, or used it yourself to explain why your graphics looked like someone else's? In one sense the statement is true. Everything we design is a variation on something we've seen, experienced, or heard about. As people and as artists, we are the sum total of our experiences. So what makes an original artist? Good question—it will only take your entire life to figure that out. Meanwhile, here are a couple of hints: paint and learn, and never stop doing both. Kustom painters don't retire, they die. (Did you ever hear of Picasso or Dali retiring to play golf?) If other professionals retire to become artists, how the heck can an artist retire? We just keep on painting. The more you know and understand this, the better you will be able to come to terms with your choice to be an artist. This industry is already full of part-timers who get out as soon as the going gets difficult. Can you make a bundle as a kustom painter or an artist? Sure, but if that's your sole motivation, you're in it for the wrong reason. You have to love the kustom industry to be good at it. Only then is it worth the effort.

The kustom industry is very personal. Each of us must find our own way of making the journey, and making it our own. Nevertheless, a little help along the way is always nice.

To begin with, many artists get confused by all the copying going on, so this becomes a gray area. If you're supposed to copy to learn, where do you draw the line between artistry and theft? It's simple if you stop and think about it. If you steal somebody's design and palm it off as your own, that's theft, whether or not you're caught. If you give credit where credit is due, all that trouble can be avoided. I'm not talking about copyright infringement or any of the legalese associated therewith—I'm talking about the basics.

Still, how can you come up with something that hasn't already been done—in other words, something original? The trick, paradoxically, is to copy—but to copy from as many artists and kustom painters as possible. The more varied your influences, the more original your work will look. If you learn from only one or two artists, your work will look like theirs, usually a bad imitation at best. If you absorb 30 or 40 artistic styles, your work will have such a broad base of influence it will look different enough to be considered truly original.

First, you need to be well versed in just about every technique you can lay your hands on. While you're at it, consider becoming what I call a "triple threat" kustom painter. A triple threat is someone who can lay and spray graphics, airbrush murals, and pinstripe. If you can do all three decently, you will never be captive to someone else's deadlines. You will be a valuable commodity. But to become original as well, you'll also need to start thinking beyond copying to process painting. Process painting is breaking down the kustom paint job into its basic elements to understand why one job works and another doesn't. This takes time and is not easy; but knowledge is the only way you'll advance to the next level. You'll need to understand color theory—why certain colors work together and others don't. You'll need to understand design and compositional theory, and how color theory works with them for the complete paint job. Last, you'll need to understand negative and positive space. Negative space is basically the area not occupied by your graphic. Many people don't consider it important because it's the area you're not painting. Yet negative space will determine whether your paint job looks busy or flows. Negative space includes the bodylines and style of the car. It's the reason killer graphics look best on the car they were designed for. When you slavishly copy another artist's work, you never have to worry about the thought, time, theory, and effort that went into it. Now is the time to start becoming the one doing the thinking.

The way I approach a task—whether a paint job, set of graphics, logo, or mural—is always the same. Graphically, they all operate under all the same rules of design. I've broken down my approach into three steps that will enable you to become the thinking person's kustom painter. Not because I told you what to paint, but because these steps will force you to use your learning, creativity, background and personality to create truly original work.

READING THE CLIENT AND REVERSE ENGINEERING

First, find out what the client wants. This can be more difficult than it seems, for all too often, clients don't really know. As a kustom painter it's your responsibility to help them decide. Many times clients will tell you they like everything you paint, and that you should do whatever you like. This is excellent if it comes from a regular client who trusts you; usually, however, it comes from clients who can't envision what they want, so they let you decide. The downside is that they'll change their minds the minute a buddy points out something different. So it's imperative that you find out what they truly want before you start the work. Only then will you have the ideas and materials to create the best paint jobs possible for them. If they can't decide on colors they like, ask them what colors they hate. Clients always feel freer when talking about what they dislike than what they like. Either way, you must get the information you need.

The term "reverse engineering" has two meanings. Figuring out your client is one form of reverse engineering. You're taking the ideas in your client's head, breaking them down, and reassembling them into a plan of attack for yourself. As for the second meaning, let's assume you're coming up with a paint job, no client involved. Maybe you really like what you saw in a magazine. You want to create something as arresting, but don't want to be labeled a copycat. Well then, start reverse engineering. Break the design down into its simplest components, then put it back together, hopefully with your own twist, to create your own work of art. In the product industry that's often referred to as "thumbprinting"—reversing the technology, then figuring out how to make a uniquely new and improved product. Here we are at the very heart of kustom painting. Start with the colors used, the number of individual graphics, and any recognizable graphic style. Are there flames? Are the graphics tribal in nature? Are all the graphics equal in importance, or is there a root graphic the others play off of? Is the base color of the vehicle dominant in the design, or does it play a lesser role? Do the graphics use the bodyline of the vehicle to arrive at a contrasting or complementary pattern? (If so, you will need to alter the design to suit the vehicle it's going on.) These are the kinds of questions you must answer to reverse-engineer a design and make your own version.

THE SHOPPING LIST

The shopping list is exactly what it sounds like. After you've discovered what your client wants, or what you want to paint, you need to come up with this list. It comprises more than just paint materials; it also includes the techniques that need to be mastered and the applications involved in creating your kustom paint job. The list will specify what you'll be able to do yourself, who you'll need to bring into the game to finish the job, and how much it will cost you. The list is essential to figuring out the price for your client. Only through reverse engineering can you determine the elements and techniques needed to complete the job, and only through the shopping list will you be able to go on to the next step, which is your plan of attack.

THE CHESS GAME APPROACH

Now, don't freak out if you don't like chess. I could have just as easily called this the football approach, because both games make intensive use of strategic planning. You plan a setup from the beginning, like a series of opening moves in chess, or the opening series list the coach shows up with on game day. But every good active strategy also has contingency plans, things to do when plans do not go...well, as planned. A contingency plan is just as important for a kustom paint job as it is for any football game or chess match. A good kustom painter will visualize the completed job, apply lessons learned from past mistakes and achievements, and keep these under consideration as he works. The result will be a well-planned, well-thought-out, well-executed paint job.

So, for starters, you need to have a plan of attack. This plan should take into consideration which of your graphics you'll spray first, which second, etc., etc. This can greatly reduce the amount of materials and time you waste, not to mention give a huge boost to the job's overall quality. The reason for contingency plans is that nothing ever goes quite as first planned. When you're basing a paint job on a rendering, you should never be surprised that applying a two-dimensional drawing to a three-dimensional object involves modification along the way, usually the addition of another graphic. Even with scale drawings the design tends to look quite a bit different in person. An unhappy client can't be pacified by your insisting that the rendering he approved is exactly what you painted. As kustom painters, we should not depend solely on our original rendering or on an initial plan to finish a job. Design doesn't end with the concept rendering; it ends with the final clear coat. You need to be constantly redesigning, reconsidering, and modifying so that your paint job becomes what you envision, not what you settle for.

I wish I could explain everything and answer all your questions, but I can't, and neither can anyone else. Still, if this chapter gives you even a slight advantage by adding a few tricks to your arsenal, I've done my job. I titled it The Zen of Kustom Painting because I understand Zen to be a sublime state of being that, while never truly achieved, should always be the goal on the horizon for all of us.

In that spirit, I wish you good luck and happy painting!

THE FINE ART OF SELF PROMOTION

This chapter is basically a modified version of my college architectural thesis entitled The Art of Client Manipulation. As readers responded to the posting of it on my website, I continued to modify and add to the original. The current version attempts to answer one of the most commonly asked questions in the kustom industry today: "How do you get your name out there?" As such, the article examines the need for, and describes techniques used in, self-promotion. Since it got such a good response online, I decided to include it here. I changed it somewhat from the original, so even you Internet types can enjoy it all over again. Peace.

All artists need self-promotion. Effective self-promotion is the bridge to greater exposure and a vital tool in building your business. Magazines, galleries, and art clientele need and seek artists, so it's your job to make sure they know you exist. Being well informed about your industry and constantly aware of your position in it enables you to keep your finger on its pulse.

When I began airbrushing more than 20 years ago, I observed three distinctly different artists' personalities. There were the hardworking painters who cared little for publicity and who focused narrowly on production to maximize their earnings; there were those who were obsessed with their art for its own sake, and then there were those who were more outgoing, sometimes even flamboyant, who—often no less hardworking—had charismatic personalities that they channeled to promote their work. Needless to say, all three categories included good and bad artists. My most striking discovery, however, was that the professional longevity of artists turned out to be only in part due to the caliber of their art. In my career I've seen aggressive artists with lesser talent be far more successful than highly talented artists who knew little to nothing about marketing and business. Aesthetes and production workers little concerned with publicity would often burn out, while the business-minded, marketing-geared painters could sustain their longevity with better profits and cash flow. To sum up, you reap what you sew. If all you want is money, and all your work is geared solely to financial gain

or security with little concern for the industry or your own continuing education, then money's all you will get—and often precious little of that. Production-minded artists concerned only with the bottom line are the first to be replaced by cheaper labor or automation. The artist obsessed with art who gives little or no thought to the bottom line, to the state of the industry, or to clients, will eventually go under as well. He may be another Van Gogh; but if so, the sad likelihood is that he will be appreciated only after death, if then.

Like it or not, ego and money are important components to an artist's career and success. If you can successfully balance the two, your chances to succeed improve greatly. Believe it or not, recognition is largely within your grasp as an artist.

REACHING THE MEDIA

Attaining public attention is easier than you may believe, yet too many people feel they will fail before they even try. The trick to getting attention typically boils down to one thing: persistence. There are currently two primary ways to represent yourself and your work: directly and indirectly. Since few of us have direct personal contact with journalists or gallery owners, the indirect approach is the most practical: phone, e-mail, or snail mail. And don't think that one is more important than the other; all three should be employed. Normally you can use e-mail for the initial contact and follow up by phone. Then you can go to the post office to mail CDs (if you or a client doesn't have an ftp site to upload high-resolution digital files to), photos (if the client doesn't have a computer), portfolios, or work transparencies (again, if the client doesn't have a computer; but let's face it, traditional photo development formats are all but dead, and digital is where it's at). Currently, other forms of contact are available through artists' forums and Internet web-rings—the now and the future of networking, and an absolute must for artists who want their work seen. Because these systems cost little or nothing to use, I highly recommend getting involved with as many as possible.

Magazines are always seeking new editorial—step-by-step articles, news releases, reader galleries, feature stories, etc.—to fill their pages. A great reference source for finding just about every magazine known to man is the SRDS (Standard Rate & Data Service). Because these directories and online subscriptions are cost-prohibitive ($500 or more), your local library is the way to go. SRDS is divided into consumer and business publications. All listings include important contact information (publisher, editorial staff, e-mail addresses, telephone numbers, etc.), submission info, circulation data, and advertising rates. I recommend first sending an e-mail with low-resolution images of your work, and then following up in a couple of days with a call to the editor to confirm that he received your message and ask whether he or she is interested. Of course, you can look up individual publications on the Internet or find editors' names on the masthead of the magazine itself.

And be sure to always show your best, most distinctive work, something that stands apart from the average representation. Entering your work in a readers' gallery, going on readers' rides, or participating in contests sponsored by magazines are other effective ways of grabbing attention. It bears repeating, persistence is the key. I'm not talking about being obnoxious or becoming a stalker; just be sure to get people at the magazine to connect a voice, a face, and personal references with the artwork they receive. Remember, you're one of hundreds calling and sending material, so anything you can do to make yourself stand out is a big plus. Here's an interesting factoid: 90 percent of people who submit their work never follow up. Make sure you do, and your persistence will very likely pay off.

Galleries can be a bit more elusive and picky because their primary focus is on making money for you and themselves. Can't blame them, really, but it doesn't mean you can't send in your work. Just be sure it's your best. Also, it's best to know them in person. If a gallery doesn't reflect your style, they probably won't be interested and wouldn't represent your work adequately. I also advise participating in group shows. A group show is usually themed or geared to a particular genre of art, in which one or two pieces per artist are shown. Not only are these shows fun, they're great for networking and for getting valuable feedback from professional critics and fellow contributors. You don't have to come up with 20 or more pieces of work, and if the show does badly, it's not necessarily your fault. Remember, if you're accepted for a gallery show, there's nothing worse than missing a deadline; don't bite off more than you can chew in the excitement of the moment.

PHOTOGRAPHING
AND REPRESENTING YOUR WORK

All the best contacts in the world won't matter if your notes can't be read and your photography is amateurish (i.e., poor lighting, distracting reflections, focus issues, low resolution, bad composition, etc.). The best and easiest way to proceed is to hire both a professional photographer and a publicist, but if you're like me, such expense is not practical. Fortunately, even if your writing and digital photography aren't up to snuff, all magazines filter your text through a copy editor and pics through an art director for correction and retouching.

I figured it would take at least a decade for digital imaging to replace film, but boy, was I wrong. In fact, I can't even remember the last time I used a 35mm camera. For those of you still shooting slides, understand that most magazines (if not all) no longer process or even scan slides. Digital is an absolute must. If you're looking to buy a digital camera or just doing work for your website, I recommend a minimum of six megapixels for the desired higher resolutions that magazines require. (Nowadays, however, eight megapixels and higher is the norm, and is relatively inexpensive to boot. I wouldn't even attempt a cover shot or poster image with anything less then an eight-megapixel camera.) In selecting a digital camera, your choice of brand (Canon, Nikon, etc.) should hinge on the lenses you already own. If you have a Canon film camera with a removable lens, it's likely that lens is compatible with its digital, or DSLR (digital single lens reflex), counterpart. And for still photography, a good tripod will hold the camera steady for the shot, and also enable you to keep the frame of reference and angle of photo consistent. Because I shoot the majority of my photography and want to appear in many of the shots, I'm constantly using the camera's timer. So a tripod is a must.

When taking stills of artwork, a black backdrop or piece of dark carpet is the best way to minimize background interference and make your work stand out. The black background also makes it easier to crop the shots later, if need be. I like to work outside if the weather permits, with the sun at either nine or three o'clock in the sky, but not at twelve. Overhead sun is apt to make hotspots on automotive graphics; and while shadows may look good, the light is a bit harsh. I personally love a slight overcast, or a strategic cloud overhead; clouds filter out glare. Since none of us can predict the weather with certainty, studio shots are often the norm, and studio interiors require lighting.

You can purchase expensive photo lights, but I discovered quite by accident that combining overhead fluorescents (present in most shops and offices) with tungsten lights, or preferably halogen spotlights, provides a good balance between yellow and blue. Heck, a lot of the new digital cameras can accommodate just about any type of light source, and their instant-review capability takes a lot of the guesswork out of photography. If you want to get a little tricky, set up whatever lights you have (halogen, tungsten, mercury, sodium, cigarette lighters, mood candles), then shoot a couple of shots moving the lights around, trying different f-stops and shutter speeds. (Most of us just set the camera on "Auto" and start shooting. I'm not going to delve into settings deeply here. It would take a separate chapter even to scratch the surface of camera settings, and I'm not the biggest expert on that anyway.) Today's digital camera can be programmed to shoot a rapid set of three images, two being automatic brackets. Pretty cool! When thinking about lighting, also consider filters for your camera. You can often get a dealer to throw in a small set of filters with the purchase of a camera. These can be great for eliminating hotspots, especially when shooting at outdoor shows. And ultimately, you can use the Adobe Photoshop computer program to color-correct and manipulate your photos endlessly.

As I mentioned earlier, when photographing a how-to, I mostly use the camera's timer, focusing on the area to be shot, then stepping into the picture to pose. Imagining yourself in the shot beforehand takes some getting used to, but you can always use reference objects in the background to avoid cutting off your head. My new Cybershot has a pivoting LCD screen so that I can see whether I'm actually in the frame before the camera clicks. (In addition to a black background, it's equally important to have a background set when shooting tech stills. The more information in a tech photo, the better.) Although the subject matter, your painting, must be the focus of the article, you should also include photos of yourself working on the painting. That helps direct the reader's attention to what you're talking about in the text, and gives scale to the work itself. There's nothing more boring than a tech article with no one in it. Alternate close-ups with wide-angle shots help the reader comprehend overall progress, yet still see detail. Because I'm right-handed, I prefer to have the camera over and above my left shoulder, at about a 30- to 45-degree angle. I have a spotlight slightly behind and above the camera to eliminate any shadows I might cast. I use fill flash to eliminate any other shadows and punch out what I'm working on. I also have the camera at an angle to prevent flash from bouncing back into the lens. You can accomplish the same thing by bouncing the flash off the ceiling if it's low enough. Simply experiment with flash and camera angles to your satisfaction. When using a flash, I keep the camera within 15 feet of the image. I also like to use a telephoto lens, so I keep the camera a minimum of six feet away to be able to zoom in on details. This eliminates the need to move the tripod and lighting when going for full-frame shots.

Whew! Hope I didn't overload you with all of this. If I did, feel free to drop me an e-mail or visit my forum so I can clear up anything I muddied. For more information on digital photography, search for local workshops (camera stores, community colleges, photography clubs, etc., are likely to offer training), instructional DVDs, and books.

THE TEXT AND NECESSARY
BIOS

Everyone knows that the info in a tech article is important, but how many of you know the importance of the bio? It's the part of your presentation that describes and represents you when you're not there in person. It ought to reflect yourself, as well as your work, accurately. Standard biographical notes should include a brief history of your career in art, along with any additional specifics you deem necessary. The length of your airbrushing or painting experience is often put in, but that's really up to you. A client list is nice, and I personally like to read about what tools, materials, and media the artist prefers. Other than a bio piece on yourself, it's also quite common to include a history of each submitted piece; i.e., materials used, artwork size, date of completion, and even price, if the piece is for gallery consideration. If it is, by the way, remember that the gallery will assign its own price. The price you specify is what you want out of the work. Don't be surprised if the gallery doubles it. That's quite common and shouldn't really matter if you were happy with the price you quoted. Gallery clientele realize this and don't have a problem with it. Later they may approach you privately to commission pieces. If you have no agent, it's OK to negotiate on future work yourself. But never try to sell behind a gallery's back. That's a professional ethics no-no. After all, the gallery did expend resources on advertising, display space, mailers, opening and closing parties, and paid staff. It deserves its cut.

As for the text in a how-to or feature, write as well as you can. Most of us are literate, and many editors are quite adept at deciphering what comes in. If, however, your work is going to be edited for content as well as quality, make it a point to request and read a final proof. This will eliminate most misprints, misquotes, and misunderstandings. I have never come across a professional editor who had a problem with this; just make sure they understand how firm you are about being involved up to the last moment before publication. My best advice is to write the way you speak. Read your work aloud to yourself, and if it sounds bizarre or dry, add a little more life. Often, a friend's proofreading can save the frustration of future rewrites. (My wife is my proofreader, and she hates the way I punctuate. When she objects to my run-on sentences, I tell her that's the way I talk!) If you write the way you speak, then your words will convey not only your content but your personality as well. That's important if readers are to connect with you. Finally, I'm going to assume that everyone reading this has access to a computer with word-processing and spell-check capabilities. If your work looks professional, you'll be treated like a professional.

THE ART OF THE FOLLOW-UP

The art of the follow-up is literally that. The only reason I'm giving it a separate category here is to remind you of the importance of following up contacts with phone calls, e-mails, snail mail, or skywriting—whatever works. If new contacts don't return calls right away, or ever, don't take it personally. However, if you're well acquainted with them and they don't call back, you have a right to fume. Realize that you're one of thousands who phone and send in their work and letters. In this industry it's often the squeaky wheel that gets the attention, so go ahead and squeak. Heck, all they can say is no. Once, I pretty much got ignored for the better part of a year; it didn't stop me, and it shouldn't stop you. Your artwork, portfolios, and transparencies are valuable; make every effort to be sure that they are at least looked at. Again, I'm not talking about being obnoxious, just persistent.

If you'd like any of your work returned, never assume that a company will do so out of kindness. Postage is not necessarily the issue; the obstacle may be the entire chain of work needed to return anything. I personally never send one-of-a-kind pieces, and I always include a self-addressed, postage-paid package along with the work. I also recommend including a separate letter or note requesting that the work be returned. If the company states that they keep all submissions, don't be upset; this is not necessarily because they're lazy. Often they simply wish to keep work on file for future reference. That's why you should always send expendable items, such as duplicates of transparencies, rather than originals. I've gotten many jobs from magazines and galleries that have kept my work on file. I consider that a compliment.

THE REALITY OF IT ALL

To sum up, here are the tools; the rest is up to you. It is a basic fact that publicity is important to our industry and that self-promotion, while requiring considerable effort, can be satisfying when it truly represents the artist. As I always say, there are no guarantees. But, hey, if I can do it, there's no reason you can't. While it's true that the magazine and fine art/gallery industries are rife with politics, the same may be said about most enterprises of mankind. Whenever you have two differing viewpoints, you will have politics. This is fine if you're a politician, but as an artist...well, let's just say that what I treasure is my art, the field of art that I consider a home, my family and friends, and fellow artists I meet along the way. The politics are just there to be dealt with. If you want something, and it's worth fighting for, it will be worth far more in the end than whatever was simply handed to you. Try to view any pitfalls and criticisms along the way as inevitable character-builders, and you and your art will be the better for it. The important thing is to try.

GETTING DOWN TO BIZNESS
"REMEMBER, MONEY IS RARELY LOST. IT USUALLY JUST GOES TO SOMEBODY ELSE."
—Anon. Stockbroker

Some of the most common requests for advice at my kustom paint workshops are not about any technique, airbrush, or brand of paint. They're about the business end of kustom painting. It appears that while the kustom paint industry is alive and well, it's just not too sure of itself financially. Now, I can't tell you what to charge—not by the job or by the hour—but I can steer you in the direction of figuring out what you're worth at the moment, and what you can get for that. The important thing to remember is, no matter where you are in the world or which economy you're in, never charge more than the market will bear.

I can't give you a rate, because I'd first have to set one; and I don't believe in price standardization, especially in the kustom kulture industry, where every artist is unique. Heck, that would be like asking Picasso or Salvador Dali what they charge by the hour. The problem is that, as kustom painters, we constantly straddle the fence between the artistic aspect of kustomizing and the practical aspect of automotive refinishing. That's why at Air Syndicate Inc. I charge by the job, not by the hour. Every job is different, and some techniques are so specialized they should never be billed by the hour. This still leaves the question of how much to ask for. Well, sometimes the answer is simply "whatever you owe." I owe rent, so the charge for the next big job is the same as my rent. What a coincidence! Of course, if you run your business paycheck to paycheck like that, you'll eventually go bankrupt—or die of an ulcer. Still, generally speaking, think about basing what you charge on your needs. This requires a budget and knowing your monthly needs, which vary from painter to painter. You'll need to replace and upgrade materials and tools, pay utility bills, put something aside for shop maintenance, and cover basic living costs. Sit down and figure out your expenses, then break them down by month, week, and day. That won't give you an exact amount— your field is art, not accounting—but it will give you a rough framework for computing what to charge.

Another good frame of reference is the amount the competition charges. This should never be your sole reference or a copycat amount, but merely a rough gauge. In fact, you'll need to look beyond what the competition charges to see what they're doing for the money. You'll need to become familiar with the quality and quantity of their work and the time it takes them to do it. If you're just as good but slower, you'll need to offer clients something extra. I recommend not going down in price if you can help it. You never want to be known as the bargain basement guy; plus, you probably won't stay in business long if you keep beating everyone else's prices. Nickel-and-dime crap like that can drive painters nuts. Don't let it get to you! Instead, approximate the competition's price, but give your clients more. Offer what the competition can't—your own personal style. You do need a standard level of competence to fit into the industry, like the journeyman piano player who sight-reads, plays in several styles, and knows some cover tunes. But offer clients something in addition, something only you can do. That's the easiest way to beat the competition. They can always come back and underbid you, but they can never be you! Remember, you're not just selling a completed job, you're selling a style and quality distinctively your own. Someone else could do the job, no doubt. But it could never be truly identical to yours. Nor could someone else offer what you're about to come up with next!

From a business perspective, the kustom industry resembles a stool whose three legs must achieve a degree of balance. All three require attention, and each is affected by the others:

1. Cost
2. Time
3. Quantity

There's also a crucial fourth element. Set atop the three legs and holding them together is their reason for existence, the crowning element that gives the stool purpose, utility, and viability. I refer, of course, to the seat, which in this metaphor stands for Quality. "Ifs" and "ands" abound in the kustom industry, but Quality is where you should immovably plant your butt.

Historically, kustom painters have been playing musical chairs with these four elements, trying for that perfect balance to keep their businesses from crashing. Their mistake lies in messing with quality as if it were one leg of the stool. They rationalize that they need the money. However, no amount of money is worth a bad paint job leaving your shop with your name on it. If you need money that badly, take a job delivering pizza. At least it won't mar your reputation as a kustom painter! Seriously, folks, always keep quality high and on the level. If you must mess, mess with cost, time, or quantity. Say a customer is quoted $5,000 for a job but needs it in half the normal time. What do you do? Well, if he forces you to mess with time, it's going to cost him more. Why? Because you'll have to move other jobs aside and possibly give discounts to other clients to compensate them for delays. Or you'll have to stay late, possibly all night, to get it done. (Personally, I would rather pull a few all-nighters than get a reputation for asking other clients to extend deadlines.) What if he can't pay more money, or refuses to pay more but still demands the accelerated deadline? Then offer to do less work—perhaps one fewer graphic, five skulls in the mural instead of ten. Offer a reduction in quantity, never quality. Keep quality where it belongs—up top, above all other considerations. Do this, and you will never have to answer for a bad paint job or worry about your reputation as a quality artist.

What about the constant haggling over price? Some painters enjoy it, others hate it. Regardless, time is always lost in the bargaining process, and time is money. I lived in Florence, Italy, for more than a year, and I learned an interesting bargaining technique there. I call it "the price variant," and here's how it works. After you and the client have discussed what he wants and the time required, you would normally quote a price. Let's say it's a helmet, and you quote $500. What's the first thing the client says? "Will you do it for $400? The guy down the street is cheaper. That's more than I paid for the helmet alone, blah, blah, blah!" The bargaining begins. But now let's go back and start over. It was a mistake to give the client a firm price; in doing so you asked to be abused. Give him a range instead. Tell him, "For the helmet you want you're looking at between $500 and $750." His first question will likely be, "What's the difference between $500 and $750?" He doesn't realize it, but you just took control. He now believes that his cost will lie between those two numbers. You have him. Tell him that the difference is in the number of pearls you'll use, or extra skulls, additional details, special techniques, etc. At the very least, he'll never stray below $500, which is all you were going to charge him in the first place. I know it sounds simple, and that's the beauty part: it is. It's not merely simple, it's honest; and it will keep you making money without losing the respect of your client base. Just give it a try.

Now, what if the guy does not have the $500, only $400, but still wants you to do the job? That's when you ask him for more time. I will happily go down $100 on a two-week helmet job if I can extend it to four weeks. That way I still get the job, but I work on it between other jobs. The client is still paying, but now with time instead of money. A lot better than sending him out the door and down the road to another kustom painter, don't you agree?

My next suggestion is not solely money-oriented, but it will help you focus on your ability and constantly improve your art, which is always good business practice. I've been following this basic philosophy for quite a few years, and it has worked for me. Just think of your kustom paint ability as having three steps or levels.

Get good.
Get fast.
Get smart.

Let's start with the most important point, "Get good." I know this sounds simplistic, but think about it. Getting good at your work is the most important thing you can do as a kustom painter. I know tons of airbrushers who are fast but also suck! If you offer quality, however, you can always rationalize unassailably from that position. If you do a killer paint job, so what if you're a little slow? People will wait. Who wants to be in a hurry for a paint job that sucks? "Sorry, your car came out like crap; but, hey, I got it done early!" Get the point? When you first start on a new technique, trick, tool, whatever, you're going to suck at it. Work hard to master it. The harder you work, the more worthwhile the time spent will be. Nobody can ever fault you for being good, or attempting to be. So just do it. Get good.

The second point, "Get fast," should be your focus after you feel you've gotten good. Trying to get fast keeps you from getting cocky. Speed up your technique about 10 percent at first, and you'll be surprised how fast you end up back in the "suck zone." Keeps you humble! Plus, think about it: when you first start airbrushing, your abilities may improve 20 to 30 percent the first month. Think this rate of improvement will continue? No way! Acceleration gets exponentially more difficult the faster you go. If you could get better at that rate every month, it wouldn't take you long to reach the speed of light. Not going to happen. Think of getting fast as a sort of cross-training. Increase your speed but keep quality high. Not as easy as it sounds. But if you manage, you'll discover that speed can make you qualitatively better in some respects—continuity of line, for example. Speed is not just about efficiency and time saved, it's a technique unto itself. Getting fast forces you to analyze your approach to technique. In the long run you'll not only get faster, you'll get better. Get good. Then get fast.

So, what about the third point, "Get smart"? This will come automatically if you keep quality high while trying to get fast. While getting faster, you'll be forced to analyze your approach to painting, reverse-engineer your technique, and troubleshoot the way you paint. Making the effort will put you in the mindset of believing you're constantly in need of upgrading. Indeed, you do upgrade yourself with each new technique learned or bad habit eliminated. Getting smart is realizing the difference between cutting corners and discovering a true shortcut. Getting smart is discovering that you can do five jobs at once in the time that it used to take to do three one after the other. Getting smart is noticing that, while working on those five jobs, your quality has gone up because multitasking is more entertaining to the creative side of your brain than assembly-line work. Getting smart is, basically, getting smart—not just about painting, but about really looking at your work, planning ahead, realizing that kustom painting is like a chess match you play with yourself, becoming so good at the process that you win every time.

GET GOOD, GET FAST, GET SMART!

Finally, you need to run your business in a professional manner, and that means invoicing every activity in your shop. If you don't want to pay for custom-printed invoices or four-copy work orders, buy generic at your local stationary store. It really doesn't matter what they look like. What matters is that they're legal, that you itemize each aspect of the job, and that you get the client's signature on the work order. In California, it's illegal to work on a vehicle without a signed work order. You won't go to jail for not doing it, but you may get a nasty fine from the B.A.R. (Bureau of Automotive Repair); and without a signed work order, you don't stand a chance in a court of law should a customer decide to sue. Even if you have a signed work order, you'll need to be careful about last-minute changes. If your client makes changes, you'll have to either amend and have him initial the changes, or start over with a new work order. Handshakes and verbal agreements are nice in westerns and gangster movies, but in reality always have a signed, itemized work order. Period!

That's about it for my business suggestions. There are certain commonsense things I haven't discussed here, to say nothing of what's only applicable in certain states or countries. To cover everything would take too much of your time and mine, and sacrifice too many trees. However, if you do have business-related queries that are not addressed above, feel free to e-mail them to me at fraser@gotpaint.com, or drop by my forum at www.kustomkulturelounge.com. I would be more than happy to help you out, or at least try. The forum has well over 6,000 members who will not only network with you but give you dozens of answers to choose from, no matter what the question. You'll never suffer from too much information, only from a lack of it—so get networking.

One last thing: I make it a point not to recommend many books because I rarely come across an author I agree with totally. But one book that's pretty cool and fairly interesting is Sung Tzu's *Art of War*. The way I've approached business in general, and the kustom industry in particular, owes much to this book. It's hundreds of years old and is still probably used by more military strategists and Fortune 500 companies worldwide than any other reference text. Full of competitive common sense, it makes a fine mental tool to add to your kustom arsenal.

It is a war out there. As Sung Tzu would say (if he were here), "Lots of luck!"

CRAIG FRASER

The in-house airbrush artist and designer for Kal Koncepts, Craig is also the sole proprietor of Air Syndicate, Inc. With a background in architecture and aerospace engineering, Craig splits his time between kustom painting and instructing for the esteemed Airbrush Getaway workshop program and other established information forums. Author of Automotive Cheap Tricks and Special FX, a best-selling book, Craig has also been featured in more than 20 instructional DVDs on airbrushing and automotive custom painting, and is the creator of 50+ stencil designs manufactured by Artool. Recently, Fraser added tattoo artist to his extensive resume, and is also active in freelance illustration, and design consulting.

DION GIULIANO

Dion, founder and owner of Kal Koncepts—established in 1986—is considered one of the world's leading automotive custom builders and painters. A third-generation car customizer, Dion remains on the cutting edge of his craft. Since 1992, Dion and Craig Fraser have partnered in building and painting some of the top customs in the industry.

BRANDON LAMBIE

Owner of Black Sheep Kustoms, Lambie brought his fabricating, painting, and bodywork skills to Kal Koncepts in 2004. A veteran mini-trucker, Lambie has been building and driving customs for more than 20 years, and is one of the founding members of Subversive Minis. Currently, he "rolls" with the Freaks of Nature Car Club with his Pinky truck, one of the vehicles featured on the cover of this book.

PAINT AND EQUIPMENT
EVERYTHING YOU WANTED TO KNOW ABOUT PAINT AND EQUIPMENT, BUT WERE AFRAID TO ASK.

Without paint, guns, airbrushes, or pinstriping brushes, we kustom painters would be like most street mimes: mildly annoying and entirely pointless. You've probably heard a million opinions on which airbrush, paint, or tape is the best. In reality, a number of excellent products are available, and choice is often a matter of personal preference. So how can you tell if your favorite painters are giving you solid advice or just the latest infomercial? Simple! Visit their shops to see what they actually use. I've met many who do incredible work with a combination of (in my opinion) the best and the worst materials.

I believe that, as kustom painters, we should shop for materials and equipment the same way we shop for high-end stereo systems. If you know an audiophile, chances are you've noticed that his system includes components by several makers. For example: McIntosh may turn out killer amps, but Nakamichi has a better tape deck; Denon markets a great CD player, but compared with Klipsch their speakers suck. Point being, it's a statistical improbability to find one company that does everything best. That said, look for what works best—not for the industry or the painter next door, but for you. Every painter is different, and luckily for us, there's lots of equipage by lots of manufacturers to choose from.

Have you ever had painters tell you a particular paint sucks, but then admit they'd never used it? Sure sounds intelligent, not! But, honestly, how many times have you judged a paint, a gun, or a technique before really trying it yourself? Hmm? Thought so. Make sure you give something a fair trial before you criticize. You'll sound more intelligent and your opinion will carry more weight if the product really is inferior. As a kustom painter, I try everything I can—mainly because I'm paranoid. I know from experience that if I try nine out of ten products, the one that works best for me will be the tenth. I listen to every painter who offers advice. I try both what they recommend and what they badmouth. Then I go back to my shop and make the decision that counts.

At Kal Koncepts/Air Syndicate Inc. we currently use a variety of products and tools because we're more concerned with the quality of our work than with keeping some company happy. I'm first and foremost a kustom painter and artist. Secondly, I'm an instructor and educator. At a distant third, I'm a product spokesperson. If you want to be taken seriously in our industry, that's how it's got to be. Though we've changed paints a few times in the past decade, we've always been a multiple paint system shop. For instance, in the past we used PPG for all our color matching and factory refinish work. Then, in the early '90s, we supplemented this system with House of Kolor for graphics and full-on kustom work. Over the years we've switched our factory refinish system from PPG to Valspar to DuPont. In the end it came down to a local jobber and his ability to match colors with the DuPont system and to always have the DuPont in stock. Currently the majority of paint used in our shop—about 90 percent—is House of Kolor. The remaining 10 percent is a combination of DuPont and a few specialty products from other companies. You can offer clients the best only when you have at your disposal the materials that have proven best for you.

Now, concerning guns and airbrushes, I know what you're thinking. If you've been following my work you know I've used Iwata forever. The reality is I've used their airbrushes exclusively since the mid 1990s, and their automotive guns for more than 10 years. While Iwata benefits from advertising and promotions based on endorsements from Kal Koncepts/Air Syndicate Inc., they've earned those benefits 100 percent. We

have no contract with Iwata, except for my promise that as long as they make the best product for our purposes, we'll continue to use it, and I'll continue to speak and write about it. They have no need for a contract, and neither do I. Be wary of a company that wants you to sign an exclusivity deal. Often, they'll lure you with promises of advertising, free equipment, and even paid retainers. They'll give you all these things because they know you wouldn't use their product unless they did. Am I paid by House of Kolor, Iwata, or Artool when they hire me to do a job, a hands-on workshop, or a demonstration at a show? You're darn tootin'! But do I get paid for using their products in my shop or for the use of my name? No. We have a firm policy at Kal Koncepts/Air Syndicate Inc. If we use your product in our shop and like it, and you ask to use our names to endorse your product, no problem. We don't take money for that. (From that point on, however, we expect not to spend money on your product for our shop.) I know of too many kustom painters who've sold their name and, along with it, their integrity and reputation. No amount of money is worth doing that to yourself. Plus, think about it: what company can expect your honest opinion if they're paying you to use their product? At least in our industry, an exclusivity deal is likely to be bad for both parties. Sooner or later it will almost certainly damage the artist's reputation and backfire on the company.

So how, on a limited budget, do you go about trying all the paints and equipment to pick the right ones for you? It's easier than you might think. Because of the huge competition in the industry, companies will go to surprising lengths to get their products into your hands for a trial. Samples of paint and clear are easily available through your local jobber. So are the demonstration guns your local supplier will let you play with. Often you can get killer deals on used demo guns if new ones are a little rich for your budget. The more you try out, the better basis you'll have for making an educated decision. The NACE show is a great place to check out the newest toys. From airbrushes to guns to paint to sanders to tape, you'll never see a bigger in-person infomercial in your life. Now that NACE has buddied up with the SEMA show in Las Vegas every November, you have no excuse for not attending.

What airbrushes do you need? Try the following three-brush system.

First: a workhorse for medium work, sketching, and filling. It should also be able to spray pearls and metallics. I use the Iwata Kustom Eclipse CS for my shop workhorse. Virtually indestructible, it has a free-floating nozzle for high-volume flow, is inexpensive to keep in tips and needles, yet also goes for three to six months without needing a needle/nozzle change. The Kustom Eclipse CS top-feed airbrush does about 75 percent of my airbrush work in the shop.

Second: a standard detail airbrush for refining, detailing, shading, and shadowing; capable of finer work than your workhorse, with less volume, but still reliable. For this tool I choose the Iwata Kustom HP-CH. The HP-C had been my workhorse for years, before the Eclipse came out. The advent of the HP-CH highline series brought a rebirth of the HP-C top feed. With fewer internal parts, a finer spray pattern, and a larger top cup, it's a higher-quality airbrush than the older HP-C, and also one of the few that let you micro-adjust air at the nozzle. The HP-CH handles about 20 percent of my work in the shop.

Third: an airbrush to be used only for ultra-fine detail and small highlights in tight-up mural work; one that shoots overreduced paints and kandies, but not metallics or pearls. My choice is the Kustom Micron-C. It also has the micro-adjustment (MAC) valve at the nozzle and a hand-matched spray head system that gives me the most precise spray lines possible with an airbrush. It accounts for only 5 percent of my workload. Now, before you conclude that it might therefore be unnecessary, remember that this 5 percent is the fine detail work that finishes off a job, the detail that's noticed first and remembered last.

Will you need other airbrushes? Very possibly, depending on what you paint and your style. But the three above are a good start.

You can apply the same rules of thumb to guns. Start with three—a primer gun, a basecoat/kandy gun, and a clear gun. The primer gun may be purchased inexpensively at any hardware store, but nowadays primers are sort of particular. So I would recommend not buying junk. I like the Air Gunza with the 2.0 and 3.4 nozzle setup. That way it can be your polyester primer/sealer gun, yet do double duty as a flake gun. Our preference for a basecoat/kandy gun is the Anest Iwata LPH-100 or 300. This is an excellent medium-range gun with killer atomization. Your choice of a clear-coat gun will depend on what you're clearing. If I cleared only helmets, murals, or bikes, I'd probably stick with the LPH-300; for anything larger I'd want the volume of the LPH-400LV. With the same nozzle sizes available as the 300, this gun has almost twice the volume for large-scale clear-coating. All these new guns come with nozzles capable of spraying waterborne and water-based products, something important to consider, since nobody likes to buy multiple guns unnecessarily. With the Iwata, all you have to do is replace the nozzle, cap, and needle. How simple is that?

Most LPH guns also have the new LV pre-atomization technology that allows better paint transfer to the surface and covers faster with less material. I should also mention here that I use a touch-up gun, the LPH-50. The world's smallest HVLP (high volume, low pressure) gun, it's excellent for small graphics, doorjambs, small fades, etc. Another new player you might want to look at is the LPH-80, which falls between a touch-up gun and a full-size spray gun. I originally viewed it as a mutt gun, useful to painters of helmets or bikes only. Then we tried it with AutoAir Colors. Turns out it's amazing for spraying water-based colors for graphics, jambs, and two-tones. Though small, it sprays just the right amount. Our LPH-400 1.0 was down for cleaning at SEMA two years ago, so we ended up spraying an entire Ford Fusion for AutoAir with this gun. Darned impressive!

Yeah, yeah, I know—I sound like an infomercial for Iwata. But, hey, that's what we're currently using, and what I currently know in this field. I will say, though, that before you buy any gun, you should test-drive it. Most distributors will let you, and it's really the best way to find the best product for you and your shop. Personal preference is the only reason you'll need to decide on your favorite gun, and I'll never argue against a decision so based—unless you have zero experience with the guns you're criticizing. At Kal Koncepts/Air Syndicate Inc. we have the opportunity to test many guns, airbrushes, masking systems, and paints. That's one of the principal reasons we can guarantee the quality of the work that leaves our shop. Think about it.

I've seen painters who spend all their money on paint and new equipment go under because of this extreme behavior. Another behavior, just as extreme, is never buying a different paint or new equipment and using the cheapest materials to finish a job. Both extremes are wrong. Remember, airbrushes, guns, tape, and kustom paints are tools, no more and no less. Don't be obsessive, but never stop searching for, as my grandfather put it, "the right tool for the right job." The searching is what's important, and the search will be your reward.

BACK TO DA' BASICS

All houses, big, small, cheap, or expensive will fall without a proper foundation.

Not a day goes by that I don't get a question, phone call, or e-mail asking me what is the best path to becoming a great airbrush artist. I've been airbrushing since the early '80s, specializing in automotive kustomizing, and teaching since the early '90s, and I have yet to find a magic bullet that will accomplish skills in a minute. Hate to say it, but the only magic bullet I know of is practice, and it takes more than a few minutes to get the job done. My mistake was that I didn't include this chapter in my first book, but hey, that's what second books are for.

When I say that freehand is king, I'm not just holding court. It's true. I'm not saying that masking, frisketing, freehand shielding, and stenciling do not have their place, but they all take second to freehand ability. To explain this, I like to use the analogy of an automatic transmission versus a standard stick with a clutch. They're both important in the industry, otherwise one would've replaced the other. All of us know somebody who can drive an automatic but can't touch a stick. Do any of us know somebody who can drive a stick but has no idea how to drive an automatic? Think about it. If you can freehand airbrush, you can always develop or fake acceptable skills concerning masking or stenciling. But it doesn't work the other way around. We will accept that both styles can develop incredible levels of artwork, but the skill levels of a freehand airbrusher far outweigh the airbrush skills of somebody who cannot freehand. This is the real "inconvenient truth."

The one thing that I've noticed with my teaching is that there are no complicated problems or mistakes, just complicated solutions. Most habitual or systematic problems that artists come across are usually basic in nature and can be traced back to beginning techniques. Like I stated in this chapter title, the foundation is the key to stability. Airbrush basics are the primary foundation of all airbrushing skills. The good thing is, there really are only three basic skills you need to master to be able to freehand airbrush. The trick is, there are only three. Which means there's little leeway for making mistakes if you have not mastered them all. In all fairness, I should add that no one will ever be finished learning all the airbrush basics, but it should not prevent you from trying.

These basics should not be viewed merely as exercises to crank out mindlessly until you cannot even stand the sight of your airbrush. View them as troubleshooting demos to help you self-diagnose your weaknesses in airbrushing, thereby allowing you to repair your techniques at will. These techniques are important for beginners and veterans alike. Your goal is to attain an automatic ability with the airbrush that would rival your ability at using a pencil to sign your name. Any artist who has picked up an airbrush knows that while you're learning to use it, your artwork suffers.

Not just with techniques, but also creatively, too. Why? Well, basically, when you're learning a new technical skill, your brain goes into learning mode. Your left brain takes over the whole game, and your right brain goes to the zoo, leaving you with zero creativity to go along with your new undeveloped skills.

The trick is to learn the technical side of the airbrush as soon as possible, then get your right brain to join the game. True creativity is not solely right brain; it's a balance between right and left. You'll only get this balance when both sides are working together on the project. Getting automatic with your airbrush is the best way to get started. I have two major exercises that I recommend using as warm-ups every day before you start spraying. They only take about five minutes, and you'll see the difference in your airbrush ability within a mere two weeks. (Geez, sounds like an infomercial!).

Before you start spraying, let's cover a few absolute basics concerning the physics of your airbrush and how to make it perform at its optimum efficiency. There's nothing worse than trying to learn on a bad brush, or using one that's set up inappropriately. Falling back on the old "My airbrush sucks" excuse will not work for long in the industry. For one thing, you need to keep that air going. Good rule of thumb to remember is, "Air on first, air on last." If you shut your air off in midspray, you'll load your needle with paint. This can result in spitting, or additional needle loading and tip clogging. Keep that air flowing, and you'll find your detail work improve and your gradations being a lot cleaner. So with all that being said, time to start your basics.

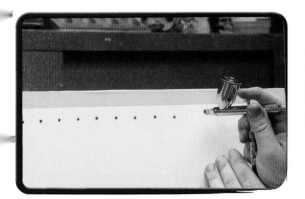

1. The first basic skill also happens to be the easiest technique that can be done with an airbrush; the dot. While easy, the trick in this exercise is to control the aspects of the dot. Make sure to keep the dots the same size, same distance, and same intensity as one another. This means keeping the airbrush at the same distance, holding the trigger back the same amount, and taking the same amount of time on each dot. If you do all these well, you should have equal-sized dots all day long. Fair warning: The simpler something appears, the more that can go wrong with it!

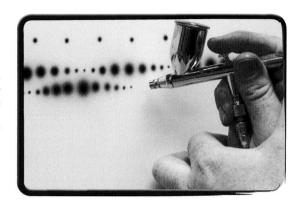

2. Once you get the dots down, then it's time to throw another challenge into the mix. Consider these exercises to be like juggling. You start out with a few balls, and you continue adding more and more as you progress. This exercise is the same as the previous one, but instead of being careful to keep the distance the same, you vary the distance to create a varied pattern of dots. The difficulty is varying the dots in the same pattern each time. Good luck.

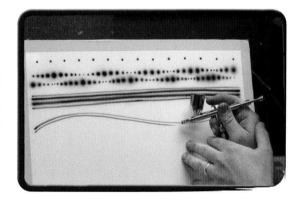

3. After a couple of lines of the varied dots, it's time to go on to the next test. (Yes, you should view these as tests. If you cannot do one of these demos, do not go on to the next one until you can.) Lines have always been considered difficult to master with the airbrush. The best way to approach line work is to think of lines as merely moving dots. I mean, the technique is exactly the same as a dot, just start moving the brush before you stop the material flow.

4. When I have students lay out a straight line, I always ask them how they feel about it. They look at me kinda funny. Feel? Yeah, how does it feel? For comparison, let's try a line with a slight curve. After laying out the curved line, every student agrees that it's much easier to do than the straight one. Upon which I ask them to try duplicating the curved line right underneath the first one. Guess what? Just as difficult. Actually, a little more so. The reason for the difficulty? Perception. Technically the lines are the same, but in your head you have a perception of the straight line that is close to perfection. Hence, more difficult. Only after you try to duplicate the curved one do you feel the same apprehension. Aside from technical skills, a lot of airbrushing is in your head.

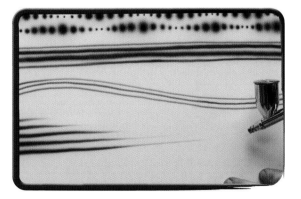

5. Well, you have done dots, and now you have done lines. The third, and last, exercise is the dagger stroke. The dagger stroke is not only the most difficult, but also the most necessary of freehand skills. Literally a "tapered line," the dagger stroke is necessary to create or render anything out there. The dagger stroke is a combination of trigger control, distance control, and speed control. As you start the dagger, you start at the widest point. As you move along, you simultaneously push the trigger forward as you close the distance to the surface and speed up. When finished, you should be a few inches from the end of the dagger, with the paint fully shut off, and the air still on (remember the air rule we talked about earlier!).

6. After you start feeling somewhat comfortable with linear dagger strokes, you may want to move on to curved ones. This is the same exercise used to train T-Shirt artists to paint faster at their cursive lettering. It creates muscle memory that allows you to gain speed and consistency with your line work. Continuous exercises will help you with necessary continuity, no matter what you paint.

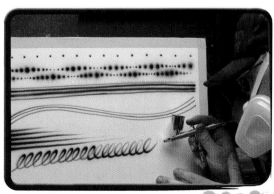

7. Now that you've finished your troubleshooting, you should be quite aware of what you're good at and what you need a little work on. Now it's time for those two exercises I was talking about earlier. The first one is called the dot box, and it uses both dots and lines to develop your automatic airbrush skills. To start with, you want to make a box using five rows of five dots each. This will give you a total of 25 dots in a grid pattern. Besides teaching you excellent dot control, this exercise will also teach you spatial awareness—something very important if you ever want to airbrush free-form murals.

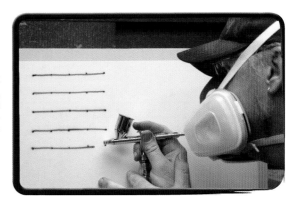

8. Of course, the next step is connecting the dots. This part is easy. Just use your line skills to create horizontal lines covering your previous dots, and ending cleanly at the last one. Because I want you to be a well-rounded freehander, try going in both directions when creating these horizontal lines. The ultimate line would be to completely cover your previous dots. Right now, I would just be happy to have a straight line ending at the last one.

9. With the horizontals done, time to start the verticals and turn the lines into a grid. Again, you want to alternate the direction from top to bottom, to bottom to top. I would rather have you start out lousy in all directions than be good at airbrushing lines in only one. One direction is useless. If anything, it will break the continuity of your work and show how bad your other techniques are. Perfection is impossible to attain, so don't worry about it. But lack of perfection is not what people see when they criticize your line work; it's the lack of continuity.

10. Lastly, the diagonals. These are tricky, because your eyes start playing tricks on you in this third step. The majority of your dots are no longer visible, so you have to see through the existing pattern to get the lines down correctly. In the "dot box" demo, the trick is to lay out all of the lines cleanly and at the same speed. If you ever find yourself slowing down for one set of lines, it's because you're not comfortable with it. This comfort level is necessary to become an automatic airbrusher.

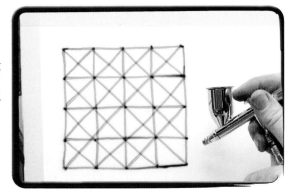

11. The second exercise is the "dagger stroke box." The same way that dagger strokes are more difficult than simple lines, this exercise is much more difficult than the dot box. To start this one, we want to create four sides of the box, with an equal number of dots on each side. The number of dots is not as important as the fact that we need a center dot for each side. Again, like the dot box, try to make all of the dots equal size, equal distance from one another, and equal intensity.

12. Now the fun begins! Time for dagger strokes. Let's consider the corner dots to be the world's shortest dagger stroke, basically a dot. Then go from short to longest, with the longest being the center dot, and then back to short again. Try to keep the longest center dagger only as long as the center of the box, otherwise you will get some overlapping from the opposite side.

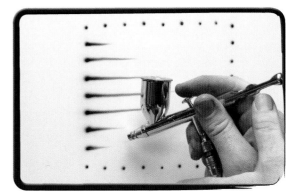

13. As you complete each side, continue on to the next one. The design of this exercise automatically forces you to airbrush your daggers in all directions, so there is no need to alternate. You will notice that while none of my daggers are perfect, they are all similar in nature. This is that all-important continuity that I've been pushing.

14. When finished, you can see the implied "X" in the middle of the box. The reason that it looks like there are many more daggers in the end is because I added more in between the existing starting dots. You might think, Why not just add extra dots in the beginning? The difference is, when you're forced to add daggers later on, it's an extra exercise all by itself. It forces you to think during the dagger strokes, remembering that this one has to be longer than this one, but shorter than the next. Anytime you can throw a monkey wrench in your exercise and come out OK, you know you've learned something.

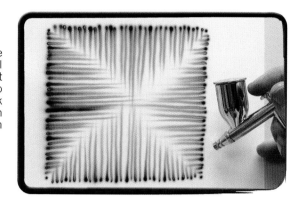

There you have it. Can't get much more basic than that! Now, I cannot guarantee you will become a great airbrusher or phenomenal freehand technician, even if you follow these exercises, but I can guarantee that you will have a very difficult time getting there if you don't know and practice these on a regular basis. The more you practice, the more automatic your reaction to the airbrush will be. The best part is, the more automatic you are with your airbrush, the less you have to think about the technical aspect of your airbrushing. With your brain freed up from this technical crap, it gives you the chance to be creative.

If that's not what airbrushing is all about, then I don't know what is.

Paint to live, live to practice your ass off! Especially your dagger strokes!

BULLET RIDDEN

STRAFING A PANEL WITH THE ARTOOL FX-2
BULLET-RIDDEN STENCIL

A fter my first book came out, one of the most frequent reader requests (thanks, by the way, for your gratifying response!) was for more stencil chapters. Well, your wish is my command. Of course, I can't include the more than 50 Artool stencils in this book—comprehensive coverage of them would probably require a two-volume tome (hmmm, now there's an idea)! For more information and instruction on Artool stencils, check out the many *Airbrush Action Magazine*-produced DVDs (www.airbrushaction.com), not to mention the Artool stencil-specific columns in *Airbrush Action*. As a matter of fact, this chapter is a rewritten version of an *Airbrush Action* tech column. I just grabbed one from the bag, and it happened to be one of my favorites.

Faux bullet holes have been a kustom industry staple for years. Whether done in One Shot or with a sticker applied over the clear, they have been a popular way to cover up chips and other paint-job issues. Another cool use is incorporating them into a paint job so that they look real from a distance. In fact, I saw some close-up on a chopper that looked so real that I thought somebody had actually shot the bike's oil tank. There was even a little drop of oil coming out of the hole! I had always cut my own stencils or used an adhesive masking system to paint bullet holes, but after seeing how many artists were using that technique, I figured that creating a stencil with Artool might be just the ticket.

1. This stencil includes bullet entrance holes, exit holes, and concrete holes in negative, in positive, and in three sizes. (Sorry, no caliber info available. Be imaginative!) I also included a shotgun blast, a broken window pattern, and smoke positives on both sides of the stencil. Everything you could hope for!

2. Selecting the big hole for demonstration, I placed a few random entrance holes across a stippled black paint panel. Using BC-26 White with a bit of silver added, I airbrushed the patterns. Silver gave the added realism of bare metal. This design is supposed to mimic the chip of paint that would fly off the surface of the indented bullet hole—leaving, of course, bare metal.

3. With BC-25 Basecoat Black, I airbrushed the bullet hole itself, using the size appropriate for the pattern. Keep the stencil tight to the surface or you'll get fuzzy underspray, making the result look more like a sprayed dot than a hole.

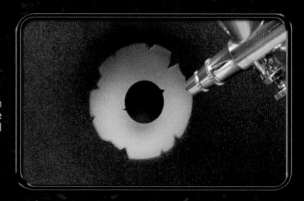

4. Using the same airbrush loaded with black, but a little overreduced with RU-311 reducer, I fogged in a subtle shadow to give the illusion that the area was sunken in. Even though my Micron C+ airbrush is more for detail work, it gave me the perfect atomization for this small shadowed area.

5. Returning to the BC-26 White/Silver and Eclipse CS airbrush, I sprayed in the metal furls on a few exit holes. These can be done before or after you spray the holes—it's really your call. A little tape on the stencil is the best way to mask off the plastic while spraying.

6. The next step is fairly self-explanatory. Switching back to the Micron with the black was a lot easier than cleaning the airbrush every time I needed to change paints. You can't beat having several guns while working on a project. The cost of the spare gun is easily paid for in just one day of time saved.

7. This is where the detail ability of the Micron C+ came in handy. With the transparent black, I airbrushed drop shadows over the background base color to create the silver/white furls that added a 3-D effect. You've probably figured out that the reason I stippled the black panel with gray was so that the true black would show up as the drop shadow. Always keep this in mind when working on black.

8. Using the negative hole on the edge of the stencil, I sprayed some pure BC-26 White, with a little overreduction, to give the smoke effect. Offsetting the stencil added a slight illusion of thickness to the edge of the hole—a small detail, but small details like this add considerable realism. Keep the smoke simple for starters—just a little overspray, really.

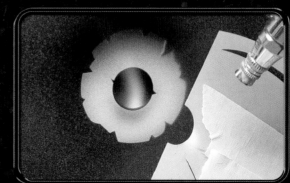

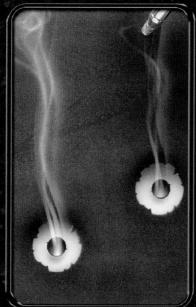

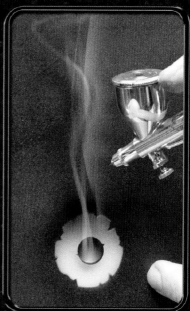

9. After masking off the rest of the stencil, I used its smoke-effect section to create nice tight edges for the furl of smoke rising from the hole. Be careful not to have white effects like this trail below the hole. The soft lines may look simple, but let your eye do the work here. Less is more when it comes to smoke.

10. It's important to incorporate freehand with the stencil for true realism in your design. Smoke rises because it's hot. As it rises and cools, it breaks up and starts to fall. You can represent this best with freehand airbrushing. That's how I produced the broken squiggle at the top of the furl.

11. Don't forget to use the transparent black for the drop shadow. I had shadowed everything so far—no sense in forgetting to shadow the smoke. Without the subtle shadow, the smoke would look bizarre against everything else.

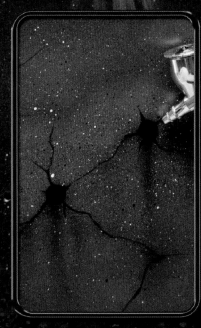

12. With my first bullet holes finished and smoking, I began work on the concrete bullet holes. Here I needed more stippling to give the true stone effect. This was done by flicking and by loading up the needles of both the white and black guns. While not practical for large-scale areas, this gives a killer effect for small spots like this.

13. Using the stencil's concrete hole, I threw a few repeats across the stone effect with the same black. At this point you learn whether you've stippled the area lightly enough. If you can't make out the black in the bullet hole, you might need a few more white or gray spots.

14. If you're going to have bullet holes in stone or concrete, then you're definitely going to need cracks. With the transparent black still in the Micron, I couldn't have asked for a better airbrush to spray fine cracks and streaks.

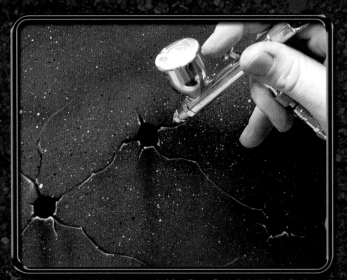

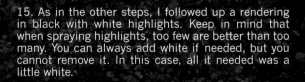

15. As in the other steps, I followed up a rendering in black with white highlights. Keep in mind that when spraying highlights, too few are better than too many. You can always add white if needed, but you cannot remove it. In this case, all it needed was a little white.

16. I sprayed the same black through the stencil to create the dispersed pattern of the shotgun pellets. The pattern looks especially cool if you spray pearl through it over a masked graphic—a lot faster than using a single-circle template!

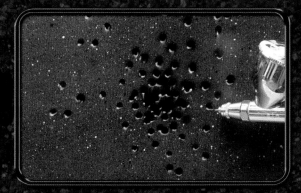

17. Now, this step did take a bit of time, but was well worth it. Not every hole needs highlighting, but try to highlight the majority. Just a little crescent is all the hole needs to take on that realistic punched-out look.

18. Switching back to white, it was time for a little smoke action. The width of the smoke-streak stencil was perfect for the width of the shotgun pellet hole. I just lined up the stencil and sprayed. Don't forget to break up the smoke with freehand airbrushing as it rises. Done right, it will look just like a photograph.

19. Grabbing the Micron loaded with black, I airbrushed the last of the *Bullet-Ridden* shot-out window effect options. I imagine that going over a pure black background, you could do this with white as well. Just be sure to finish with the opposite color to give that necessary depth.

20. There's nothing like a little freehand work to add reality to a piece. Besides connecting the lines and sections of the glass, the concentric circles I created throughout this piece emphasize the spiderweb effect we've all seen on glass. Come to think of it, this stencil would also work pretty well as a foundation for rendering spiderwebs.

21. Again, the final step was highlighting. Besides tracing thin white lines along the black lines of the broken glass, I also created bright hotspots with soft-edged halos to mimic the light reflection you would see in the real McCoy. As always with highlights, less is more.

You asked for it, you got it! This is probably the longest article I've ever written about a single-sheet stencil. No one can say I left anything out! Amazing how many different faux bullet-hole designs you can do with a simple 8" x 10" stencil. While the techniques are fairly simple and can be duplicated by a novice, this stencil is also a great tool for the professional. Next time you need a little something different, don't forget bullet holes. It will be one of the rare times your client won't mind having a ride shot up!

Paint to live, live to strafe!

blades bubbles 'n. water

Three Kool Effects That Go Great Together

When I first got into the automotive graphics industry in the early '90s, competition was stiff. Trying to stand out in the crowd of successful kustom painters was no easy trick—until I noticed that the industry was lacking in the use of the airbrush. Back then, its most popular application was murals. While many a graphic painter had an airbrush lying around, it was usually relegated to fades, a few stencils, and the occasional drop shadow. In fact, when I started working with Kal Koncepts in 1992, the majority of paint shops outsourced their airbrushing. I should know, because for the first part of my automotive career that's what I did—freelance airbrushing for other kustom painters. I figured that if we could incorporate airbrushing into every graphic we cranked out at Kal Koncepts/Air Syndicate, we would not only stand out from the crowd, we would force the industry to do what we were doing. Simply put, I was merely creating job security for myself. See what it turned into?!

In this chapter, I demonstrate a simple tribal layout, incorporating a beveled blade effect, rivets, and a background water mural. These additions will turn a standard graphic job into something truly remarkable. Who ever said that murals and graphics can't be combined? Funny thing is, the amount of time these effects add to the job is so minimal, you'll be bummed that you didn't incorporate airbrushing sooner. So, without further blah blah, let's airbrush.

1. As with most of my graphics, I established the layout with 1/8" tan 3M crepe tape. Freeform tribal work is always fun, especially in symmetrical designs. I laid in a center line, then worked on only one side of the panel. That way the entire look came as a surprise before I duplicated the opposite side. I use this technique on hoods and tailgates quite successfully.

2. Next, I pounced the design. I describe this technique numerous times in this book, but if I neglect to mention it here, someone might scream. I started the process by doing a dry-rub transfer with chalk over masking paper. That transferred the tribal to the paper for the final pounce.

3. Then I traced the lines with the 1/8" tape. During this step, I like to take my airbrush, or air hose, and blow off the residual chalk dust. That way I can still see the transfer line, and the tape has better adhesion.

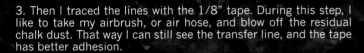

4. With the graphic laid out and masked with Auto Mask, I sprayed the base silver color with House of Kolor's MC01 Kosmic Krome Aluminum effect. The panel had been pre-sanded, and while spraying, I noticed that the scratches were slightly irregular and distracting. Not to worry; this was fixed easily. But it made me more cautious the next time I sanded a panel that would be sprayed with this type of aluminum paint.

5. Here's how to fix those random scratches: use a Scotch-Brite pad. It's that simple. No underlying scratches can stand up to the mighty power of a scuff pad! Keep the scratches made by the pad linear, and it will give you the classic brushed aluminum look. If you go a little too far and break through to the black? Just hit it with a bit more paint. (Good reason to keep the airbrush loaded during this step!)

6. Time for the bevel effect. Grab your tape of choice. For a full-sized graphic on a car I usually use ¼", but for this panel or a motorcycle, 1/8" works nicely. Follow the design edge, keeping the tape on the paint and butted against the edge of the design. Decide where the overlaps of the tribals will occur and lay them in appropriately.

7. With the beveled edges masked, I added character to the tribal using a mixture of BC-25 Basecoat Black, KK-17 Violette, KK-04 Oriental Blue, and SG-100. With this cool black kandy I airbrushed in shadow bars that gave the tribal the look of tempered metal. The trick was balancing soft edges with hard and keeping them at the same basic angle.

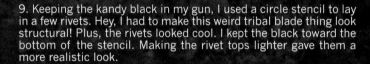

8. As I unmasked the edge, what I had planned became apparent. The edges were now much lighter than the center and looked as if they had been either machined or sharpened from the original piece of metal. Hence the term "blade" in the title of this chapter.

9. Keeping the kandy black in my gun, I used a circle stencil to lay in a few rivets. Hey, I had to make this weird tribal blade thing look structural! Plus, the rivets looked cool. I kept the black toward the bottom of the stencil. Making the rivet tops lighter gave them a more realistic look.

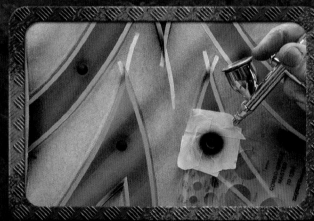

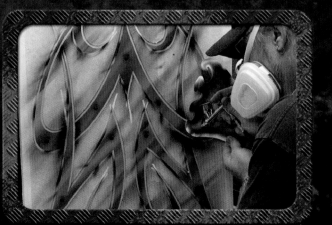

10. Simple sharp edges, rivets, tempering, and scratches alone did not cut it in this blade graphic. Had to put in some drop shadows, too. Using a spare stencil, I played "French curve" and masked off the overlaps to create realistic depth.

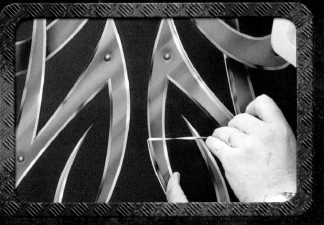

12. It was time to unmask the masterpiece. You could tell, even before the clear coat was applied, that this tribal graphic had been taken to the next level. While I normally will pinstripe a graphic, this one was an exception because of the beveled edges. But as with most things in my shop, we were not going to stop here.

13. Before you start crying "déjà vu," I was not outlining the tribal with 1/8" tape; I was tracing the inside edge. That's the best way to remask your graphic for overpainting. "Cut," you say? No cut edge can ever compare with the cleanness and safety of a masked edge. Plus, it may be nearly impossible to see a design through most transfer papers; the 1/8" tape gave me a great trace point for later cutting.

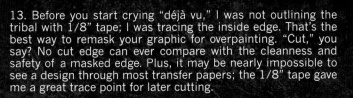

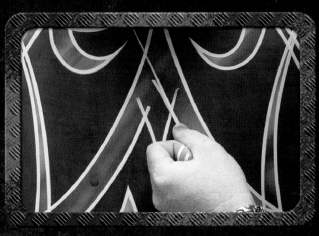

14. With the tribal protected, it was time for some background work. I started by giving myself a cool border. Then, taking the same white that had been sitting in my Eclipse, I laid out a center light source. This was intended to look as if it was coming from above and diffusing through the water into distinct beams. Freehand is the best technique for this step.

15. The bubbles were done with a combination of stippling, or flicking, and simple blowouts. (A blowout occurs when you get the airbrush too close to the surface, then overspray the paint. The point is pushed out in a circular pattern that looks like a bubble with a thin outline.) With the bubbles done, a simple wash of KK-04 Oriental Blue/SG-100 was all I needed to add color to the game.

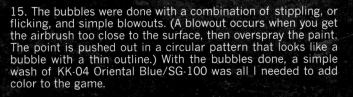

16. Remember, when working with a kandy, the more you apply, the darker the image becomes. The color will remain the same, but its intensity and value will shift. Great—because that's exactly what happens when you actually look through water! I wanted the bottom even darker, so I added a few drops of KK-17 Violette Kandy directly to the airbrush.

17. I know what you're thinking: "You already did the bubbles!" Those were background bubbles (hence the overlaid kandy). Now I had to make bubbles in the foreground. These were done the same way but with more detail. I actually rendered a few of the larger ones, highlights and all. Google "water bubbles" on the Internet; I'm sure you'll come up with more than a few good references.

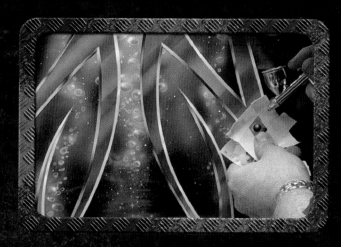

18. With everything unmasked and finished, it was time to do a little troubleshooting and a few touch-ups. The rivets needed help, so I hit them with some of the bubble white. You probably noticed the water reflections on the bottom of the panel. These gave an added sense of depth and realism that made the entire panel pop.

It's remarkable how a little airbrush work can turn a simple graphic into a masterpiece. Use your imagination! Just because something has never been done before, doesn't mean it won't work. You'd be surprised what can happen—you might originate the next big trend. Back in the '90s when I started incorporating my muralescent style of airbrushing with graphics, it really pushed the industry forward. It wasn't as if it hadn't been done in the past; if you look back to the '60s and '70s, the era of the van paint job, everything but the kitchen sink was thrown into graphics, including airbrushing. That style of painting had just been forgotten in the later mix. Whether you're inventing a new technique or revitalizing an older style, the main thing is to actually do it—it won't create itself. So next time you plan a graphic job—whether tribal, scallops, or flames—consider how a little airbrush work might add to the finished product, and to your profits.

Blades and bubbles and rivets, oh my!

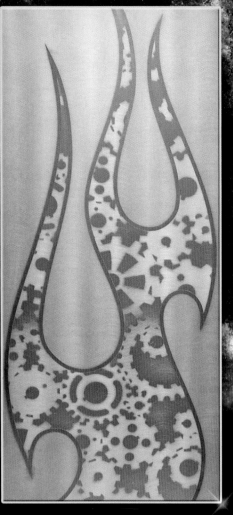
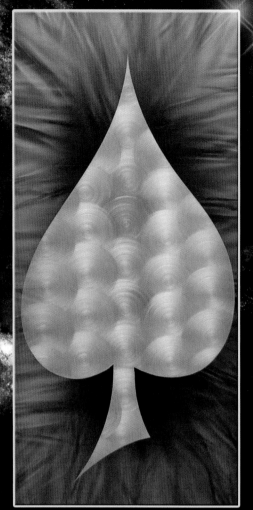
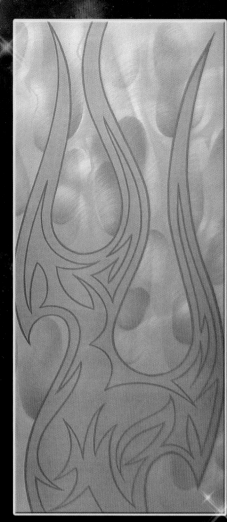

KOSMIC KROME KULTURE

Painting with the new Kosmic Krome Aluminum from House of Kolor.

One of my specialties at Kal Koncepts/Air Syndicate Inc. is coming up with tricks for new gadgets, paints, and materials. So when Alsa Corporation showed me its line of MirraChrome and Ghost Chrome products, I was fascinated. A paint composed of micro-sized 6061-T6 aluminum is cool as an abstract concept. It's even cooler when the concept is applied. The aluminum pigment is so fine that the grain is invisible, making the painted surface look like an aluminum object rather than an object coated with aluminum. When I first experimented with the Ghost Chrome—an aluminum

effect sprayed as a base coat—I was warned to sand it with nothing coarser than 1500-grit sandpaper because even the smallest scratches would make the aluminum look terrible. That got me thinking about a possible effect. If this paint was 100 percent aluminum, then done right, scratching its surface should make it look like brushed aluminum. I took a Scotch-Brite pad to a Ghost Chrome surface, and that's exactly what it looked like.

House of Kolor developed its micro-aluminum product at nearly the same time, obtaining the pigment from the same supplier, but didn't release it until much later. The primary differences from Alsa's product are the carrier that holds the pigment and the amount of pigment in the solution. HoK Kosmic Aluminum does not use alcohol as a base and has better adhesion. So while it does dry a bit more slowly, it makes up for that with better structural stability and a heavier pigment content that covers more quickly. While I personally prefer House of Kolor products to those of any other company, I still like to try out as many new products as possible. If you don't expand your horizons by experimenting with what all manufacturers have to offer, you'll miss out on tricks that could push your paint jobs to the next level. If I'd used only HoK, I never would have discovered and developed the techniques demonstrated in this chapter!

1. Although HoK Kosmic Aluminum can be painted over any color, the best and fastest application is over black. So I masked off a black powder-coated panel in an ace-of-spades design. If the photo makes you wonder what was in my hand—well, never overlook power tools for kustom painting. I figured if a Scotch-Brite pad could work wonders by hand with this aluminum paint, what might it do when hot-glued to a Rollock die grinder? Experimenting is fun.

2. Using the Scotch-Brite grinder, I carefully overlapped the circle to create a repeating pattern over the entire design. Pressing too hard or overworking any area could burn through the base color or damage masking on the surface. Be sure to work only on powder coated surface, single-stage, or clear-coated black base coat. Unprotected base coat isn't strong enough to keep the scratches from breaking down in the following steps.

3. Using an Iwata TH-3 airbrush, I sprayed on three light coats of the Kosmic Krome MC-01. The TH-3 works perfectly because of its fan-head attachment. Make sure the coats are even, and don't layer too much or it will dull out. Also, wait at least five minutes between coats to let them dry. Done correctly, you'll get a killer machine-turned effect. Amazing what a little scratching will do to this stuff, huh?

4. After spraying a protective coat of SG-100, I unmasked the entire design. The cool part about this effect is that its reflectivity shifts at different angles, just like real ground aluminum. You can layer any of the kandies over it and get a killer anodized/jeweled look. You can trim different-sized disks to give yourself different patterns. The possibilities are limited only by your imagination. At this point, the gears in your head should be turning at full speed. That's what this book is for!

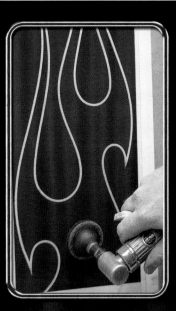

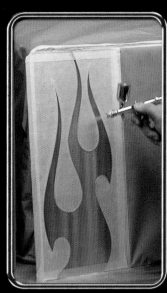

5. Another trick started with a couple of classic flame layouts. By now you've probably figured out that 1/8" tan 3M tape is my favorite. I know, I know—in my first book, I preferred blue vinyl fineline tape. Well, I'm allowed to change my mind. No matter, I'm currently digging the old crepe tape.

6. With the flame masked off, I did a number of vertical grinds with the Scotch-Brite grinder. The faster you move the grinder, the more individual grind marks you'll see. With tape covering the underlying black, the end result will be a cool etched-metal effect.

7. Using Automask transfer tape, I masked off the flame so I could spray it with Kosmic Krome Aluminum. When cutting, make sure to stay in the center of the 1/8" tape, using it as a buffer so that the tape itself will be the paint edge, not the cut line.

8. With the same TH-3 fan gun and MC-01, I sprayed the flames with two light coats. I sprayed one coat fewer than before on the machine-turning effect because I would be spraying more later. Didn't want to overdo it.

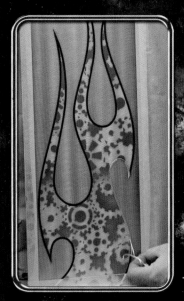

9. Another killer effect with the Kosmic Krome Aluminum is to layer in stencil designs with black. Here, I broke out the *Gearhead* stencil from the FX-1 series. I get serious mileage out of this stencil. Using it with Kosmic Krome is especially cool.

10. After the base coat was dry, I sprayed a light coat of Kosmic Krome Aluminum over the top of the stencil work. When dry, this resulted in a funky acid-etched metal effect, like the etched designs on metallicized trading cards.

11. Here the work was un-masked. See how with just a bit of masking and stenciling, Kosmic Krome Aluminum can give you an innovative piece of artwork? By creating negative space with the 1/8" tape, you leave the design as is and get a black-striped outline on the flames without having to break out the pinstripe brush.

12. Of course, if you're like me, you're never happy leaving something alone. Adding a bit more Kosmic Krome Aluminum over the entire design gave the piece a completely different look. The finished design was now truly monochromatic in every sense of the word. Just be sure to hit the finished artwork with a protective coat of SG-100 if you plan on masking back over it. Or you could just clear it and call it a day.

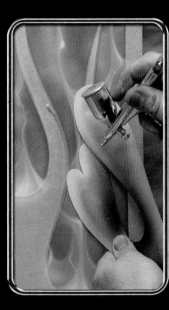

13. For the third piece I laid out the same flame design as for the first, but in reverse. That gave the panel a nice symmetrical look. Normally I would pounce a design like this, but here eye-balling was just as easy, especially since the panel was right in front of me.

14. Now for something different with the grinder. Instead of doing simple circles or vertical bars, I moved the grinder randomly all over the place. That gave the realistic look of, well, taking a grinder to the entire surface. Try tilting the grinder as you move it to produce pleasing variations in the lines. Remember, the faster you go, the more grind marks you'll see.

15. Add a little Kosmic Krome MC01, and you've got one randomly sanded piece of aluminum. When I did this on a fiberglass tank blank at a car show, I had people convinced I'd somehow laminated MC-01 aluminum over the whole thing!

16. What about realistic aluminum fire? (Remember, these effects are limited only by your imagination.) With my trusty flame stencil, I airbrushed realistic fire with overreduced base coat BC-26 white.

  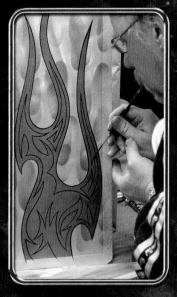 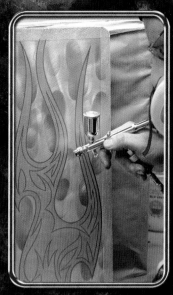

17. To finish the fire, a little black to add depth was all that was necessary. Just about any fire stencil will do; the simplest are usually the best. Try using one of the *FH1* or *FH2* stencils from Artool; any simple French curve works well, too.

18. Leaving the fire over the aluminum looked OK, but I wanted to really push the Kosmic Krome here, so I unmasked the flame and layered in some aluminum. That brought the fire back into the design and contrasted nicely with the plain aluminized flame design.

19. We hadn't done any pinstriping yet. While you can't actually pinstripe with the Kosmic Krome Aluminum (it's too thin to actually pull a line), you can pinstripe a design, and then layer MC-01 over it. For this effect, I brought out the HoK black and added Von Dutch styling to the flame piece.

20. Check out how the pinstriping took on an aluminum look when the Kosmic Krome was sprayed over it. In fact, if you use MC01 Mirror Reflective Kosmic Krome, the pinstripe will actually take on the appearance of chrome. Just be sure to add a bit of U-01 Striping Clear to the HoK striping urethane. The shinier the pinstripe, the more chrome-like the effect.

21. Here's one more effect: with my whisk broom stencil, I fogged some Kosmic Chrome Aluminum around the border. Add the aluminum and maybe some kandy through the stencil (killer all by itself) and you have something definitely unique.

Well, what did I tell you? The sheer number of effects with this new Kosmic Krome is truly amazing. Heck, I showed you eight different effects and never even used colors! While House of Kolors Kosmic Krome is an innovative product, it will be the techniques you learn that will make it invaluable to you. For more information, contact your local House of Kolor representative. A DVD is available for all Kosmic Krome products. While I mentioned only the MC-00 and MC-01 aluminum, there are three others: Bronze, Copper, and Gold. Because they're available in small quantities from Coast Airbrush, you can afford to try them all.

The central aim of this chapter, and this book, is to help you realize the possibilities that are out there. Experiment with every product you can get your hands on. Follow instructions, but go for it. Be aware that nearly every special effect in the kustom industry was at one time a screw-up. The difference between a mistake and a kustom effect is merely intent. Learn from your mistakes, never be afraid to experiment, and you'll never be at a loss for new and innovative techniques. Thomas Edison said it best when asked by an interviewer if he felt like a failure after all his unsuccessful attempts with the light bulb. He exclaimed, "I didn't fail! I just discovered 600 ways not to make a lightbulb!" Experimentation is never a waste of time; and, who knows, you just might find a killer technique that can make you a little coin.

Experiment to live, live to experiment!

OL' SCHOOL TRICKS

A few old-school tricks you always wanted to know, but were afraid to ask.

F irst of all, I don't have room here to include every last old-school trick. Honestly, you could do an entire book just on the tricks everyone has forgotten. So I'll cover only three in this chapter. Heck, the rest of the book is mostly old-school tricks that have had a bit of a face lift. I picked these techniques partly because I really like them and use them often, and also because they were requested. So, for those of you who sent in the requests, here they are! As for the rest of the tricks, be patient. I can always write another book; and by the time it's published, the first will be nothing but old-school.

Now, old-school can be defined in many ways—it depends who you're talking to and how old they are. The three techniques covered here can all be considered as coming from the elderly crowd,

because they've been around quite a while and somehow have remained secret. They are the acetylene smoke trick, water droplets, and print transfers. Of course, they don't amount to a hill of beans if you don't incorporate a little style with them. And that's where many people misfire. They spend so much time trying to discover the magic technique, they don't spend any on its presentation. I've tried to do these three justice here by incorporating them into cool tribal and traditional Maltese cross designs. (Come to think of it, I really should be careful about how I throw the term "old-school" around. I'm not that young myself anymore.)

Let's get painting before I get any older!

1. Next to black, my favorite surface to work on is metallic silver: House of Kolor BC-02, to be exact. With 1/8" 3M crepe tape, I laid out the tribal and Maltese cross designs freehand.

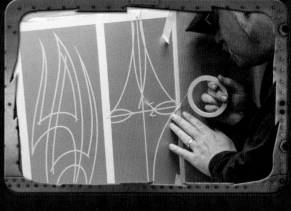

2. Nothing like getting carried away with a simple design! Well, cool techniques deserve a cool framework. In this case, instead of just masking off and painting, I began by using the tribals as negative elements in the design and painting the backgrounds. In the center piece, the tape width itself was important, since it would also be a negative part of the design. Wait—you'll see.

3. How often do you get to fire up a blowtorch for paintwork? Now, before you freak out, there was nothing flammable nearby, and I was ready with a fire extinguisher just in case.

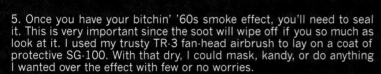

4. The trick with this technique is not to go overboard...whoops, too late, I'm using a blowtorch! Adjust the torch to go somewhat heavy on the acetylene for a sooty smoke. If you waft the flame near the design, the smoke will fall against the surface, transferring the smoke image in soot to the raw base coat. Too far away, and it won't work; too close, and you burn the sucker. Also be careful not to have the acetylene too high, or you'll have big dots of soot over everything. Luckily, they wipe off with pre-cleaner.

5. Once you have your bitchin' '60s smoke effect, you'll need to seal it. This is very important since the soot will wipe off if you so much as look at it. I used my trusty TR-3 fan-head airbrush to lay on a coat of protective SG-100. With that dry, I could mask, kandy, or do anything I wanted over the effect with few or no worries.

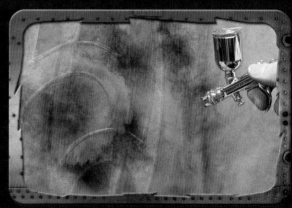

6. It still needed a little something, so I threw some Oriental Kandy over it. Ever wonder about the origin of the smoke effect? It seems pretty obvious. Someone was painting too near the welder, or the welder was working too close to the painter. Bam! Cool effect.

7. I never can get enough of that torch thing! After unmasking the tribal, it was time for more soot. That gave an intriguing look to the silver tribal design and added depth to the blue kandy by laying an effect over itself. Make sure the paint is thoroughly dry before doing this, and be sure to pull your hair back very securely. (I learned the hard way!)

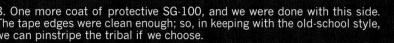

8. One more coat of protective SG-100, and we were done with this side. The tape edges were clean enough; so, in keeping with the old-school style, we can pinstripe the tribal if we choose.

9. It was looking a little flat, so I decided to airbrush a drop shadow. Instead of backmasking the tribal, try a freehand shield—it's a lot faster, and there's no risk of paint lifting. If you'd like to experiment with the smoke trick but don't have a blowtorch, try winding 3M tan tape into a wick and lighting it. Gives a nasty sooty smoke that works pretty well.

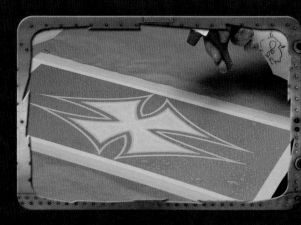

10. Turning to the water droplet trick, I started by spraying a little atomized water on the artwork. Now, I know you can't turn the side of your car on end to keep the droplets from sliding off, but if you add a bit of pharmaceutical-grade glycerin to the water, the droplets will hold on and bead up. Be sure to get a sprayer that really atomizes. That way, the more you spray, the bigger and more random the droplets will be. A bad sprayer will just make everything wet.

11. Once you have a droplet pattern you like, load up your airbrush with overreduced BC-26 white and hit the droplets from one side. The airbrush should be at a sharp angle. Then load up with BC-25 black and do the same thing from the opposite direction. That will mimic the look of light and shadow on the droplets. Wait for them to dry, and the paint will hold the 3-D effect.

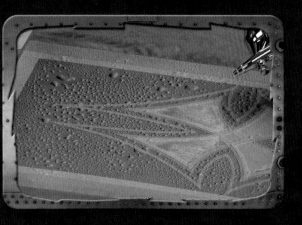

12. Of course, like the acetylene smoke, the water droplets are wimpy. A mere touch will wipe them away. So a little SG-100 is just what the doctor ordered for best adhesion. After that, I used transparent black for a drop shadow to enhance the effect. (Be sure to keep the light source in the same direction, or it will look weird.)

13. With the design unmasked, all that was needed was drop-shadows for a beveled-edge effect. The tip of the Artool *FH-1* freehand shield works great for these simple shadows, especially when the SG-100 is too fresh to mask on.

14. And now for print transferring. I'd already scanned a $100 bill and reversed it in Photoshop before printing. Don't use the prints for the transfer; copy them on a dry-toner copier and use the copies instead. With these cut out, I positioned them to see how they would look.

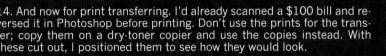

15. Now for the magic trick, which employs just a bit of Toner Release (i.e., toner cleaner). Apply it to the paper with a Q-Tip and the ink will be transferred, leaving the paper behind. This technique doesn't always work perfectly. It sometimes results in a dirty or broken transfer. When it does work, it's cool. If you can't find Toner Release, try "Oops" or another solvent-based cleaner. Test first on an inconspicoluos surface to make sure it works,

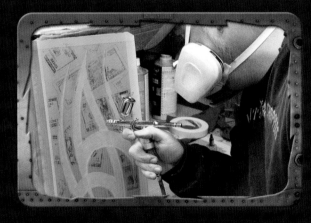

16. With the transfers done, I bathed the background in KK-09/SG-100 Kandy Organic Green. If you choose not to use kandy over your transfer, at least be sure to cover it with a protective layer of SG-100.

17. Before unmasking the design, I took advantage of the tape and added a little drop shadow using the same transparent black still sitting in the HP-CH Kustom airbrush.

18. Unmasked, the tribal needed just a little more love; i.e., drop shadow to create an overlap in the design. Remasking wasn't needed here, just my favorite *FH-1* shadow shield. If you don't have one, you're burning a lot of time!

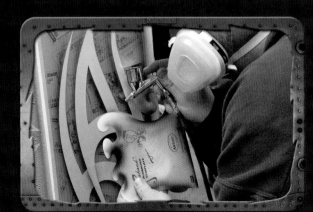

19. Well, there you have it: three old-school techniques showcased in one panel. Old as they are, they're definitely not tired. Personally, I love incorporating new techniques with classic ones. Digging up some of the more unusual, like these three, is always fun. It's important for kustom painters to balance the old and the new, in style as in technique. When you do, you create a hybrid that puts you a step ahead of the game.

Enjoy the game, and keep on old-schoolin'!

BLUE FIRE VETTE

WHAT KUSTOM PAINT BOOK WOULD BE COMPLETE WITHOUT A LITTLE REALISTIC BLUE FIRE?

In this chapter, I thought I'd also show you a variation on fire: blue flames. Done correctly, blue fire looks killer without dominating the entire vehicle. Realistic fire has been one of the hottest effects to hit the kustom community in years. It's been the flavor of the month for quite some time, though as with all popular effects, the fever for it has started to subside. I never was a fan of realistic fire as the sole element of a paint job. I've always combined it with graphics, used it in the background, or added airbrushed elements half-hidden within the flames. Another thing I like to do is to modify realistic fire colors to blend with the paint job. Giving the usual an unusual twist is a cool way to restoke the fires of creativity.

For this job, the client had a brand new Corvette in which he had just installed a Magnuson Supercharger kit. It required a new hood for clearance, so he brought the hood by our shop to be matched and painted. After realizing that his pearl blue Vette was going to be a 600-HP monster that looked stock, he decided to go with a little kustom paint. It was a toss-up between classic flames or realistic blue flames airbrushed to blend with his existing paint job. We did what we do for all our undecided clients—paint a comparison panel showing both effects. (While this takes extra time, it almost always guarantees a happy client.) After seeing both examples, he went with the realistic blue flames.

1. With the hood already matched, painted, and mounted, Jermaine sanded the clear on the Vette in preparation for the fire work. Notice that the back of the Vette behind the doors was masked off. To apply realistic fire over factory paint, we needed to reclear only the areas where the fire would be. Nonetheless, we buffed the entire car to be sure that the finish matched throughout.

2. Since fire would not be covering the front of the car, I wanted to create a visual balance between the bodylines of the Vette and the areas showing fire, such as the intake inlets on the sides. To make sure the design looked good from a distance, I took chalk and outlined the basic shape of fire on the car, then stepped back. The chalk, applied very lightly, was easily wiped off after the first application of paint.

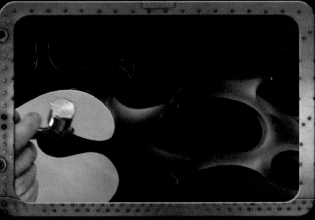

3. Using an *H* template, my favorite, I began creating the basic shapes of the fire with a transparent mixture of BC-26 White and a Kustom Eclipse CS. There are many excellent realistic fire templates on the market. The *H* template, which is fairly simple, works well for water, smoke, fish scales, and of course fire.

4. The key to using the *H* template is to border the design, then create the fire in the positive space left by the stencil. You can usually tell a negative stencil has been employed by the fact that it rarely looks like the element was painted with it.

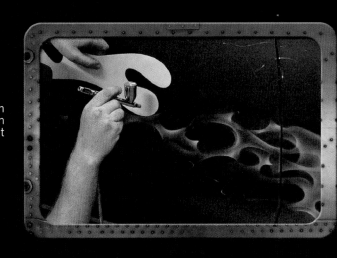

5. Once I'd filled in a chalk sketch, I continued back and forth between sections around the Vette until all the fire had been laid out and balanced. It's a mistake to try to complete one area in its entirety before proceeding to the next. Doing so endangers continuity, and you're likely to wind up with undesirable variations in quality. In the short run, you may feel like you're going faster, but in the long run, you'll spend more time repairing than painting.

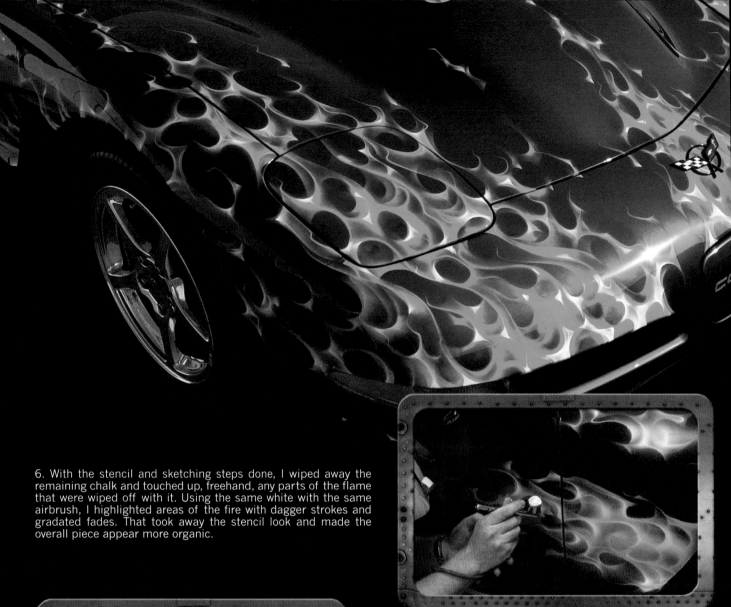

6. With the stencil and sketching steps done, I wiped away the remaining chalk and touched up, freehand, any parts of the flame that were wiped off with it. Using the same white with the same airbrush, I highlighted areas of the fire with dagger strokes and gradated fades. That took away the stencil look and made the overall piece appear more organic.

7. Now it was time to bring in some color. Using a TH-3 trigger airbrush and a mixture of KK-04 Oriental Blue with SG-100, I blended and faded in the kandy over the fire. The blending was a combination of working the fire into the background color and lightly tinting the brightest parts of the flame. The balance was delicate. Too much color and the flame would have lost depth, not enough and it wouldn't have blended properly with the background factory color.

8. To bring some of the factory color, or "inclusions," back into the fire, I mixed factory Pearl Blue with a little KK-17 Violette. That darkened the background inclusions, yet still blended with the original paint. I used the inside curve of the *H* stencil for the main inclusions. I could not freehand with this mix, since the pearl made it semi-opaque. Freehanding this color would have created lots of overspray, which would have killed the detail of my fire work.

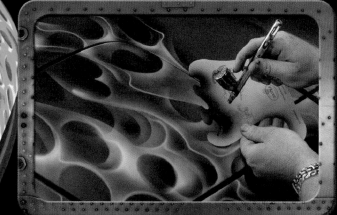

9. For the small detail work on the inclusions, I grabbed a few Artool *FH-1* and *FH-2* stencils. You will find that the majority o realistic fire work was originally done using French-curve-styl freehand shields like these. If you'd like to read up on early free hand shield work, get Radu Vero's book, *Airbrush: The Complet Studio Handbook.* Vero is the recognized originator of this style o airbrushing.

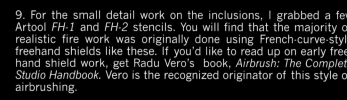

10. With the kandy and background work complete, I finished off the fire with freehand highlights. These very select highlights, done with transparent white, punched up the fire and gave the finished piece incredible depth after the clear was on. I was careful not to get overspray on my stencil work. Opaque white is the king of overspray!

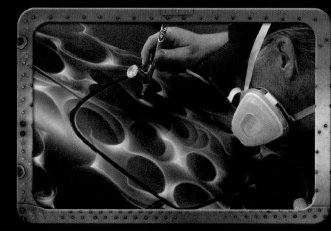

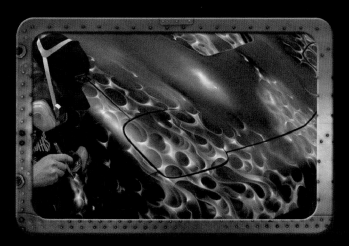

11. When the fire was finished, the client and I decided that the mirrors should be flamed as well. So, to make sure the fire on the mirrors matched those on the rest of the car, I airbrushed them using the finished car as a reference.

12. Last but not least, it was Dion's turn for the clear coat. Because the realistic fire here had been created with a low-volume airbrush, the whole car was easily cleared in a single session. Dion used an LPH-400LV spray gun and UFC-35 for the job. Three medium coats and a final flow coat did the trick. All that was left was to do was color-sand the entire car and buff it.

This Vette came out killer, the client was happy, and we had one more unique paint job to add to our portfolios. I always tell my students it's imperative that they learn to do realistic fire. Even if you don't enjoy it, learning and honing the techniques required to create realistic fire is much more important than the effect itself. It calls for the ultimate in freehand techniques, moveable masks, and negative/positive space airbrushing. Being able to create realistic fire helps prepare you for freeform mural work and even portraits. No improvement in your ability enhances only one aspect of your art; you'll see enhancement in every aspect. Plus, knowing how to create this popular effect will not only help make you a well-rounded airbrusher, it will help make you a

TRICKING OUT THE TRIM FOR A

One of our most regular clients at Kal Koncepts/Air Syndicate for the past decade has been Doug DeBerti. The original owner of Trenz Manufacturing, Doug currently runs DeBerti Designs and a number of other companies that specialize in building prototype vehicles for General Motors and Ford. You may have seen some of his vehicles at SEMA, such as the gigantic tank trucks in the Ford booth, or the tricked-out T-Bird and Mustang that won design awards in 2003-2004. One of his vehicles at SEMA 2003 was a Pro Street Custom Chevrolet S-10 that blew away everyone who visited the Trenz/Wings West booth.

Doug wanted us to do something simple on the S-10, maybe just a two-tone with a little graphic separating the colors. It's always a challenge to see what we can come up with, given a limited path. This vehicle was sponsored by GM, which is notoriously conservative about paint work; but I had an idea. Staying within the framework of a two-tone with a border graphic, I talked Doug into letting us play with some faux trim designs I'd been working on. I wanted to give the S-10 something a little radical, but not so much as to scare the GM guys. Doug wanted something that would grab attention and hold it. The problem with radical

graphics is that they usually appeal to a narrow audience whose attention, once grabbed, soon fades. The problem with conservative graphics is that, though their potential audience is large, they often fly under the radar of attention-grabbing, and the grabbing of attention is important at SEMA. We had our work cut out for us. In the end—keeping with his paint scheme of black, orange, silver, and purple—we gave Doug and GM something to be proud of.

When I talk about faux trim, I'm basically referring to simulated or imitation trim. Don't ask me how the French word got in there, but it did. Blame Martha Stewart! I wanted to create the classic look of a '57 Chevy. Suits at GM always like it when you bring up their past design successes, even more so when you incorporate them into something new—but with twists. Purple for one, and a couple of added chrome trim spears for another. What we wanted was a combination of the new and the old, a radical yet conservative appeal. Something that would beckon from a distance, yet call for extra analysis when you came closer. In sum, a paintjob that would both attract and hold your attention, be ye avant-garde or buttoned-up.

1. Starting with the S-10 already black, Dion and Nino sanded it with 600–grit sandpaper and prepped for graphics. With 3M blue fineline tape, I laid out the main trim graphic. The top of the truck was to remain black, while the bottom would be House of Kolor Tangelo Pearl. Here you see a bit of the front fender and kit already Tangelo. Meaning that I needed to keep the two-tone above the kit line in the front.

2. To begin the fun, Dion sprayed the base color of the graphic with BC-02 Orion Silver. Dion likes the LPH-400 for basecoats and for clear because of its even spray pattern and the high volume of material it transfers.

3. Using negative space design theory, Dion masked off the areas that would contain the faux-chrome spears I'd laid out earlier. By working in both the negative and the positive, we were able to save steps, materials and time in the final paintjob. Since this was for the SEMA show, we had all the time in the world. (You do realize I'm joking, don't you?)

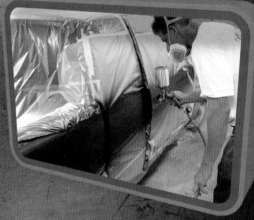

4. With the chrome areas masked off, Dion applied a kustom mix of his own. We aren't quite sure what it was, but I think it combined PBC-40 Violet Pearl with PBC-39 Passion Pearl, and who knows what else. It did look killer, though, and had lots of pearl.

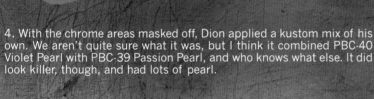

5. After letting the mystery violet basecoat cure for a few hours—I gave it a little extra time so as to guarantee no tape marks—we applied a coat of SG-100 as added insurance. To lay out the linear grooves that mimicked the machined siding of the '57 Chevy trim, I used 1/4" 3M tan crepe tape. It leaves little or no glue residue and pulls a straighter line than flexible vinyl. Remember, there are many tapes out there, and each is a different tool. Don't limit yourself by using only one type in your shop!

6. Lots of 1/4" tape later, it was time to spray. I mixed a violet kandy combining KK-17 Violet, and KK-04 Oriental Blue with SG-100. To give it serious punch, I blended in a mess of HoK Purple Haze Pearl, which simultaneously darkened the alternating grooves and made them flip-flop in the light. Oooooohhhh, aahhh!

7. The fun part (*not*) was pulling the tape. Grabbing it all together, I tried to remove it evenly, without allowing it to fall back on or lift the pearl. Not an easy trick. Always pull tape directly away from where it lies—and, if possible, away from the paint edge—to eliminate any possibility of peeling.

8. With the tape safely removed, I used a combination of BC-26 Basecoat Black and pure Violet Kandy without the pearl to lay in drop shadows beneath the still masked silver spear graphics. That gave them added depth and dimension. Always take advantage of existing masked areas to airbrush without danger of overspray.

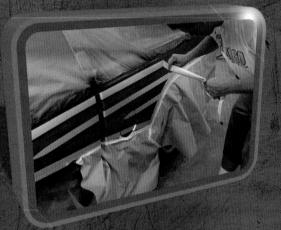

9. As Dion pulled the tape, the Orion Silver spears really popped. They would look killer once they were airbrushed as faux chrome trim. Whenever you have lots of tape laid over basecoat, be sure to apply light coats of SG-100 on the artwork as a safety precaution. That way, you can wipe it down later to get rid of any glue residue.

10. Splitting the trim down the middle, I backmasked the areas to be sprayed and airbrushed a subtle black horizon line the length of each spear. When airbrushing faux chrome trim this small, I like to keep it simple to promote realism. Get too many goodies going on the chrome and it starts looking like a cartoon.

11. Next, I backmasked the top half of the chrome in preparation for its white/reflective horizon line. Laying 1/8" tape down the middle to separate highlight from black horizon, I also over-reduced the white by ten percent to keep it from spitting. I wanted this white to be very fine and to gradate evenly.

12. The final airbrushed touch is always the highlights. A white highlight evenly placed along the center gives an added sense of realism. Just don't get too happy with highlights. Too many airbrushers don't know when to quit; their work ends up looking like a mall-airbrushed T-shirt! Now, please don't send me nasty letters about this comment. I'M KIDDING! Geez.

13. With my airbrushing done, we backmasked the entire affair, and Dion laid in the bottom color of the two-tone. Although Tangelo is considered an opaque, it does look quite a bit brighter over white. So, as you see, Dion sprayed the area with basecoat white first. The advantage of doing this after the graphic, instead of before, was that now the graphic and Tangelo butted up against each other and made less of an edge when cleared. Ah, hah! You're starting to get it!

14. Now it was Nino's turn to carefully remove the tape. We inspected the entire area for bleeds and blemishes, then wiped it down for clearcoating by Dion. Using HoK clear; we leveled the entire paintjob in preparation for striping. Many painters don't like to stripe faux trim, but I always think it looks rough and unfinished if I don't. I stripe with a similar color to clean the edge and pop it out.

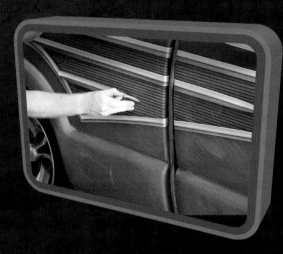

15. Starting with the top line—didn't want to drag my finger through a wet bottom line while doing the top, I used a mix of HoK Silver and White urethane striping paint. With my Mack #10 000 Sword Striper, I pulled some nice straight lines right on top of the graphic edge. The silver/white pinstripe simultaneously popped the graphic and highlighted the chrome trim.

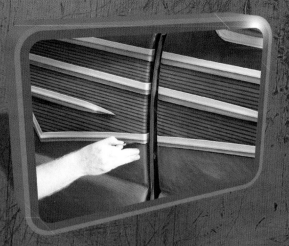

16. The second line was painted with black striping urethane. The black stood out against the drop shadow because the airbrushed drop shadow I'd done earlier was not pure black, remember? Otherwise, a truly black pinstripe would have gotten lost.

17. In the end, almost all good paint jobs are clearcoated. Here we used an LPH-400 spray gun loaded with UFC-35 HoK clear. We don't vary much from what works. Dion is the expert, and as long as he cranks out killer clear jobs, we don't question his choices. Plus, he keeps the guys at Iwata and House of Kolor happy.

Turns out the faux-trim graphic on the S-10 spread happiness all around. Doug was happy, GM was happy, and attendees at SEMA were happy. What more could you ask? We've used this faux trim effect many times since, and are continually modifying and playing with it for different effects. By the way, I came up with the idea for Doug's truck literally in the middle of a discussion with him about what to do for the paint job. I happened to glance at the side of his Mack tool box, which had a '57 Chevy motif. Sometimes you get the best ideas on the spur of the moment or when you least expect them. As painters, many of us have a bad habit of straining to come up with something original. It's like waiting for a pot to boil. Actually it's worse: if you wait for a pot to boil, eventually it will. If you sit down with pad and paper, creativity may skid to a halt. As John Lennon remarked, "Life is what happens to you while you're busy making other plans." Well, sometimes kustom paint creativity is what happens to you when you're not trying too hard to be creative.

Other Examples !!!

FLAMIN' OUT A KILLER SKULL

From the Artool *Horror of Skullmaster* Stencil Series

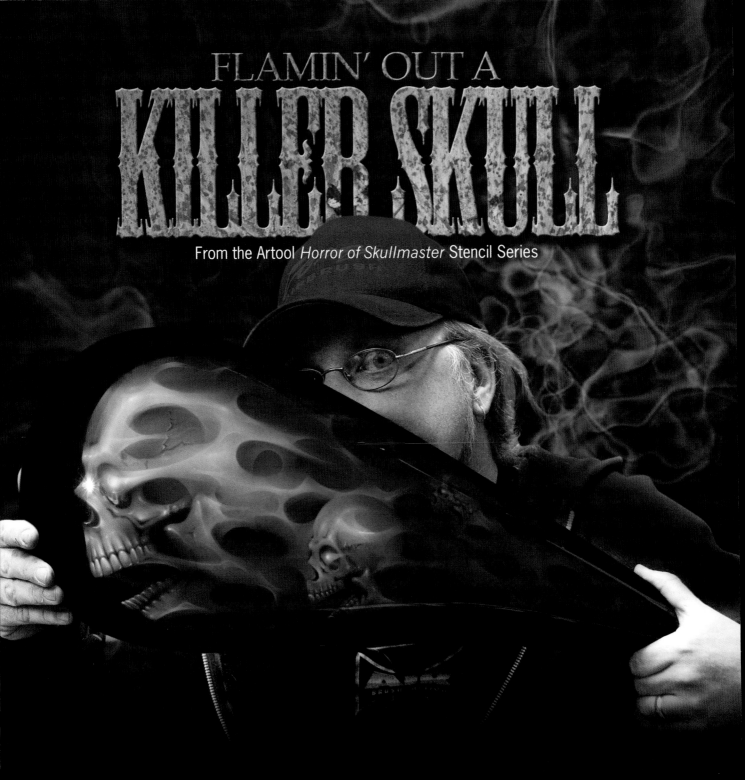

In this chapter, I'll demonstrate three different techniques: stenciling, freehand airbrushing, and realistic fire, all tied seamlessly together in one design. I'll paint on one of Coast Airbrush's fiberglass tank blanks, which make the perfect canvas for a custom paint job and are also light enough to hang on the wall for display.

The stencil for the skull mural was one of the first of my designs to come with both a positive and a negative sheet, affording complete control over all aspects of the design. The *Horror of Skullmaster* was also the first time I'd gone for a more anatomically correct skull. With all the stylizing I'd been doing over the years, it was about time. Unfortunately, too many artists view stencils as appropriate only for beginners or cheaters. Truth is, stencils are just another tool. Certainly, if you can only airbrush using a stencil, you're no better than a remedial airbrush artist. But if you paint an entire car with 1,000 skulls and do them all freehand, you're probably an idiot. My point is, right tool for the right job. Use stencils when you need them.

1. Coast Airbrush's tank blanks come already gelcoated. I first sanded the gelcoat with 220-grit sandpaper, then primed with base-coat black and clear-coated with UC-35 House of Kolor clear. Artwork always comes out nicer when applied over sanded clear. Here you see the two stencils for the profile skull in both negative and positive form.

2. Using tape to hold down the stencil and prevent overspray, I lightly sprayed SG-101 Lemon Yellow for the base color. I emphasized the outside edge and details of the stencil, leaving the center alone until later. The center area is so big, it's better to spray it with the stencil off because using the stencil would get overspray on everything, when spraying from a distance.

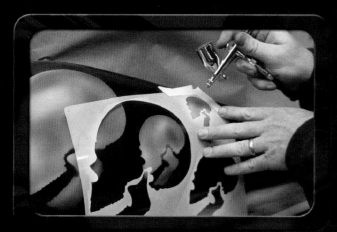

3. Taking advantage of everything the stencil has to offer, I threw in a few profile skulls of different sizes, aiming to use the realistic fire effect to tie the overall design together. With the jaws in the open position, you can always mask them off in the stencil, then reposition them any way you want. Cool, no?

4. With the yellow sprayed in the negative, I turned to the positive stencil to lay in the details with the same yellow. Normally I would have used a darker color for the details, but don't forget that these skulls are on fire! Note that Artool gives you four registration marks at the corners to line up their designs easily. These work great when you use the negative and positive stencils in conjunction with each other.

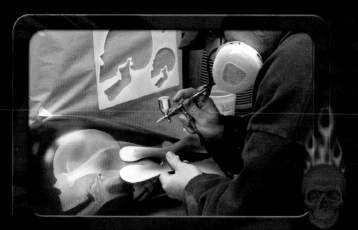

5. Using one of my *H* stencils. I started bringing in the realistic fire effect to connect the separate skull elements of the design. This stencil let me bring in long, sweeping flames, yet also tie in the tight radius of the flame licks. The trick with all realistic fire is to keep the flames random. Funny thing about realistic fire: the best versions I've done used stencils that looked nothing like fire. Hmmm.

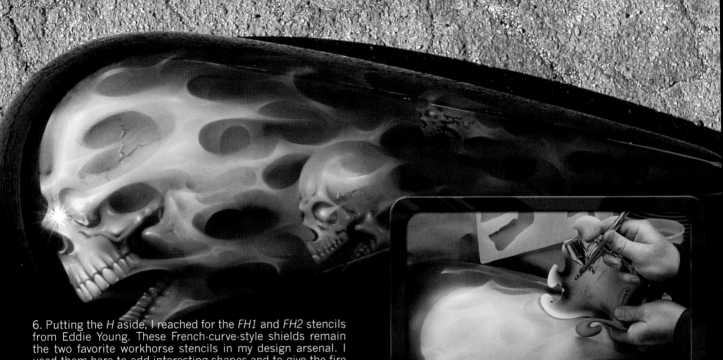

6. Putting the *H* aside, I reached for the *FH1* and *FH2* stencils from Eddie Young. These French-curve-style shields remain the two favorite workhorse stencils in my design arsenal. I used them here to add interesting shapes and to give the fire a bit more chaos.

7. With the yellow sketching completed, I mixed separate batches of KK-08 Tangerine and KK-11 Kandy Apple Red. (Be sure to mix them only 20 percent by volume to the SG-100 intercoat clear before reducing.) These kandy base coats were then layered over the yellow to give added color and intriguing depth to my fire.

8. Keeping tangerine in the gun, I added some KK-17 Violette Kandy and a bit more intercoat clear. These gave a nice reddish-brown that allowed me to darken details without killing the colors with black. Even when painting a mural over black, I rarely use black; colors are so much cleaner to darken with. The positive stencil let me bring back details that disappeared with the airbrushing. Best part about stencils: when your design changes, they never do. They're always there to fall back on.

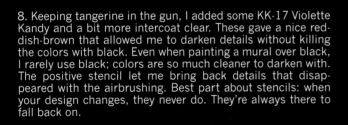

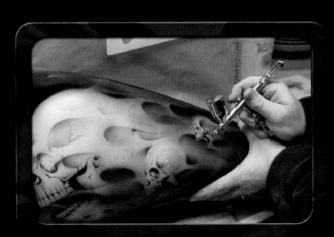

9. With the same Violette/Tangerine Kandy mix in the gun, I used the Iwata Eclipse CS Kustom airbrush to detail the skulls. You want to connect and soften all the stencil lines so that the final image doesn't look like a stencil. The aim in stencil work is for the final result to look freehand. That's important for any artist who wants to work smarter, not harder.

10. I switched back to Kandy Apple Red to blend more color into the flames. This also softened the tight details and eliminated any leftover violet that may have been showing through. Health tip: even when working on small projects, don't forget to wear a good dual-cartridge active charcoal respirator.

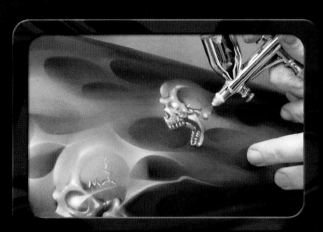

11. Switching colors and guns, I returned to SG-101 Lemon Yellow and my detail airbrush, the HP-CH Kustom. I can get killer detail with this airbrush and also dial the air pressure right at the gun to eliminate spitting. Initially, the yellow killed depth with opaque overspray, but in the long run it enhanced the overlapping fire look I was going for.

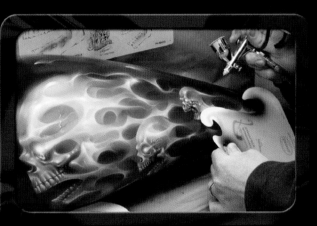

12. Along with a little freehanding, I brought the stencil back in, too. Together, they let me create those killer soft yet sharp edges necessary for showing the anatomy of a flame. The absence of the air cap on the airbrush enables me to see if it's going to spit from paint buildup on the needle and lets me get closer to the surface for better detail. Otherwise, I keep the cap on to protect the needle.

13. To knock down some of the yellow overspray and really bring back the brightness and rich color of the fire, I airbrushed a mixture of KK-12 Pagan Gold and SG-100. This color is one of my favorites for brightening a mural. If you want something less orange, you can also go with Spanish Gold Kandy. Or, if you want a green tint, as in lime-green flames, Limegold Kandy is killer. Any kandy used properly will eliminate the clouding of overspray and liven up your mural.

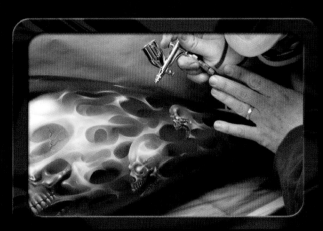

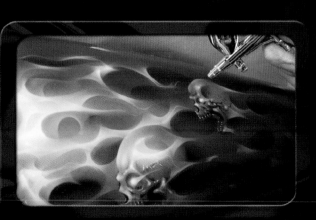

14. The last highlights are always the final touch. I added them here with an overly reduced mix of SG-101 Lemon Yellow and just a drop of white. Use this mix sparingly because it can create lots of overspray and undo all your hard work with the kandy. I often use this mix to create smoke, too, since the white dominates.

The *Horror of Skullmaster* stencils, with their designs of varied sizes, are perfect for bikes and cars. They're what I like to call "rendering stencils," acting as great sketching tools, freeing your style and creativity for whatever your imagination can come up with. Remember that a stencil is only a tool; your use of it must reflect your own ability and creativity. It can speed your work and enable you to achieve better continuity in your designs, but it can't replace freehand airbrushing. That's why I always incorporate additional effects and freehand work in my demonstrations of stencils. I hope you enjoy using them as much as I enjoy making them.

Paint to live, live to paint...sometimes with stencils!

FAUX FINISHED

KUSTOM PAINTING A SET OF HEADLIGHTS FOR A
TRICKED OUT FUNNY CAR

The most requested kustom treatment for race cars or bikes today is not flames, graphics, or even lettering, but faux painted headlights, taillights, and grills, and basically in that order. Faux (pronounced "foe," it means "imitation") finishing is not just for interior wall murals or exterior wall treatments. It can take the form of wood grain on the sides of a car, an airbrushed vent that's not really there, chrome trim, water droplets, bullet holes, or the aforementioned headlights. The trick lies in the balance between sharp detail and what's not in focus, trying to mimic reality, and in reality not everything is in focus—so you need to translate that balance into your faux-finish work. Probably the best tool for faux finishing is a good reference, such as a photograph or even an accurate memory of how something looks. Give your viewers just enough information for their eyes to take in, and their brains will do the rest.

In this chapter, I describe faux-finish work on a funny car we painted for Steve Romanazzi a few years back. Any fiberglass race car is fun to work on because such a variety of appliances and so much of the trim have to be faked to minimize weight and cost. The only drawback is the static electricity ever-present in a fiberglass or carbon-fiber shell. Static electricity can wreak serious havoc when you're attempting a clean fade or blend. Think you can just wipe it away with a dry cloth? Think again. Even a slight movement of air can cause static electricity. Instead, try grounding the body with a set of jumper cables attached to the booth. A chain draped over the frame and left to lie on the ground works, too. And keep a water-dampened towel handy.

The body here happened to be a stretched retro version of a '57 Chevy Bel Air. The work needed on this kustom was a heck of a lot more than a couple of headlights. I include here a few of the sundry other items we painted, but I'll focus mainly on the headlights and taillights.

1. We started with the fiberglass body already single-staged in black and sanded. Using blue fine-line tape, I laid out the chrome bumpers, headlight rings, and trim. While I originally intended to demonstrate only the technique for headlights, I quickly realized I couldn't show just a headlight without the surrounding trim. Also, if you're wondering why I used vinyl tape for this job, it was because I would be wiping it down a lot with a damp towel to combat the static electricity; I needed tape more waterproof than crepe.

2. After masking off the line work, I base-coated the masked areas with a 50/50 mix of Orion Silver and Basecoat White. That gave me a good base for the chrome and stainless. After letting the silver/white cure for an hour, I masked off the center bar and logo in the grill area. Transfer tape might have worked, but remember the wiping down with a damp towel? Transfer tape is highly susceptible to water damage.

3. For the proper chrome cast, I fogged a mixture of KK-04/SG-100 Oriental Blue Kandy over the silver/white areas. A little blue on the pure white headlight was also needed to mimic the natural reflection of the sky on the headlight lens. The biggest mistake you can make on faux chrome is to go nuts with the blue. Too much, and your chrome and headlights will look cartoony.

4. With the blue done, it was time to render the horizon line reflection with BC-25 Black with an Iwata Eclipse CS airbrush. Reference photos came in handy during this step, since reflections on a compound curved surface rarely make sense. This is also a step you don't want to overdo. Too much horizon or too much black, and you're back to the cartoony thing.

5. Using 1/8" crepe tape, I backmasked areas where I wanted beveled or highlighted edges to show up. Side-vent trim pieces have these sorts of beveled edges. Combining masked painting with freehand airbrushing gives a realistic reflective look to chrome. Check out the reflection of the headlight that I airbrushed on the chrome right below the lens. You want this to look real, not rendered.

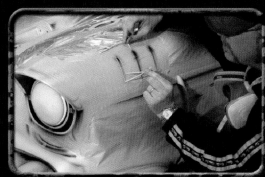

6. While the overall color and reflective properties of chrome are important, details are what truly define a good faux finish. With 1/8" tape, I rendered the exhaust resonators on the back bumper with transparent black. To make the black transparent, I added more reducer to the BC-25 and a little SG-100 to keep the paint from becoming binder-poor.

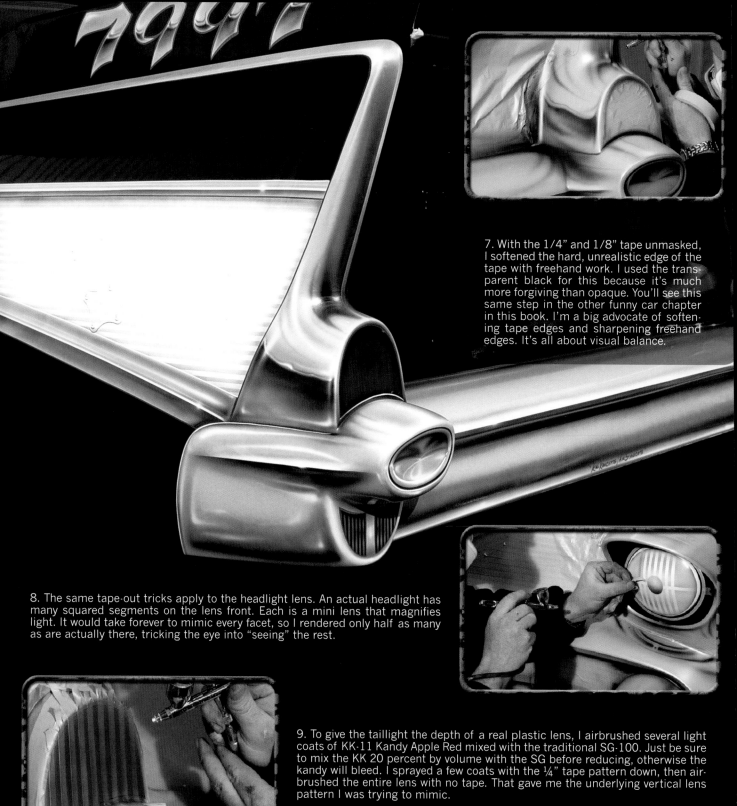

7. With the 1/4" and 1/8" tape unmasked, I softened the hard, unrealistic edge of the tape with freehand work. I used the transparent black for this because it's much more forgiving than opaque. You'll see this same step in the other funny car chapter in this book. I'm a big advocate of softening tape edges and sharpening freehand edges. It's all about visual balance.

8. The same tape-out tricks apply to the headlight lens. An actual headlight has many squared segments on the lens front. Each is a mini lens that magnifies light. It would take forever to mimic every facet, so I rendered only half as many as are actually there, tricking the eye into "seeing" the rest.

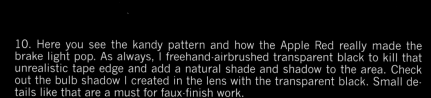

9. To give the taillight the depth of a real plastic lens, I airbrushed several light coats of KK-11 Kandy Apple Red mixed with the traditional SG-100. Just be sure to mix the KK 20 percent by volume with the SG before reducing, otherwise the kandy will bleed. I sprayed a few coats with the ¼" tape pattern down, then airbrushed the entire lens with no tape. That gave me the underlying vertical lens pattern I was trying to mimic.

10. Here you see the kandy pattern and how the Apple Red really made the brake light pop. As always, I freehand-airbrushed transparent black to kill that unrealistic tape edge and add a natural shade and shadow to the area. Check out the bulb shadow I created in the lens with the transparent black. Small details like that are a must for faux-finish work.

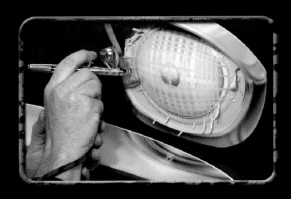

11. Back to the headlights, I continued to use my tape-out trick to create a realistic lens pattern with a combination of white and transparent black. Another freehand trick added the reflection of the headlight on the chrome bar beneath. I saw this in a photograph of an actual '57 Chevy front end. Remember what I said about using reference photos? They really help with detail accuracy.

12. Again, a little freehand airbrush work softened those tape edges. Don't worry about making a mistake when freehanding. You can always come back with tape and fix anything. Note how I used white and dark-gray pinstriping to outline and emphasize the highlighted edges on all chrome trim.

13. Here are some of the other trim goodies I did on this funny car. While most of the fuel injection and side trim was detailed with lettering quills and striping brushes, it was the balance between airbrushing and brushwork that gave the final image its realistic 3-D look.

14. The final step in good kustom work is the clear coat, and this job was no exception. Dion threw on a few good wet coats of UFC-19. Today, he'd be using UFC-35. You'll probably find that the majority of products mentioned in this book will be modified within a few years of publication. Regardless, the techniques will remain valid.

There you have it—classic use of faux finishing to give a fiberglass funny car the look of a much heavier vehicle. While you may not find yourself doing as much chrome trim or grill work in your kustom paint career, I can almost guarantee you'll be called on more than a few times to crank out realistic headlights or taillights. When people ask me if a vinyl sticker wouldn't be faster, I always answer that I can do a set of headlights and taillights easily within an hour. If all headlights were the same shape and design, then, yes, a sticker would probably be more viable for a race car that's always being worked on or repaired.

I never try to talk people out of using vinyl when appropriate. Kustom paint will always be called for, however, when quality and originality outweigh budget and quantity.

Faux on!

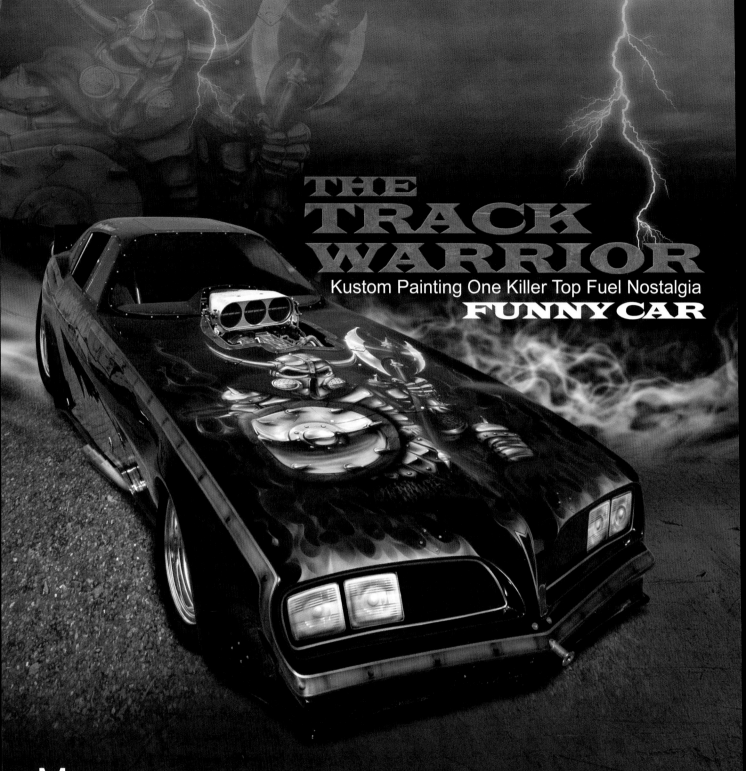

THE TRACK WARRIOR

Kustom Painting One Killer Top Fuel Nostalgia
FUNNY CAR

Most kustomizers can cite a part of the racing industry as being influential in their career, and I'm no different. My favorite racing events when growing up were the quarter-mile events at the world-famous Famoso Raceway, in Bakersfield, California. Out of all the quarter-mile monsters, the ones I always waited for and built models of were the funny cars. They were just the coolest looking things out there. All muscle, yet always sporting a bitchin' paint job.

Steve Romanazzi is one of the rare breeds in the industry who owns, builds, and drives the cars. You'll recognize one of the first

funny cars that we painted for him in another chapter in this book—*The Faux Headlight* chapter. Steve approached us with this raw Pontiac body that he had just received from the shop and wanted a paint job that was reminiscent of the old school airbrushed customs that were roaming the NHRA circuit back in the early 1970s. Because the name of his funny car was the *Warrior*, and his logo was a stylized Viking warrior, putting a huge kustom Viking mural on the hood was not just an option, it was an imperative! After a few phone calls, we got House of Kolor on board as a paint sponsor, and we were ready to go.

1. With the body being fresh from the mold and covered with mods and ugly reinforcing glass, Dion and Lambie wasted no time taking down the gelcoat and raw glass repair with a combination of 80- and 220-grit sandpaper on a DA sander. With the gelcoat sanded, and the bodywork taken care of, the entire body was primered with a coat of catalyzed polyester primer/sealer. In the pic, you can barely make out a stippled black texture. This is a guide coat of black paint that is stippled over the entire body, so when blocking it out, you will see the high and low spots. This is the only way to get a body straight, and for black, this is a must!

2. After the bodywork was completed, and with everything lying flat, Dion sprayed the entire body with a nice coat of BC-25 HoK basecoat black. Normally we would immediately clearcoat the basecoat, then sand in preparation for the graphics. In this case, we applied a two-tone effect, and then we clearcoated.

3. This may be hard to see, but I already sketched the logo, "Warrior," on the sides of the car, on the split line for the two-tone. For this paint job, I wanted the name to actually be part of the separating graphic. With the name drawn out, I used ¼" 3M crepe tape to mask off the top edge of the logo, and continued the two-tone line down the car.

4. To save steps, I jumped ahead of Dion spraying the two-tone. It was sprayed using the HoK MBC-01 Coarse Black Diamonds. This is a killer metallic pearl that when cleared literally looks like black metalflake. We cleared the entire vehicle at this stage to lock in the bodywork and gave ourselves a good base for the graphics and murals to go on. After sanding the cleared two-tone with 600-grit sandpaper, I masked off the rest of the logo, along with the separating graphic, in prep for the next color.

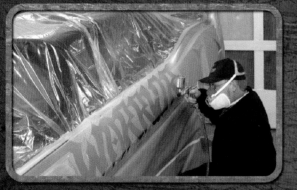

5. I wanted this graphic to look like a riveted strap of metal surrounding the body to reinforce the whole war-wagon Viking theme. To start this effect, I sprayed a nice coat of HoK MC-01 Kosmic Krome Aluminum effect with the LPH-50 touchup gun. Even with the graphic sanded, you can see how reflective this aluminum paint can be. Made of pure 6061 T-6 aluminum, this graphic doesn't just look metallic, it now is!

6. After scuffing the aluminum even more (hey, I wanted this sucker to look worn!), I grabbed my ¼" tape again and proceeded to inlay the tape all along the graphic and logo. This would give me a masked bevel area all around the inside edge of the original mask. Very easy yet effective technique, as you will see.

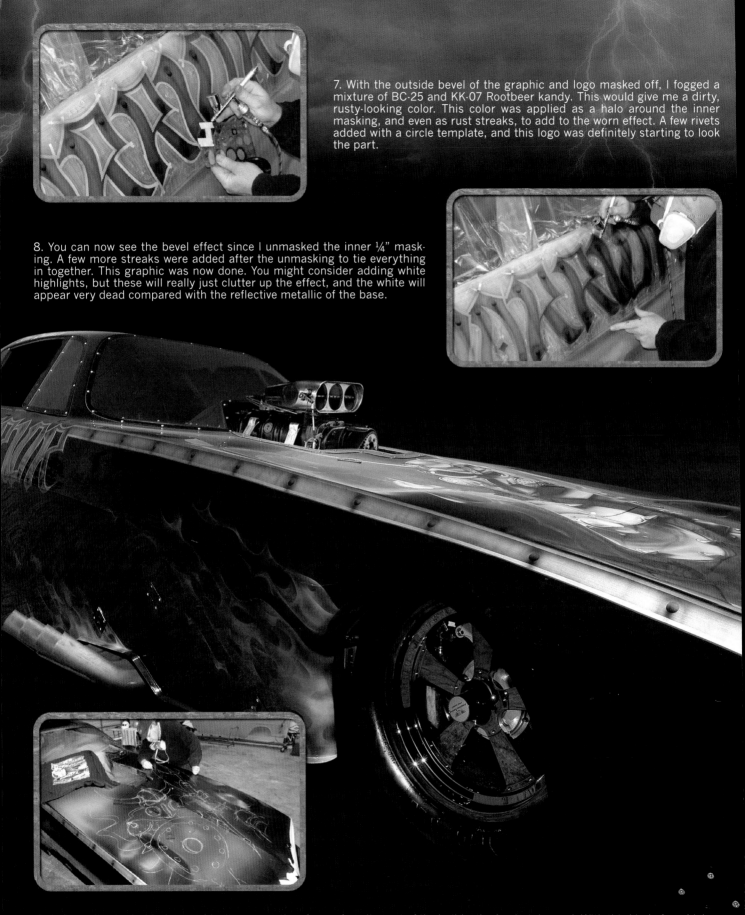

7. With the outside bevel of the graphic and logo masked off, I fogged a mixture of BC-25 and KK-07 Rootbeer kandy. This would give me a dirty, rusty-looking color. This color was applied as a halo around the inner masking, and even as rust streaks, to add to the worn effect. A few rivets added with a circle template, and this logo was definitely starting to look the part.

8. You can now see the bevel effect since I unmasked the inner ¼" masking. A few more streaks were added after the unmasking to tie everything in together. This graphic was now done. You might consider adding white highlights, but these will really just clutter up the effect, and the white will appear very dead compared with the reflective metallic of the base.

9. As I was finished with the graphic, it was now time for my favorite part of the build—the freehand mural. With this kind of a vehicle, and the angle I was working at, it was almost impossible to predraw, or project, the image onto the surface. This is when freehand sketching becomes necessary. Using just a piece of chalk and the Kenny Youngblood T-shirt design that Steve gave me as a reference, I began laying in the monster. The chalk was great because if I made a mistake, a nice damp rag made all the evil go away!

10. I proceeded the same way as with most of my freehand murals. When the chalk design was finished, it was time for the BC-26 white. I sketched the entire design, tracing my chalk sketch, and when the outline was done, I wiped all the chalk off and began the shading, rendering still using the white. This was one of those designs where you have to move back and forth a lot to see if you're getting the right perspective. You can easily work yourself into a corner if you stay too close for too long!

11. It may look like I was spending a lot of time on this white step. You would be right. It's the single most important step since it's the base and foundation for all your kandies and details to come. And because you're working with a fiberglass body, it's important to constantly wipe down with a damp towel to get rid of overspray and remove static charge.

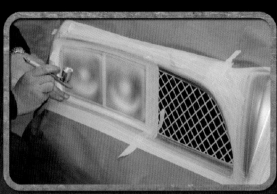

12. Before applying the next color, I like to use the white on any other areas of the car that might need it. In this case, the headlights. Hey, guess what? You get another faux headlight and grill demo for free! Using the masking to keep the black where I wanted it, and basing everything else in white, I started rendering the headlights and grill with the Eclipse CS airbrush.

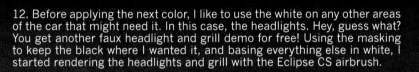

13. Even the Pontiac logo got some love in this paint job. Basing it first with the same MC-01 Kosmic Aluminum, I sprayed Kandy Apple Red over the silver with 1/8" tape reliefs to mimic the original red plastic laminated logo.

14. A little black layered over the white gave the final headlight some depth and eliminated any of the white overspray. These were the base colors before we came back in with the masking tape.

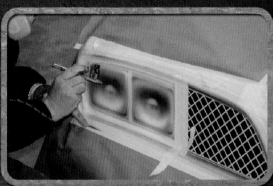

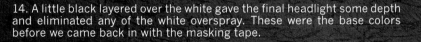

15. With the 1/8" and 3/4" tape, I created the reflective lens patterns, then sprayed white back over them. After unmasking, a little more white sprayed in softened up the tape edges and really punched out the headlight effect.

16. The Kosmic Aluminum really gave the grill a nice realistic effect. All that was left was a little pinstripe outline, and we were done with the front end. Nice thing about using just white or black for the headlights is that any touchups are easily done. This is something to consider when painting the front end of something that goes this fast.

17. Bored of working on grills and headlights, I returned to the mural. With the white finished, I tinted all of the metal areas with a nice mixture of KK-04 Oriental Blue and SG-100. This was just enough to give a chrome effect and not make everything look day-glo blue.

18. Time to start coming in with more colors. First, I mixed a combination of Euro Red and Blue Blood Red, then painted in all the cape areas. While I normally come in with transparents over my white, I really wanted the red to punch out and not go too black, so I went to my opaques.

19. After laying in some KK-07 Rootbeer kandy over the wooden areas and helmet horns, I started airbrushing the details with transparent black. The nice thing about airbrushing a mural this size is that I can do the entire piece with the same airbrush. The Kustom CS works for all the large areas and the details.

20. What better way to finish off a killer Viking mural on a funny car than with a little realistic fire. Since I was going to do this realistic fire all with kandies, I started it off with basecoat white using the H stencil and, you guessed it, Eclipse CS airbrush.

21. With the white completed on the fire, it was time for the color again. For the volume of kandy I needed for the flames, I switched to the TH-3 airbrush. This is probably the highest-volume airbrush out there, and with the fan-pattern head, I could really get the kandy to lay down nicely. In this case, I based the white with kandy Pagan Gold KK-12/SG-100. Don't worry about the overspray; it'll look like reflections of the fire on the background of the mural.

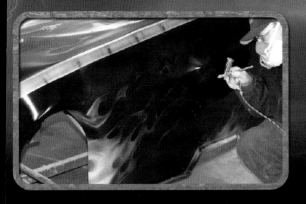

22. A little bit of KK-08 Tangerine and some KK-11 Kandy Apple Red, and our fire was finished. Normally I would come back in with a little lemon yellow for the highlights, but I liked the dark look I ended up with here.

23. Taking a little break from airbrushing, I finished the pinstriping with a mixture of Cardinal Red and Roman Red using a Mack 10 000 sword striper. This blood red really made the logo and metal strap graphic punch out.

24. The last few hours of any paint job are normally spent running around the vehicle and touching up any and all goof-ups, oversprays, and tape bleeds. The great thing about working over a black paint job is that you can easily blend just about any problem back to being black. I just had to be careful over the black diamonds with the pure black.

25. The last little touch is the final highlights. Using some overreduced white, I punched out the small highlights in the chrome and throughout the entire mural. Final highlights are one of those things that can really create a nice finish, but if overdone, will kill your mural.

26. With all of the artwork done, Dion hit the body with three good wet coats of UFC-35 clear. A good trick to keeping the static down when clearing is to run a ground wire from the body to the booth and keep the floor wetted down. Otherwise you can get some seriously weird patterns forming in the clear when drying.

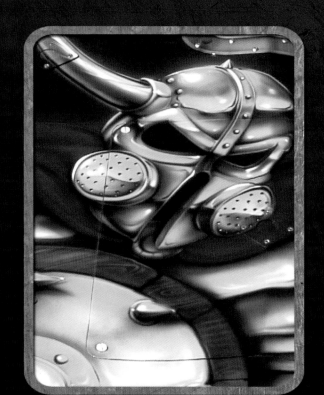

After a good night of curing, a little sanding and buffing, this body was ready to be put on the car and taken to the track. One of the coolest things about funny cars is that the builders can take the car and work on the setup and motor without us being stressed about how long we have to work on the paint job. They just leave us the body, and we roll it around on a dolly and paint it. Granted, there are still pretty tight deadlines whenever you're dealing with a racing series.

In this case, if you were wondering, we had 10 days to prep, paint, and clear this bad boy. Luckily for us, the only lettering Steve really wanted was the "Warrior" name. Funny cars are known for their sponsors, and in many cases I will spend a few days just painting them. In this case Steve, being the owner, kinda kept the sponsors to a minimum.

Well, hope you dig the paint job. While I don't get the opportunity to paint funny cars every week (bummer), they're a blast, and they give you a chance to paint something that's truly insane. And it's not just the paint job—pretty much anybody that will strap himself in and barrel down the track at over 200 miles per hour is not in the normal category!

STEAMPUNK GUITAR

CREATING A NEO-VICTORIAN, RETRO-TECHNICAL TONAL RENDERING CHORD CONTRAPTION

I was a fan of steampunk long before it acquired its current moniker. Whether it be the inventions of Crackitus Potts in *Chitty Chitty Bang Bang*, or of Captain Nemo in *20,000 Leagues Under the Sea*, it seems I've always loved the clunk of vintage technology and the art that represents it. And I've not been alone. Even today, technological concepts that go back as far as Jules Verne and H. G. Wells continue to fascinate many a science fiction author and fantasy artist.

For several years now, I've been airbrushing steampunk into fine art as well as motorcycles and kustom graphics. So when Mike Kotzen of Fender Musical Instruments Corporation and its Jackson Guitars subsidiary called and told me I had free rein on a new design for the Jackson custom shop, I knew exactly what I wanted to paint: an electric guitar manufactured in the 1890s and run on DC current from the local Tesla power plant.

The steampunk of today is based on the artisan need for embellishment that sprang from 19th and early 20th century industrialism—you know, back when a radio was art furniture and not just a disosable earpiece made of plastic. To create the effect accurately, you must embrace a number of faux finish techniques —bronze, wood, brass gears, marble, leather, tweed grills, porcelin knobs, etc. So with these concepts in mind, I set about making a current model Jackson guitar look more than a hundred years old.

1. I started with a stock Jackson Warrior "neck-through" guitar body. The guitars are shipped to me from Fender/Jackson already prepped, painted in black lacquer, and sprayed with P-Tex polyester resin as a final coat. I discovered that while P-Tex does not like basecoat urethanes, it does adhere to sanded urethane clear even better than traditional lacquers. So when I finish a guitar, it has a light, leveling coat of UFC-35 clear that may be re-sanded for the final coat. Here, I was masking off the areas that were to remain black for the moment.

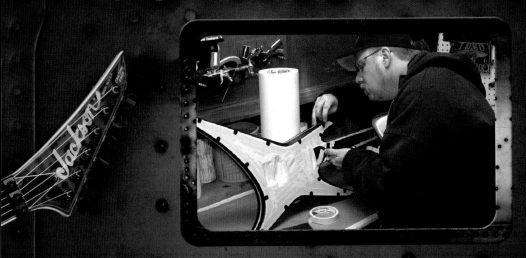

2. I do most of my masking with regular 3M automotive #233 masking tape. That's because it sticks the best in this situation, is the most durable, and leaves few if any tape marks. I also need tape that can stay on a job for a number of days, and masking tape fills that bill. The tabs I cut into the masking tape were to be faux bronze with screws added later on. When masking a job like this, visualize the finished guitar, then sequence the steps in your head to make it happen.

3. With the black areas masked, I sprayed the rest of the body using House of Kolor's MC-04 Gold Kosmic Krome. This unique paint is made of golden anodized aluminum particles. When sprayed, it looks literally like metal, with no discernable grain. What you must be careful about are sanding scratches. The pigment in MC paints is so fine that it amplifies the slightest imperfection. For a streak-free coat, I sprayed the Kosmic Gold using a TH-3 spray gun with the fan head.

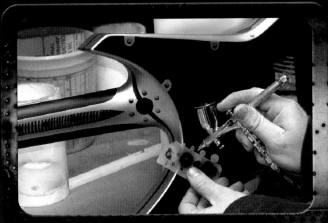

4. This photo shows the dramatic contrast between the Kosmic Gold and the black lacquer. Using a set of Scott MacKay's business-card-size stencils, I added screw heads, which started out merely as shadowed rivets. If you don't have one of these handy little stencils, use any small-circle template. The black I sprayed was standard BC-25, with twice the reducer added to make it weak or transparent.

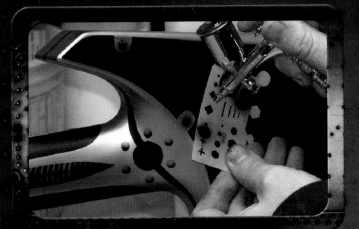

5. With another stencil from Scott's set, I airbrushed a *Phillips* screw head pattern, completing the effect. Yes, I do use stencils other than my own. I strongly encourage experimentation with the stencils of other artists, as well as with those you make yourself. Balance freehand creativity with practical aspects of time-saving so that you can base decisions on what actually looks best, rather than on conventional wisdom. (Soap box now safely tucked away). That said, keep an eye out for my new Artool *Steampunk* stencils. Slated to come out before this book hits the shelves, they offer many additional elements of the SP style and reflect the substantial number and variety of SP jobs I've done.

6. I wanted to bring color into this piece besides the metallics I'd just sprayed. With steampunk, you always want to think retro, vintage, antique, or classic. Going with a metallic olive drab seemed right to me; no bright obnoxious colors here. I created the color by combining HoK's PBC38 Limetime Pearl with Pagan Gold and Root Beer KK Kandy. Amazing what a few complementary kandies can do to a bright, vibrant, green pearl! Olive drab contrasted well with the metallics without detracting from the overall look.

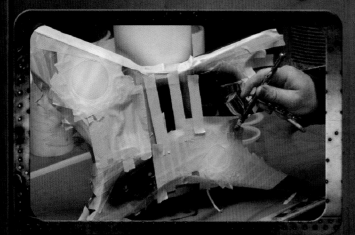

7. What would a SP design be without a few old-fashioned gauges? The olive drab pearl area was supposed to look like a painted dash piece, bolted on to cover some of the underlying technology. I'd taken the gauges into consideration when laying out the panels. Using BC-26 at full strength, I sprayed a pure white round lens.

8. Shifting gears, I grabbed the lettering quill and started adding gauge details using HoK striping red and black. An airbrushed screw head, along with transparent shading and shadowing, really finished off the gauge nicely, giving it killer depth. At this point, I might have been tempted to computer-cut a few numbers or gauge gizmos, but the freehand work mimicked the old-time, hand-painted gauges better. (In some cases, computer cutting actually can slow down a one-off custom).

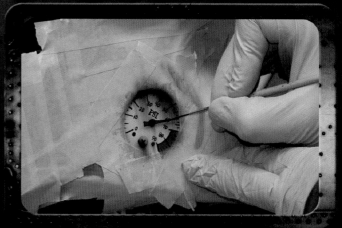

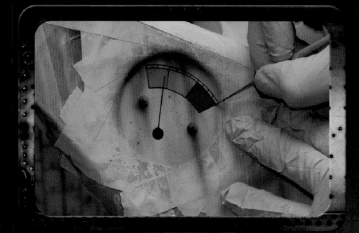

9. As a Guitar Hero fan, I couldn't resist painting a steampunk version of an applause meter. With a few airbrush streaks and some stippling, this gauge was properly aged to match the rest of the vintage-looking contraption. Also, note that the shadow on the upper side of the gauge gives the illusion of depth to the glass gauge face. Photographs or actual gauges in your shop can act as great reference for this step.

10. After masking off the border, the green panel, and the gauges, it was time to airbrush some of the background gears and other mechanisms. Using a combination of the original *Gearhead* stencil from the FX series and the new *Sraeg* (gears spelled backwards) negative stencil, I filled in the technical gaps using MC-03 Kosmic Krome Bronze effect. Together with transparent black freehand work, stippling, and shading, this filled up the background in no time at all. Half-hidden gears and underlying clockwork are what give steampunk its mystical allure.

11. This close-up of work done with the *Sraeg* stencil also shows some of the other clockwork airbrushing that filled in the blanks. The same shadows I airbrushed in the gauges I repeated here to create depth. With everything masked off, take care to keep track of your light source. If you don't, the drop shadows will look goofy.

12. Going back and forth with black and Kosmic Bronze, I continued to layer in details, adding depth to the background. White highlights here would have looked terrible because of the metallic bronze background. So if I'd gotten an area too dark I would've had to come back in with the Bronze or Gold. It's important to use a stencil or tape when re-highlighting, otherwise overspray will kill the detail.

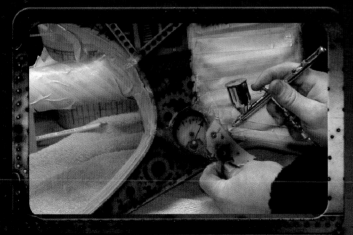

13. The one place I did use a white highlight was on the glass lenses of the gauges. Just a couple of streaks across the face gave the illusion of light reflecting on the glass, incidentally adding still more depth to the piece. This is yet another example of how overspray can be a tool, not just a nuisance.

14. With everything unmasked, I set about pinstriping and outlining the graphics. The stencil areas didn't need pinstriping, but it benefited the masked areas, such as the border and the olive drab panel. I chose a gold pinstripe for the panel to give it that vintage gold gilded look and make it really pop. Because of the tight curves needed for the pinstripe, I used a lettering quill instead of a standard sword striper.

15. The back of the guitar got the same treatment as the front, including pinstriping. I outlined the main gold border with black to punch it out from the surrounding stencil work. For the long black lines, I used a Mack-10 sword striper to make them especially clean and even. I then switched to the lettering quill for the tabs, since those radius curves would have been a nightmare to pull with a striper.

16. The final touch on the guitar before clearcoating was to paint the pickup covers. I painted the borders a matching green, but when I got to the dual coil covers I wanted to give the pickups the old Filtertron look, complete with exposed coils and allen head adjustable magnets. A little masking and airbrushing, and the piece was complete.

After we give them a single protective clearcoat, these guitars are shipped back to Fender/Jackson, where the final resin clearcoat is applied and buffed out. Then the guitars undergo final assembly and quality-control inspection before being shipped to the distributor. The steampunk-issue Warrior shown here was designed and built for the Jackson booth at the 2008 NAMM show. The response it received has caused the company to consider making it a limited-production artist's edition. Luckily, most of the work I did is easily reproducible with existing stencils. As with other limited-edition guitars I've done for Fender/Jackson, I'll probably make them all similar, but each with unique differences. Those will not only make them more valuable, but more interesting for me to paint.

If you like the SP style, I highly recommend researching it for your airbrushing repertoire. Not only is it highly creative, it can be modified to fit just about any type of kustom work. High-tech "Terminator," macabre/gothic biomechanical, and vintage steampunk are similar enough as styles to be mastered as a group, yet each has a distinctively different look. To learn more, Google "steampunk" and check out the article in Wikipedia. Also check out www.brassgoggles.com, and doctorsteel.com, the patron saint of steampunk culture.

You'll discover that steampunk is more than a graphic style; it's also about sculpture, music, and fashion in clothing and accessories. It's a sub-culture all its own.

Keep on innovating 'cause everything old can be new again!

FORMULA DRIFT

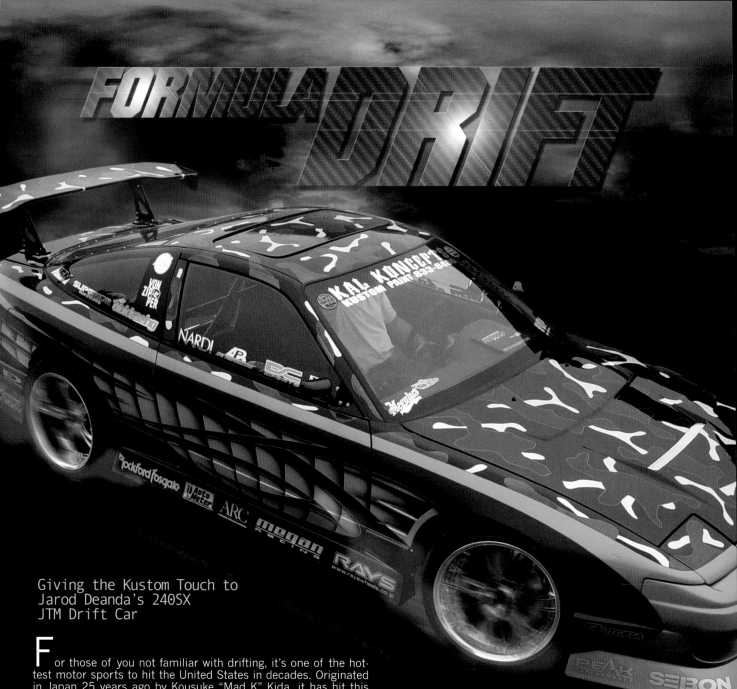

Giving the Kustom Touch to Jarod Deanda's 240SX JTM Drift Car

For those of you not familiar with drifting, it's one of the hottest motor sports to hit the United States in decades. Originated in Japan 25 years ago by Kousuke "Mad K" Kida, it has hit this country hard, with two factions operating their own race circuits, D1 and Formula Drift. A few years back my partner Dion and I were tapped by the Mad K people to paint a full-race Skyline car. Not only did we wind up painting two of their drift cars, but they flew us to Osaka, Japan, to do it. The average person's knowledge of drift racing is usually limited to the 2006 Hollywood film *The Fast and the Furious: Tokyo Drift*. Unfortunately, the reality of the drift scene is missing from the movie, and there's no mention at all of the professional aspect. (The orange Skyline racecar we painted does make an appearance, but a chick in a G-string and miniskirt is looking into the engine compartment. So when we point out the car, the majority of guys watching tend to ask, "What car?")

The skyline returned as well to go on an exhibition circuit demonstrating Japanese-style drift at many events. The SEMA (Specialty Equipment Manufacturers Association) show has been showcasing drift in many different venues ever since. This was about the time we met Jarod Deanda. Jarod is an editor at *C-16* magazine as well as an image consultant for Meguiar's car products, and is one of the key guys behind the Gumball 3000 international car rally. (You have seriously got to Google that on the Internet!) Jarod turned out to be a huge fan of drifting who, besides being one of the most sought-after announcers and color commentators for the sport, was building a car of his own. Historically, one of the most highly

regarded vehicles for drift racing has been the Nissan 240SX, not just because of the mandatory rear-wheel drive, but because of the styling options, suspension, and great horsepower-to-weight ratio. Drifting is not just about sliding your car around and doing burnouts—it's about controlling every aspect of the slide and directing the car around the course as accurately as a surgeon. The type of car that works well depends more on those requirements than on how much money you throw into it.

One of the coolest things about drifting is that the sport hasn't outgrown the shade-tree mechanic in affordability. Unlike in NASCAR and many other sanctioned racing circuits, it's still possible to build a drift car in your garage and be competitive in the open classes. The last time that was done in Indy-class racing was back in the '70s with Li'l John Buttera, and it was rare back then. In this car he already had an optimal platform and had even gotten hold of a JTM turbo engine direct from Japan. With the roll cage installed, all he needed was a new suspension, interior, body kit, and killer paint job.

This is where Dion, Nino, and I came in. Jarod needed his car painted, we needed a feature vehicle for the House of Kolor booth at the SEMA show in Las Vegas. With Meguiar's as a major sponsor, this appeared to be a perfect match. So after settling on a body kit and sketching the paint scheme, it was time to get this sucker under way. Did I mention that before we received the car a tree fell on it and that we had just three weeks to do the entire build? Oh yeah, I must have forgotten that part (block out the bad, block out the bad).

1. Actually, things didn't look too bad. The tree had fallen on the top of the car, blowing out the sunroof and collapsing the passenger side about two inches lower than the driver side. After seeing the car, Doug DeBerti, the famous designer/customizer/inventor, was quoted as saying we were screwed, and he almost never says things like that. (By the way, he was the first person to see the car after it was finished.) Well, we quickly set about un-screwing ourselves to make a SEMA show car out of a stock scrapper.

2. Luckily for us, we were replacing more than 75 percent of the bodywork with new panels, not just for looks but also for weight reduction. The kit was a prototype, never seen before, direct from Japan. The fenders and new front end were all fiberglass, with a very cool carbon-fiber induction hood thrown in. This bolt-on stuff was done by the end of the first day, so we were pretty stoked.

3. The fun part came with the rear fender flare part of the kit. This was a 1½-inch wide part that needed to be trimmed, fitted, and epoxied on. Sorry, no pictures of the epoxy job; too many of us were flipping off the camera, including me. Here Nino was drilling mounting holes in the carbon-fiber rear hatch for the wing. At this point, our bodywork guru, Pinga, had already used a porta-power to jack up and level the bashed-in roofline.

4. Here, Pinga was doing what he does best, bodywork from hell. With lots of love, a heck of a lot of Evercoat filler, and hours of blocking, he brought the bodylines back and blended in the kit to make the car look as if it had come from the factory that way.

5. Bodywork completed, we pulled the carbon-fiber panels and painted the 240SX with catalyzed polyester primer. Although the body was now nice and straight, the first coat of primer was guide-coated and blocked out to remove fine sanding scratches. Hardcore SEMA fans will probably recognize the fenders in the background—they were from the 200HP Hayabusa trike we painted for the Iwata booth that year.

6. Finish-sanding completed, it was time for the first color. This was also the base color, BC03 Galaxy Grey, that we used for the faux carbon-fiber effect. Dion sprayed it on with an LPH-400 spray gun. Don't ask me what Nino was doing in the background wearing his helmet.

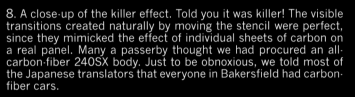

7. Using a rubber grid tool drawer matte from Harbor Freight, I started applying the carbon-fiber effect. It was simple: I just sprayed transparent black base coat through the matte, trying to get more on the car than on my hands. It was much easier as a two-person job, so I had my assistant help hold the matte.

8. A close-up of the killer effect. Told you it was killer! The visible transitions created naturally by moving the stencil were perfect, since they mimicked the effect of individual sheets of carbon on a real panel. Many a passerby thought we had procured an all-carbon-fiber 240SX body. Just to be obnoxious, we told most of the Japanese translators that everyone in Bakersfield had carbon-fiber cars.

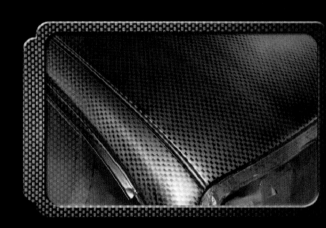

9. With the carbon-fiber effect masked off and the base coat of BC-02 House of Kolor Orion Silver sprayed on the rest of the body, it was time for me to lay out the graphics. I started with 1/8 " crepe tape, but the lines were sagging, so I switched to 3/4" for the long, straight part of the graphics.

10. The main graphic color having been laid out and masked off, Dion applied a few coats of HoK PBC38 Limetime pearl. I never cease to be amazed by the brilliance of this color. The key is the high amount of gold pearl mixed in with the paint. It looks as if a light is shining on it all the time. I don't have to tell you what it looks like in the sun!

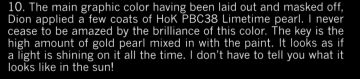

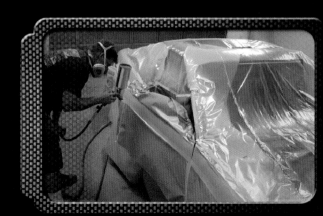

11. I continued laying out the progressive graphics systematically, working from the back forward in the design. Note the rendering taped to the window for reference. While I do use renderings for guidelines, I always tend to add more to the actual car. The result is more significant than a preliminary concept sketch would suggest.

12. The quickest, most accurate way to transfer a design is the pounce transfer technique. First, I rubbed a relief of the layout onto masking paper and ran a pounce wheel over it to create the small trace holes. Then I transferred the image to the other side using a chalk bag. Old tricks are often best.

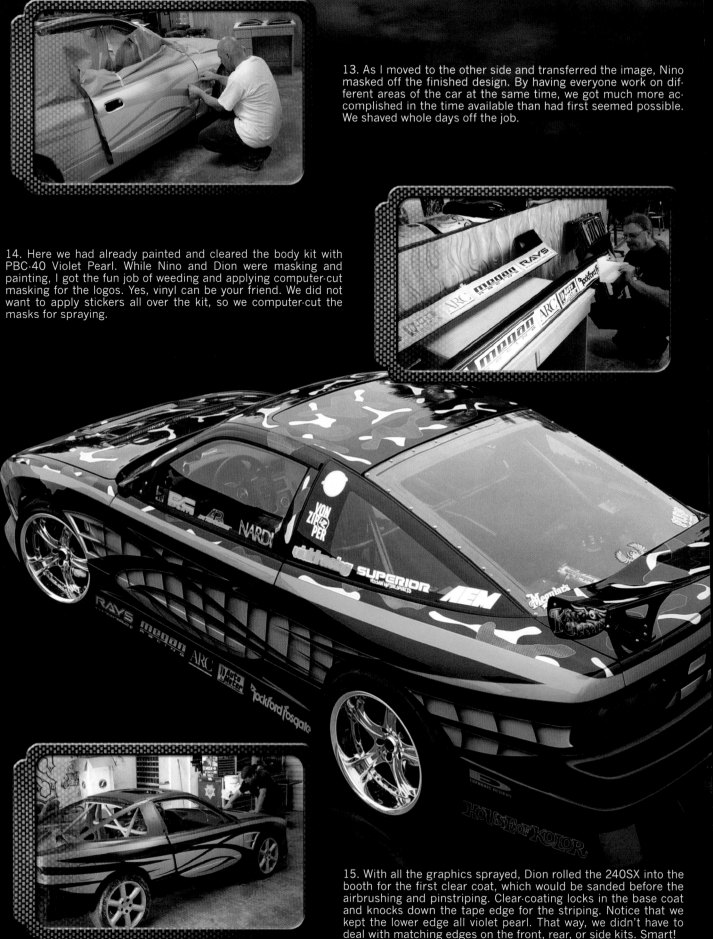

13. As I moved to the other side and transferred the image, Nino masked off the finished design. By having everyone work on different areas of the car at the same time, we got much more accomplished in the time available than had first seemed possible. We shaved whole days off the job.

14. Here we had already painted and cleared the body kit with PBC-40 Violet Pearl. While Nino and Dion were masking and painting, I got the fun job of weeding and applying computer-cut masking for the logos. Yes, vinyl can be your friend. We did not want to apply stickers all over the kit, so we computer-cut the masks for spraying.

15. With all the graphics sprayed, Dion rolled the 240SX into the booth for the first clear coat, which would be sanded before the airbrushing and pinstriping. Clear-coating locks in the base coat and knocks down the tape edge for the striping. Notice that we kept the lower edge all violet pearl. That way, we didn't have to deal with matching edges on the front, rear, or side kits. Smart!

16. With all that Orion Silver in the middle, I just had to airbrush something there. I decided it would be cool to create a faux inner bodyline and indentation to mimic some of the high-end Veilside kits out there. It also lent a biomechanical look to the finished job. All of the line work and shading was done with transparent black with my trusty Eclipse CS Kustom airbrush.

17. Alternating between sides to achieve balance as I worked, I continued to darken the indents to mimic scalloped vents. For the actual vents in the front fiberglass fenders, I airbrushed in a fake drop shadow to duplicate the shadows I had airbrushed previously. The airbrushed accenting of existing indentations makes the faux ones look even more real.

18. After I had used ripped tape for the camouflage layout, I masked off the areas to be left carbon fiber. The areas of real carbon fiber made the camouflaged faux carbon-fiber areas look more real. That may sound bizarre, but the result was great. Judging by the many cars that came out with the effect after SEMA, I guess a lot of painters felt the same way!

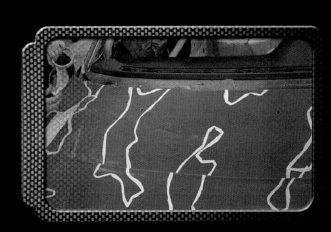

19. We went for a triple color combination on the camouflage. The base was a sprayed black diamond, using the MBC Metajuls over Basecoat Black. Carbon fiber was used as one of the patterns, and the smallest pattern was a silver/white with platinum diamonds. Pretty bling-bling for camo, but it worked. Dressed for casual Fridays, Dion sprayed all the masked patterns with his trusty LPH-400 spray gun.

20. After all the camouflage had been unmasked and cleared, the job needed something more. You guessed it—a pinstripe. For contrast—and to make the pattern really pop—I used a mixture of white and silver HoK striping urethane. That was in keeping with the monochromatic color scheme of the camo and actually appeared as different shades, depending on which element was striped.

21. I kept the rest of the striping fairly conservative, with a process blue for the violet and orange for the green. For these long graphic pulls, I often just grab one of my Mack 10 sword stripers, usually 00. In this case, I went with a trimmed-back green-ferrule Mack sword striper. Much less expensive than the series #10, this brush has more hair, and when trimmed properly, pulls long lines very nicely.

22. After painting the roll cage a marbleized Kameleon, mounting the tires, and installing the Line-X interior components, the Fosgate stereo, and the adjustable coilovers, it was time to assemble the rest of the car. We normally pride ourselves on being a one-stop shop. This time, Jarod's 240SX really proved it.

23. Here's my favorite picture. It was taken a few hours before we mounted the tires and loaded the car on the trailer for Las Vegas. The intercooler had finally shown up at the shop. Too late to install? Not for Nino Brown. While it couldn't be hooked up to the turbo, Nino got that sucker mounted so that it at least looked pretty. Heck, the car was to be shown closed-hood anyway.

With no time to spare and detailed to the max, the 240SX JTM Drifter showed up at the House of Kolor booth at the SEMA show. To say it was a hit would be an understatement. Even the Mad K people from Signal/Show-up gave us a thumbs-up. When they learned we had done it in less than three weeks, they wanted to look under the hood. We strategically hid the hood latch. Heck, our job was to put it together and make it look pretty. It was up to Jarod's guys to make it run pretty. I highly recommend that you check out a drift race. It's the X-games of the automotive industry. Besides being cool to watch, the vehicles make great billboards for kustom paintwork. After all, every extreme sport needs extreme paint to go with it.

Drift on!

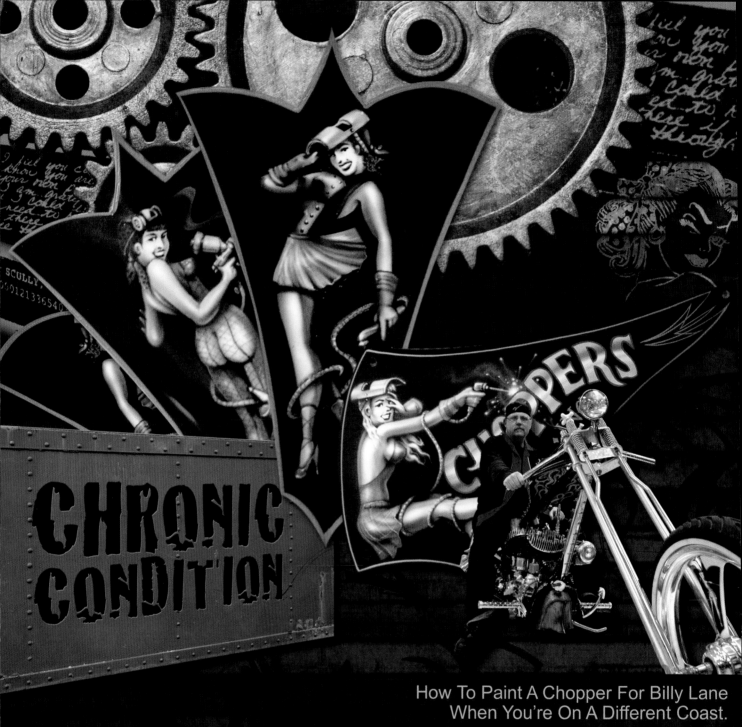

CHRONIC CONDITION

How To Paint A Chopper For Billy Lane When You're On A Different Coast.

I've admired the designs of Choppers Inc. for quite a while. So when Billy Lane asked if I wanted to do the artwork on one of his hubless bikes, the answer was easy. ("Hubless" refers to his signature rear-wheel engineering, Where the rear wheel literally has no hub.) Billy has long been a fan of the pin-up art of Gil Elvgren and George Petty. If you've ever seen Choppers Inc. logos, you know what I'm talking about. Billy's chopper *The Chronic* was being worked on at his shop. He had created floating panels attached to the tank by wing nuts to show artwork. The bike also had a custom-made billet front wheel with three spokes wide enough to have individual pin-ups painted on them. As part of the terms of the deal, the artwork on the panels and the wheel had to be unique to *The Chronic*, and I was allowed to create the art in California while Billy worked on the bike in Melbourne, Florida.

Inspired by the pin-up concept, I checked out a number of George Petty's illustrations. I liked the way he had incorporated machinists' equipment and other tools with his "Petty Girls" in ads throughout his career, an approach well suited to Billy's bikes. Using Petty's style I created a pin-up sketch that incorporated Billy's logo. At that time, Choppers Inc. had built only six hubless bikes, and I did the artwork on the last three: *The Chronic*, *Miss-Treated*, and *King of New York*. All three are radically different in design, yet all have the floating-tank-panel artwork and, of course, the hubless rear drive train. (Competitors have imitated the bizarre appearance of this engineering, but unlike Billy's bikes, theirs are not rideable.) Billy prides himself on building choppers that are not only works of art. But also driven daily.

About a week after our phone conversation, a package arrived from Choppers Inc. containing the wheel, the side panels, and a half pint of green/black metallic paint of mysterious origin that was to be the bike's frame color. I had a week to come up with something in time for Billy to enter *The Chronic* in a show.

1. After sketching the design, I transferred and re-outlined the lettering for the panel onto a sheet of Automask. Unlike frisket film, Automask doesn't react with urethanes, and it constitutes a great adhesive trace system for painting. Just be sure the surface is clean or the transfer tape will seriously delaminate.

2. Using my trusty X-Acto razor knife, I cut out the lettering. Be sure to use a fresh blade when cutting on paint. The sharper the blade, the less chance of scoring the surface. Even though I didn't plan to reuse the letters, I saved them in case I needed to re-mask for touch-ups.

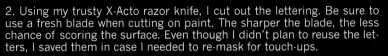

3. After airbrushing the letters lightly with House of Kolor BC-26 Basecoat White in an Iwata Micron airbrush, I sprayed streaks of pure white and black to achieve a reflective metal effect. The black was a transparent blend of BC-25 Black, SG-100 Intercoat Clear, and a small amount of Root Beer Kandy. This gave a cool aged sepia look.

4. For the considerable cutting to be done in the following steps, I used the loose-mask technique. Basically, this meant cutting the artwork out to use as a stencil. I didn't use the original but instead used copies for a series of fresh templates. Luckily, I keep a copier in my office. (Make more copies than you think you'll need; you'll end up carving them all!)

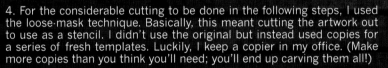

5. Holding down the template with one hand, I lightly airbrushed Basecoat White to establish a good base to work from. Had the design been larger or more complicated, I would have cut small openings around the artwork and laid tape tabs to make the stencil hands-free. Had the metal been ferrous, I could have used small magnets to hold the design down.

6. With the foundation for the girl sprayed in, I cut more details out of a fresh copy. The nice thing about cutting apart from the design is that if you make a bad cut, you just grab another copy, no repainting needed. Of course, I later wished I had used a cutting board; to this day I can still see all these designs cut into my favorite clipboard. Oh, well.

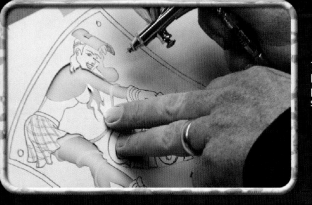

7. Because I had used only a light coat of white initially, I continued to layer only in white to create the subtle separations and details in the pin-up. Remember to layer carefully. You don't want to reach pure-white status until you're done stenciling. Otherwise you lose details.

8. After completing the foundation details in white, I used an Iwata Kustom Micron-C+ airbrush for touch-ups. Freehand detailing is the best way to soften harsh stenciled edges. I write a lot about that in this book; it's a matter of the balance between masking and freehanding.

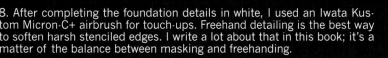

9. Going back to my first cutout, I continued to cut out additional details, using the girl's body as a reference to spray in her facial features and other accents. This was done with the same transparent black/root beer mix. (Aren't you glad you kept all your cut-outs? Don't forget to keep them as well for the other tank panel. Flip them over for the reverse image.)

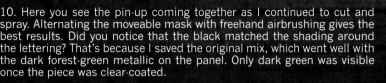

10. Here you see the pin-up coming together as I continued to cut and spray. Alternating the moveable mask with freehand airbrushing gives the best results. Did you notice that the black matched the shading around the lettering? That's because I saved the original mix, which went well with the dark forest-green metallic on the panel. Only dark green was visible once the piece was clear-coated.

11. To prevent overspray, I masked the pin-up with the original cutout and resprayed the background color. That cleaned up the image and really made the artwork pop. No super-fine detail needed here, so I switched to my HP-CH airbrush, allowing me to keep the Micron dialed in with the black for any detail touch-ups.

12. Mixing a batch of transparent white with SG-100, I sprayed the final small highlights and details. For details and line work this small, it's important to strain and overreduce the paint. As you can see, the Micron did a killer job on the details, considering the scale of the work. I reduced the pressure to 20 psi to prevent hyper-drying of the white and to achieve a nice, even flow.

13. With the airbrush work done, I used a liner brush to outline the letters. That not only cleaned up the edges but made the letters really stand out and match the paint job back in Florida. I stuck with standard HoK striping colors so that striping could readily be added to the rest of the bike, if desired.

14. The final touch was a metallic gold border stripe with a little Von Dutch styling. I chose this color because it has a classy look when combined with the background green, and because Billy had mentioned that a few pieces on the bike were to receive gold metal flake work. These two striping colors imparted a killer retro feel to the paintwork overall.

After giving the striping an hour to cure, Dion cleared both of the panels with UFC-35 HoK clear. A quick buff job and they were ready to ship back to Choppers Inc. for installation. The similarity between the right and left tank panels was achieved by using the same cutouts for the pin-up. Only the lettering had to be changed by hand.

The techniques used on the panels were also used on the wheel. After the entire wheel had been polished, I masked off the panels on the spokes and sanded them with 600-grit sandpaper. I then sprayed the sanded panels with AP-01 adhesion promoter, based them in the same green, and proceeded with the artwork. At first I was worried about the durability of the paint/clear on the wheel, but a year later the artwork still looks great.

Panels and wheel reached Florida in time to be assembled on the bike for the show; and, most importantly, Billy dug them. I'd

been wanting to paint something for Choppers Inc., and after the opportunity with *The Chronic* I had the chance to work on a few more projects with Billy. While I'm quite proud of the bikes and cars we crank out at Kal Koncepts/Air Syndicate, it's always cool to paint something really different for another shop. As a kustom painter, you must constantly challenge yourself with new styles, techniques, etc. If you don't, you and your artwork will burn out. I finally got to see *The Chronic* in person when I flew to Florida for the TV show *Biker Build-Off* last year.

For the build-off, we worked on *Miss-Treated*, another hubless chopper, which later had a bit of an issue on the way to Laconia, New Hampshire's Bike Week. But that's another story for another article!

SKULLS, CHICKS & FIRE
WHO COULD ASK FOR MORE!

Putting everything but the kitchen sink into a chopper mural.

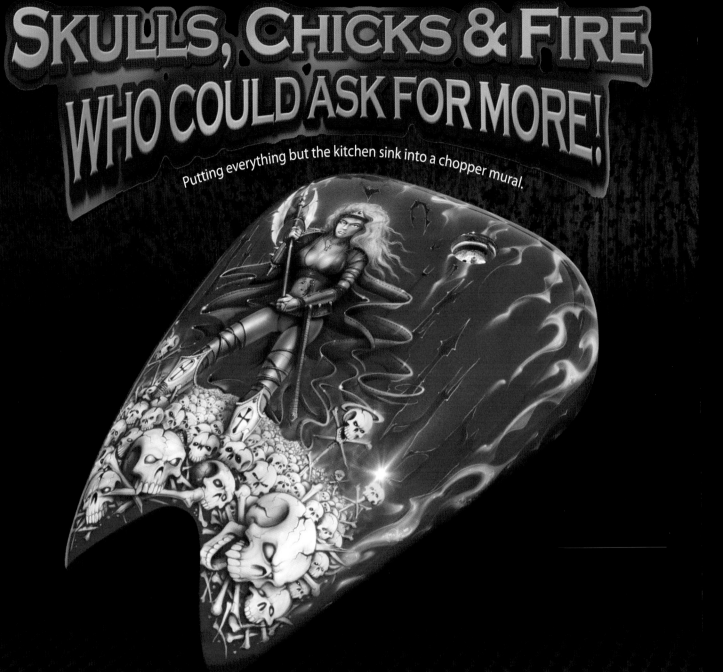

What goes together better than skulls and chicks? Add realistic fire and barbarian weapons on a chopper, and you'll have everything you could ever want, all thrown together in one chapter. In reality, the client had a specific goal in mind. He had a red bike that he wanted to remain red, but he wanted serious airbrush artwork on it, too. He also wanted a barbarian chick in a setting of skulls and fire. Using references to Frank Frazetta and Boris Vellajo, we talked about the mural and what color schemes to use. In the end, he left that up to me—with the directive to make it badass, but not too evil. No problem.

The best part of this project was that I am the consummate Frazetta fan. I've tried to capture in my murals the feeling and depth he's been able to achieve in oil paintings. As with many an airbrush artist, Frank's work is what got me motivated to enter this industry. Interesting, considering he's never airbrushed. Not surprising, for the other greatest influences on me have been Robert Williams, who doesn't airbrush, and the late Rick Griffin, who didn't either. While I've enjoyed working on and doing studies of Frazetta's work, what I really love is attempting to get the look without copying. I've always been more interested professionally in a favorite artist's style than in his work, while personally remaining a devout fan of the work. So this bike project was more fun than work and, at the same time, more of a challenge than some more technically difficult pieces I've done. I included it in this book because it reminded me of the barbarian mural painting in my first book and was just as challenging. To add to the challenge, I wanted to do this piece entirely freehand. No masking, no cutting, no stencils.

I don't consider myself a purist, but there's a certain look to pure technique you can't get with mixed media. Not better, just different. And I definitely wanted this mural to be different. Did I succeed? You be the judge.

1. As always, I started with chalk sketching. I included a sketch of realistic fire because it was to be important in the design. I made preliminary sketches on paper and used those for reference as I chalked in my mock-ups.

2. As you've probably heard me say, I believe chalking to be the best method for laying out artwork. Chalk is completely inert and won't react with paint of any kind. It easily wipes off, leaving no residue to come back and haunt you.

3. Sketched with basecoat white and an Iwata Eclipse, this fire would be different since I was laying it out over a red base. I was also proceeding freehand, without stencil help. I wanted it to look more like a stylized comic book version than actual fire. While realistic fire is the current flavor of the month in kustom painting, being able to modify it in support of your artwork is important, and keeps the style current.

4. Taking a break from fire rendering, I began playing with the huge pile of skulls the barbarian chick was standing on. I lost count of how many I airbrushed on this tank, all freehand. (Feel free to count and e-mail me the number if you like!)

5. Because it was to be a completely freehand mural, I rendered in every detail with white. I would be working predominantly with kandies in this design, so all the detail work now saved hours later and added incredible depth to the finished piece.

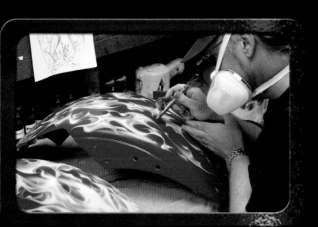

6. After the white, I moved to the next lightest color on the spectrum, yellow—actually, KK-12 Pagan Gold, closest to a yellow kandy in the HoK palette. I could've used Lime Gold, but that has too much green for my taste. To each his own.

7. I was careful about how I used Pagan Gold Kandy in the mural. Much of the white I wanted to leave as a base for other kandies. Blue, for instance, would look killer over the white, but the yellow-toned Pagan Gold would turn it green. Always take transparent color theory into account when layering kandies. Everything depends on the previous color.

8. KK-04 Oriental Blue layered nicely over the white I'd left behind, giving metal areas of the mural a cool look. I also let a little Oriental Blue overspray bleed into the skin areas, since there is a bit of blue in flesh tone. That's one way of having overspray work for you. Heck, if you can't beat it, use it! Overspray can be a great tool if you think ahead. Remember, one man's overspray is another's gradated fade!

9. The next color along the spectrum was Magenta KK16 Kandy for the barbarian chick's clothes. Magenta looks different depending on what it's layered over. On white, it's the pure magenta; on yellow, it can appear kandy apple red; over red, it will appear a brilliant pink burgundy. Recognizing the possibilities for such secondary and tertiary colors beforehand can save lots of time in painting and paint mixing. I always try to dry-mix colors on the surface rather than wet-mix beforehand.

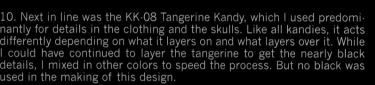

10. Next in line was the KK-08 Tangerine Kandy, which I used predominantly for details in the clothing and the skulls. Like all kandies, it acts differently depending on what it layers on and what layers over it. While I could have continued to layer the tangerine to get the nearly black details, I mixed in other colors to speed the process. But no black was used in the making of this design.

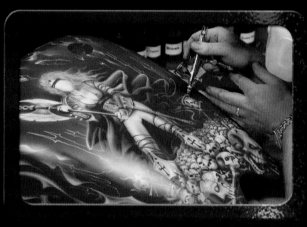

11. After adding KK-09 Kandy Organic Green to the mix to give her green eyes and a few green gems in her weapons, I mixed some KK-07 Kandy Root Beer to continue darkening the skull details. Because the wearing of respirators when airbrushing has become so habitual in our shop, I often don't think to mention it until late in a chapter. Please make it your habit, too, even when doing minor airbrushing. A dual-cartridge, active charcoal respirator rated for organic vapors is our protector of choice.

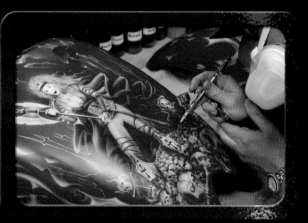

12. The design really started to come alive when I brought in violet. The violet kandy I used combined KK-17 Violet with KK-04 Oriental Blue, giving me a blue/violet perfect for rendering facial features and final details, and replacing black as my darkest shadowing tool. For the fine details, I used the Micron CH airbrush.

13. Only the Micron CH airbrush can render individual eyelashes on a face smaller than my thumb. Check out the necklace, too. The Micron used with HoK kandies can give you details like this all day long. At this point the face was gaining detail but remained more severe than I liked. Adding color softened it, achieving the effect I wanted.

14. The hyper-reduced violet mix was also perfect for detailing the skulls. Note how the skulls that were left white took on a hue of violet from the detail overspray. If I'd used black for these subtle details, the skulls would have been dulled out.

15. Since the violet would have looked purple over the background red, I added KK-07 Root Beer to the mix. That grayed out the violet, giving me a nice dark burnt color to use for the background mountains, castle spires, and whatever you call the things I was throwing back there. In any good mural, the background is as important as the foreground, just not as detailed.

16. Besides compositional balance, you need color balance in your artwork. With a powerful color, such as a red background, keep a careful eye on the balance between the brightest and deepest chromas, as well as the lightest and darkest values.

17. Taking a break from the mural, I wandered back to the fire, which I wanted to be a balance between realistic and cartoon. The anime, or comic art is a favorite reference for my murals. The use of color and loose detail I get from my hero, Frank Frazetta. If the fire is too realistic, it won't suit the mural. Too cartoony, and it will just plain suck! In art, as in life, there is a balance to be found.

18. Bringing more white and Pagan Gold into her face and hair enlivened her a bit. She was looking a little too severe and evil with the previous colors. Amazing what color, here and there, can do for a design! Remember, when approaching something you're not happy with, you're often just a nudge in either direction from a repair. Don't nudge too hard.

19. Going closer still, check out how fine the Micron CH airbrush rendered induvidual hairs and the difference highlights make in punching out details. For highlights I use HoK White Basecoat, reduced 200 percent. Only the extra grinding HoK puts their pigments through can guarantee clean lines this thin, with white this opaque.

20. With the hyper-reduced white, I added final highlights to the fire. On a whim, I also added a few mini-skulls. From a distance they look like highlights in the fire, but up close they look molto cool!

21. The airbrushing done, I lightly wipe down the tanks with water, then tacked for Dion to clear. There was no need for pre-cleaners. I'd used no tape, so there was no pesky residue to contend with. Dion used an LPH-400 and a batch of UFC-19 to clear. Without tape edges, striping, or graphics, there was no need for more than one session to bury the artwork and leave plenty of clear to color sand and buff. Don't fall prey to the urban legend that the more clear you apply, the more depth you'll get. That's not how it works. The colors under the clear determine depth. Once you've buried your artwork, the clear's job is done.

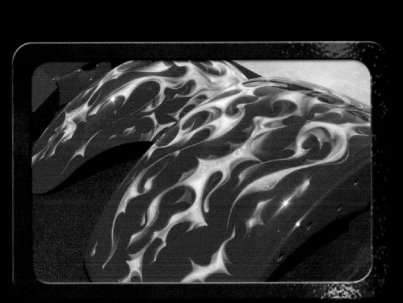

This set of tins came out killer after Dion buffed and we got them in the sun. I'd forgotten the Gold Ice Pearl in the underlying red; it really came through after clearcoating. Working with transparent kandies is the only way to go if you want ultimate depth over a pearl or metalflake. You'll finish in half the time with many fewer millimeters of paint buildup.

The client got exactly what he wanted, and loved it: a barbarian warrior chick, a mess of skulls, and everything tied together with some seriously ragin' fire. Yet the bike was still red and matched the frame perfectly. Good painters give their clients exactly what they want. Go beyond what they think they want to give them what they can only imagine, and you'll approach greatness.

HOMAGE À GIGER
BIOMECHANIZING
BRANDT'S BEHEMOTH

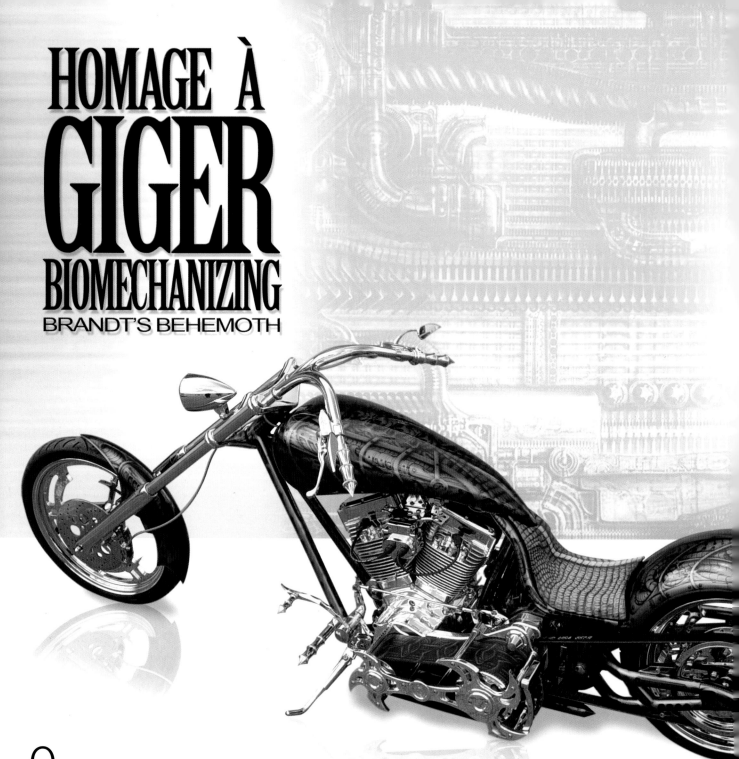

One of the artists whose work I've been asked to imitate most over the past 20 years is Hans Ruedi Giger, better known as H. R. Giger. He's best known by the public for his designs for the movies *Alien* and *Species*. The first artist ever to win an Academy Award (*Alien*, 1979), Giger has been heralded as the king of the macabre for pioneering the biomechanical style that combines man and machine into something out of a nightmare. My first book also included a biomechanical tribute chapter to Giger, and I believe this second book deserved another. Also, I've modified my approach enough that I feel you might benefit from a new demonstration of an old favorite.

Our client on this bike was Perry Brandt, the original stunt producer for the hit TV series *Fear Factor* and for a new show titled *Stunt Junkies*. He's an extreme character who, after he retired as a stuntman, went into production work and remains active in the film and TV industries. He likes to build his own choppers, too; and after finishing this incredible bike, he searched for a shop that

could give him exactly what he wanted. After talking with Mike Ortiz, owner of Psycho City Choppers (a current regular client of ours), Perry gave us a call. (See? It pays to keep your clients happy; they bring in other clients!) He wanted biomechanical work much like Giger's, but without the psycho-sexual aspect often found in his gallery work. Perry also wanted to know if it was possible to do all the biomechanical work in kandy, so that the bike wouldn't be just black and white. We told him we could do an underpainting over a silver base and paint whichever kandy he wanted over the top—and that it would look killer. He liked green, which was perfect, because Giger has actually done a series of green paintings. After looking at some of our completed paint jobs on the website (another way to attract clients), Perry brought over the bike.

With a modified frame from Amen Design and Engineering, Inc., the assembled bike looked more like a sculpture than a bike. Because the tank, fenders, and oil bag had all been custom made, there was lots of shaving, molding, and filling to do to get this bad ▶

boy ready for paint. Don't let anyone fool you: no matter how good your airbrushing, paintwork, striping, or clear-coating, your paint job is completely at the mercy of its foundation. Getting everything ready for paint was easily a week's work. Try rushing it, as on those reality shows, and you'll have a pretty paint job that cracks, delaminates, or otherwise sucks within a month. Take the time to get the prep right.

1. With the bike based in fine silver and clear-coated, I began the basic design layout using a combination of crepe tape and chalk to sketch out and mask the artwork. I didn't want cut marks to show through in this design, so all masked areas were laid on, not cut out. Most of the design was done freehand, and all of the art was monochromatic, much like Giger's originals.

2. Here you see the reference images from one of Giger's books, *Necronomicon*, that I used to imitate his style. I'm careful never to duplicate images exactly from a reference, but rather use the pictures to create an original piece of artwork. Set the mood.

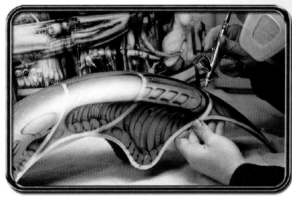

3. Airbrushing with an Iwata HP-CH, I began rendering the design I'd chalked out. Chalk is inert and won't affect airbrushing. I used a mixture of overreduced House of Kolor BC-25 black and SG-100 intercoat clear. The intercoat clear gave me a transparent black without the loss of body or the adhesion characteristics of the base coat.

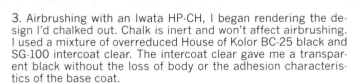

4. As I painted, I moved back and forth between the tins to maintain continuity in the artwork. On the tank I airbrushed a stacking of skulls that Giger uses in some of his sculptural elements. The ability to see most of both sides of the tank from the top helped keep the symmetry nearly perfect—not an easy task when freehanding, but the tape layouts helped.

5. Many people don't know this, but most of Giger's pieces are created using stencils. They're not the type of stencils you'd expect—they're actually metal templates used in etching circuit boards. These patterns help Giger create incredibly intricate repeating designs in his airbrushing. Without his templates, I needed a bit more freehand airbrushing to get a similar effect.

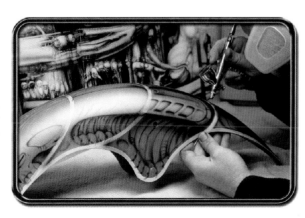

6. Since this piece was to be monochromatic black on a silver base, I wasn't able to correct or highlight the work with white. Even silver would have resulted in too much overspray, had I gone back over the black. Because of this you have to be very careful not to make mistakes; if you do, they must be small! Note that I had removed the outer air cap from the HP·CH airbrush, allowing me to get close for the really tight details.

7. Normally, I wait until the very end of a job to add my signature, but this skull was just begging for it. Though Giger was my inspiration here, I also had to throw in a few of my own goodies. As an artist, it's your responsibility to give back to the creativity pool by adding to it. That's what has kept art going all these years. Don't just imitate, innovate.

8. With the tape removed, note how the negative space of the silver contributed to the overall design and gave the artwork a framework to fall within. The rivets added a nice touch, accenting depth as shown by the airbrushed drop shadows.

9. Taking a break from the tank and moving to the rear fender, I positioned the seat where it would be placed so that I could figure out how to tie in the graphics. The seat was albino alligator, airbrushed to match the bike. Since I'd be painting the seat, I could take the opportunity to bring the design from the bike into the seat, and vice versa.

10. Laying out the seat border in tape, I continued to sketch the rear fender with chalk in preparation for airbrushing. The rear fender and tank were the most important elements of this bike because they would be seen the most. Also, the preliminary sketches I had sent in were of them, so I had to be sure to stick with my initial designs.

11. The rear fender design was more mechanical than biological. It had lots of airbrushed struts and vents, but no skulls. I tend to airbrush lots of skulls in my biomechanical work, so I wanted to see if I could tie the entire bike together with as few as possible—enough to make the bike look cool, but not so much as to make it look like a set from *Tales from the Crypt*. Giger uses skulls, but more as emphasized points in the piece, not as haphazard backgrounding.

12. Here's the patterning I created to mimic the alligator-skin seat. Since the alligator pattern was barely noticeable, I used the same base-coat black on the seat to emphasize it. This worked out killer because the skin was stretched at an angle, and I had to realign the design for the backbone—basically a small improvement on Mother Nature.

13. The frame got the same treatment as the rest of the bike. While the result may not look like much, airbrushing a frame is a pain in the ass. If you count the time that Pinga, our body man, took to shave the frame; Dion to base it, clear it, and sand it; the airbrushing; and Dion to kandy and clear it again, we worked longer on the frame than on the entire rest of the bike. Think about that the next time you quote a price to your client.

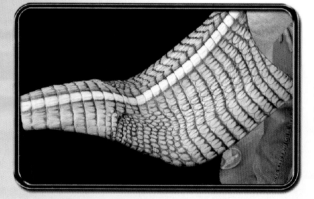

14. Because Dion was going to be in the booth for quite a while on this job, he donned his special monkey suit. It took more than eight coats of Kandy Organic Green UK-09 and Pagan Gold UK-12 to get the color we wanted. All good kandies are like that. Just remember the number of coats you applied in case there are extra parts to do later.

15. The many coats of kandy gave the artwork quite a different look, don't you think? This is the oil tank, which got the same airbrush treatment as the rest of the bike. After the kandy, a light coat of urethane clear protected it, allowing us to color-sand the surface without streaking or otherwise damaging the underlying color.

16. Here's the albino alligator seat I told you about earlier, but with all the airbrushing. The patterns on the seat matched the artwork on the bike perfectly. While I did use base-coat urethanes on the seat, I didn't use catalyzed clear. That would have created breathing problems with the skin, causing it to dry, crack, and discolor in time. A light coat of SG-100 intercoat clear gave the seat all the protection it needed and made for easy touch-ups later on.

17. Even the primary drive belt got a little airbrush treatment. As with the seat, you don't want to clear-coat these belts. They'll delaminate if you do. In preparation, I recommend wiping down the entire belt with acetone to strip away any logos and oils before going over it with AP-01 adhesion promoter, the base coats, and the SG-100. As long as nothing scrapes against the belt, you'll be fine.

18. Voilà!—one highly biomechanized bike. Whenever you can accent your artwork with a kandy, or accent a kandy with underpainted art, go for it. Not only did this bike win a healthy number of awards, it was used as the Amen, Inc., billboard bike in Las Vegas. Wherever this bike goes it attracts a crowd. It's a perfect example of what we always say at Kal Koncepts/Air Syndicate Inc.: "The paint job is the first thing they see and the last thing they remember." The client was more than happy, and we've since biomeched his wife's bike as well. Satisfied clients are like a virus—they multiply and spread. So keep 'em happy.

And keep on innovating!

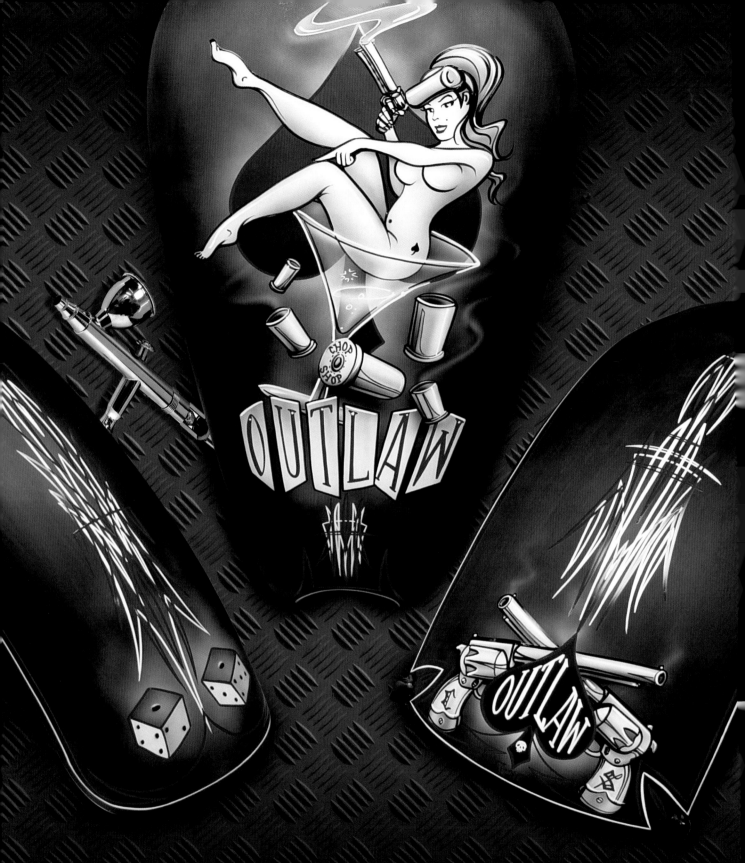

RISE OF THE RETRO CHOPPER

Choppers, Pin-ups and Pinstriping... Oh My

What do you get when you combine three of the most popular elements of the kustom industry in one ride? You get a retro-styled "Ratrod" paintjob, with a pinup, on a chopper. For the past decade, the Ol' School Hot Rod look has been getting more and more refined. One popular trend is the "Suede" or "Rat Rod" paintjob, done traditionally with a flat primer base, simple graphics, and pinstriping. That used to be the way to go because the builder needed a quick and dirty way to paint and touch up his track car or street racer. Flat lacquer primer was about as cheap, easy, and quick as you could get. Times have changed, and while today's builders can easily afford a decent paintjob, the look is what intrigues them. Before you go making fun of this trend, think about brand-new prewashed jeans with holes in the knees, and about thousand-dollar shabby leather jackets. A trend in which a look trumps practicality is nothing new in the fashion industry. If you think about it, the automotive kustom culture itself is an underground fashion movement...

When he approached us to paint his bike, the client wanted a flat black look and artwork he wouldn't have to "feel." He wanted a paintjob that would last more than a year in the elements. He also wanted a pin-up on the tank, with matching pin-striping and subtle graphics. The design was to be black, white, and red. Period. Not for budget this time, but for effect. As for the pinup, he didn't want a WWII type or realistic Varga girl; he kept pointing to artwork by Coop, Shag, and other artists in the present-day Kustom Kulture scene. They are known for stylized versions of art that mimics the screen-print art of postwar 50s America. While currently a popular trend in illustration, it was originally an advertising art that emerged from the prewar industrial age. After playing around with sketches and concepts, we finally hit on what he wanted. So with the discussions with him in mind, our sketches in hand, and a couple of new paint products to play with, we got on the job.

1. I would be incredibly remiss if I didn't give a shout-out to one of the fastest body men I've ever met. His name is Pinga, and the guy can do the work of three body men in half the time. No matter how nasty the car or bike we give him, he always responds, "I fix, no problem." Here he was smoothing out a West Coast Chopper tank in preparation for paintwork.

2. With the bodywork and tins smoothed out, Dion sprayed on House of Kolor's Blackbase/Sealer. HoK was one of the first to come out with a catalyzed primer/sealer of such high quality that it could double as a basecoat. It eliminated any need to paint the tanks black later, saving big on time, materials, and labor.

3. With a sanded coat of UFC-19 HoK clear as the base, I laid out the preliminary design. Using Coast Airbrush's Automask transfer tape, I squeegeed out all the bubbles and got the paper to lie flat.

4. I sketched the design on the Automask using a soft pencil. The cool thing about Automask is I can sketch and erase all I want without damaging the underlying basecoat. Try that with a Stabilo!

5. While there are a number of different brands of transfer tape, Automask is one of the few you can use a Sharpie pen on without the ink bleeding through. The bleeding of transfer tape is a warning that the paint will bleed through as well. I used a Sharpie pen to define the final design lines I'll be cut on.

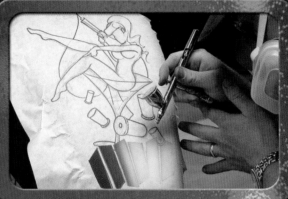

6. Starting with the brightest area, I began airbrushing in the logo cards with HoK BC-26 Basecoat White. I kept the taped edge low by using my Iwata Eclipse instead of a spray gun. Plus, I could more accurately control the gradation and amount sprayed.

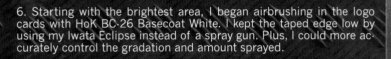

7. With the cards done, I cut, removed and sprayed the pinup girl's body parts. Note the subtle gradations of white created with the Eclipse. Subtle as they are, they're all you'll need to discern the details later on.

8. After finishing the pinup's body, the cards, and the shells, I removed most of the Automask in order to work on the background. By airbrushing in the negative space, I used the masked-off black areas to define the darker elements of my design. That gave me the vintage silk-screened look I wanted.

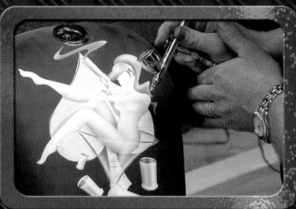

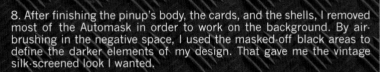

9. Removing the tape revealed the added effect of the black base as an important element in the artwork. I then freehanded in swirling smoke to add depth and fill in the design.

10. With similar artwork, I allowed other parts of the bike to catch up with the tank. A little black basecoat defined a few shaded and shadowed areas, such as the shells and the hand gun.

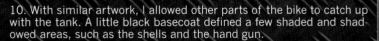

11. Taking a break from the airbrush, I picked up my Jenson liner brush and began outlining and lettering with House of Kolor Roman Red Striping urethane. The name of the bike was to be "Outlaw," but I also threw in the name "Chop Shop" to give props to the company that built the bike. I even put initials on the gun grips. Little details like these are invariably the best remembered.

12. Switching to Black Striping urethane, I continued to outline the design and render major details. This style is radically different from the freehand airbrushing you may have seen me do in the past, but a successful kustom painter must be able to adapt to any style.

13. Important as white highlights are in airbrushing, they are even more important in brush artwork, especially when you're trying to mimic a silk-screened retro piece. The white can make or break your work.

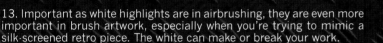

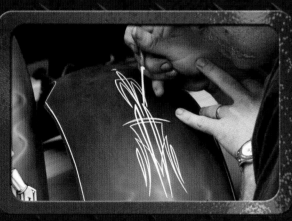

14. Pinup art done, it was time for a little Von Dutch style hot rod striping. What retro piece would look finished without this classic? Staying with the minimalist theme, I brushed in the first symmetrical design with HoK striping white.

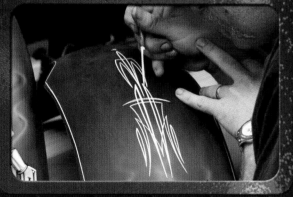

15. The final color in the striping was the same red as in the artwork. Although the color was the same, the brush I used was much different from that for lettering and outlining. It was an Excaliber 000 sword striper—not optimal for lettering, but kicks serious butt for hot rod pinstriping.

Finally, the Retro Rat-Rod Chopper was ready for a coat of flat clear. In case you're interested, the flat clear we've been really digging lately is from House of Kolor. It's actually an additive for UFC-35 clear. And there's a trick to using it. Take the additive, which is known as FA-01, mix it really well, then reduce it 1:1 with RU-311 reducer. Stir this mixture very well and set aside. Now, mix up a batch of UFC-35 clear, two parts clear to one part KU-150 catalyst, and add it 1:1 to the additive/reducer mixture. The stuff is amazing: goes on glossy, then starts flattening out. Because this product contains micro glass beads that rise and dull the finish, it's not only very flat but tough as nails. Thanks to Brian Lynch for the killer tip!

While many kustom painters are mimicking the Rat Rod look in their retro paintjobs, they often make the mistake of using old techniques to create the old look. With today's micro-textured urethane clears, we're able to create the ultimate flat look in retro-work without discoloration, graying, or streaking. The graphics are also buried beneath the clear, where theyre protected. While the old school graphics and pinstriping on top of primer looked cool, they would fade quickly, delaminate, and discolor. As kustom painters we have a responsibility to give our clients the look they want without sacrificing durability or quality.

Radio Control

Trickin' out an RC Truck Body, Air Syndicate Style

While the RC industry has been around since I was a kid, it has only come into its own in the last decade. The brushless motor and more efficient batteries have made electric cars just as competitive as the nitro burners, and more affordable for racing. Just for clarification, RC stands for "radio controlled." These model cars and trucks can range from 1/24th scale all the way up to ¼" scale in size.

Painting RC bodies is a lot like painting the gelcoat racing boats of yesteryear, or even today's flaked-out bass boats. The similarity is in the way the paint jobs are applied. On mould-released boats, the graphics are taped off and sprayed on the inside of the mould in a reverse fashion, so when the boat is pulled the graphics are already on it. This reverse way is preferred for graphics on the transparent Lexan bodies popular in the RC industry. The upside is that the naturally shiny exterior of the Lexan acts as the clear, and the paint job is much more durable when dealing with exterior damage. The downside is that it takes time to figure out reverse painting.

The trick is that the last thing normally applied in a standard paint job becomes the first thing on a Lexan body. Confused? Don't

be. Just think backwards. If you want highlights over a graphic that has a kandy fade and stencils in the base color, after masking it off, spray the highlights first, then the stencil effects, then the fade, and then the base color.

Simple, huh? Sometimes it's best to write out what you want to do, figure out the individual steps, then calculate which should go first. It will take a while; but once you get into it, it becomes second nature. The hobby industry offers many different products, brands, and tools. I recommend trying as many as you can before deciding what's best for you.

Our shop uses House of Kolor paints primarily; not just their automotive line, but their Kustom Kolor Hobby line as well. I personally favor bringing as much technology from the automotive industry to hobby work as possible. There's less relearning, and it's far more comfortable to use familiar technology with different applications.

1. Once acquired, a Lexan body must first be trimmed to fit the car in question. If you wait until after painting, you'll end up damaging your work. For this chapter, my friends Frank Amestoy and Kent Beale at Racers Haven in Bakersfield hooked me up with a body, which they trimmed and fit to a much modified Revo owned by Rodney Bowser. I wanted to use his car as an example because it's a killer setup. Heck, Rodney has more money in this RC than most people have in the car they drive. All it needed was a tricked-out paint job.

2. I've always used a Dremel Tool to drill holes in RC bodies—badly at that! Kent used a reaming tool that not only starts the hole but lets you make it as large and symmetrical as you want. Pretty neat gizmo, and it doesn't split the bodies either. Plus, with Kent fitting the car's body, I didn't have to worry about the tool going through my hand—or any other part of my torso!

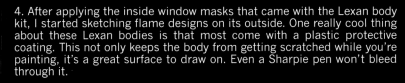

3. With the fender wells trimmed, the mounting holes cut, and the excess flashing removed, the body was fitted to the model chassis for a final check. Now don't go thinking the guys at your local hobby store will trim and fit a body for free. Still, I imagine if you've been spending as much as Rodney has, they'll probably help you out.

4. After applying the inside window masks that came with the Lexan body kit, I started sketching flame designs on its outside. One really cool thing about these Lexan bodies is that most come with a plastic protective coating. This not only keeps the body from getting scratched while you're painting, it's a great surface to draw on. Even a Sharpie pen won't bleed through it.

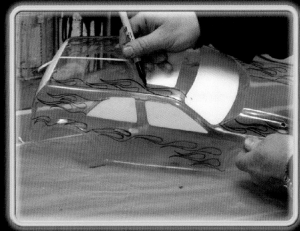

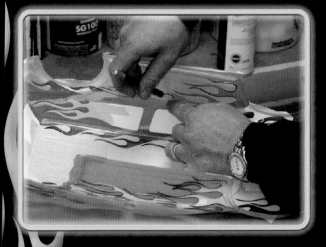

5. After sketching the design with a Stabilo pencil (you can wipe off Stabilo marks if you change your mind), and finalizing it with a Sharpie, I laid in masking tape on the inside of the body. While there are lots of different masking materials to use on RC bodies, I prefer good old-fashioned #233 3M tan masking tape. Fits the tight contours, leaves little residue, and cuts nicely with an X-Acto knife. The new V-Tape is killer, too.

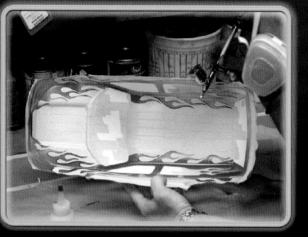

6. With the tape cut and the edges pressed back down, I wiped the inside surface with a mixture of water and KC-10 precleaner. (Gets rid of any tape residue and finger oils on the Lexan.) I always keep one airbrush nearby loaded with AP-01 adhesion promoter. Just a light coat keeps the paint from delaminating. Although House of Kolor's Kustom Kolor hobby line paints don't need an adhesion promoter, I find the AP-01 is necessary because I use a combination of Kustom Kolor and standard HoK paints.

7. Remember when I mentioned doing things backwards? For the flame graphics, I wanted the tips to have a Hot Pink fade over a Tangelo Pearl base color. While normally this fade would be applied last, it had to be sprayed first here. With a mix of Kandy Violet, Hot Pink, and SG-100, I airbrushed just the tips and the inside mouths of the flames. Don't spray too much, or you won't be able to see the Tangelo through the fade.

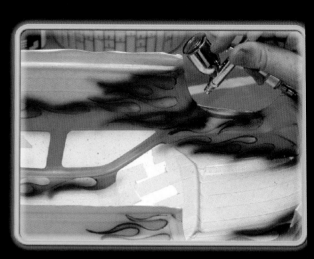

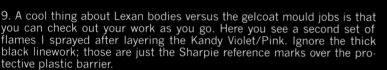

8. After spraying an additional stippling of Pink Pearl on the flames, I layered in a few substantial coats of PBC Tangelo Pearl Basecoat. Instead of spraying too many coats of pearl to get solid coverage, I recommend spraying a final coat of white over all of your base colors. This makes them very bright and prevents subsequent graphics from bleeding through. A few drops of catalyst in the BC-26 Basecoat White make it set up harder.

9. A cool thing about Lexan bodies versus the gelcoat mould jobs is that you can check out your work as you go. Here you see a second set of flames I sprayed after layering the Kandy Violet/Pink. Ignore the thick black linework; those are just the Sharpie reference marks over the protective plastic barrier.

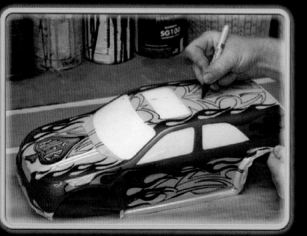

10. I like to design graphics progressively, drawing the new design after the previous one has been painted. Otherwise, it can make for a very confusing bunch of scribbles. For the next step, I laid out a KGB (Kustom Gone Bad) ace of spades hood logo with tribals to go with it.

11. With the KGB lettering backmasked, I hot-glued a piece of Scotch-Brite to my Dremel Tool grinding head. I use this to create a machine-turned effect in the actual Lexan. Scotch-Brite gives the subsequent coat of HoK Kosmic Krome MC-01 Aluminum Effect a radial turned pattern to amplify, creating the illusion. You've seen me do this on other paint jobs in my shop, and in this book. I always enjoy tricking out standard effects to use on other projects.

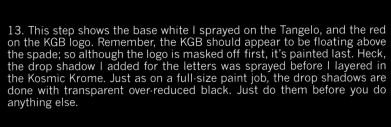

12. Here, I sprayed MC-01 Kosmic Krome Aluminum. Unless you're going for a mirror effect, I recommend using the aluminum. Because it adheres better. (Hint: with the Lexan's shiny top surface and the back-painting method, you can achieve some amazing chrome effects on these cars. Just be sure to airbrush the chrome with black basecoat lightly as a base).

13. This step shows the base white I sprayed on the Tangelo, and the red on the KGB logo. Remember, the KGB should appear to be floating above the spade; so although the logo is masked off first, it's painted last. Heck, the drop shadow I added for the letters was sprayed before I layered in the Kosmic Krome. Just as on a full-size paint job, the drop shadows are done with transparent over-reduced black. Just do them before you do anything else.

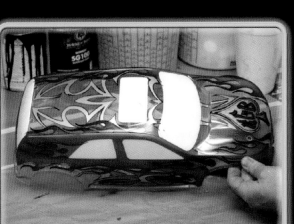
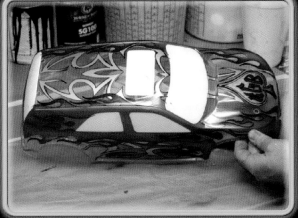

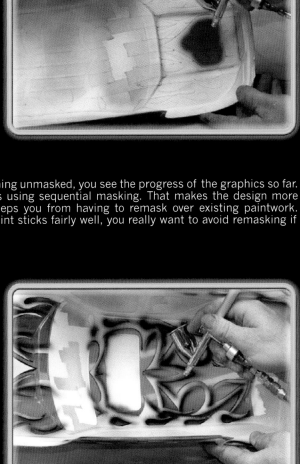

14. With everything unmasked, you see the progress of the graphics so far. I like to do cars using sequential masking. That makes the design more efficient and keeps you from having to remask over existing paintwork. Although the paint sticks fairly well, you really want to avoid remasking if you can.

15. As always with back painting, think drop shadows before spraying the next color. There's no way to add them later. (Don't try wiping with reducer or precleaner to remove paint. You'll only mar the surface and cause more problems.) Luckily, the bodies are not that expensive. The few I really messed up while learning I just resprayed on the outside. They became the thrasher bodies slated for really hard use.

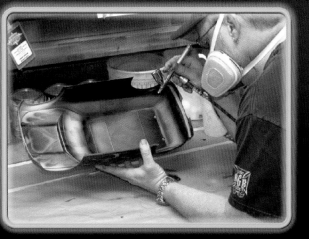

16. My next color was actually a series of colors, with an Ice Pearl top-coat. I started with a coat of SG-100 mixed with Violet Ice Pearl. Then I layered in a front-to-back fade of PBC36 Trublue Pearl and PBC40 Violet Pearl. I left the front and back transparent so that the final coat of white would give the front and back a lighter pastel look.

17. After applying an undercoat of white to lighten the colors, I added a coat of BC-25 Black to the entire underlying paint job. Not just for protection; with the masking window removed, it gave the interior a more realistic dark look. Some people like to add a coat of spray-can clear. That's a good idea, especially when building a body for a nitro car, since the fuel can really mess with the interior paintwork. A little added protection is always a good idea.

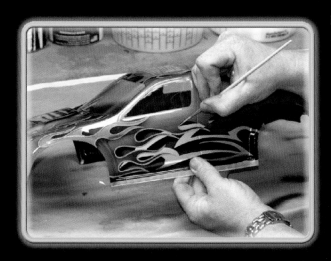

18. Unmasking is one of my favorite parts because the paint job really comes to life with all the dirty, sketched, and cluttered plastic coating removed. If this had been a traditional masked RC car paint job, I might have wanted to stop here. The cuts had been clean and the masking pressed down, so the paint job looked amazing. But in this case, I added a little pinstriping to the outside of the Lexan to tie everything together.

19. I didn't outline everything; that would've been too much work, and given the clean-cut lines of the underlying graphics, unnecessary. For the Tangelo flames, I mixed a batch of HoK Lime Green striping urethane. A few drops of catalyst in the reducer, and the striping really bites into the surface. Even a precleaner wipe-down won't faze it. The graphics were too small for a striping brush, so I used one of my favorite Kafka lettering quills.

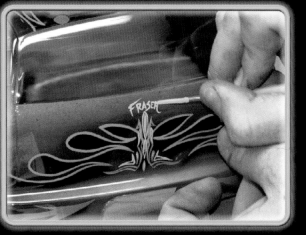

20. Besides outlining, I just had to add a little Von Dutch striping—and my name, of course. While not traditional in RC car painting, I really like adding the pinstripe effect. It takes a steady hand but is lots faster than reverse-masking thin stripes from the backside.

21. The outline of the windows, the spade, and the KGB lettering got the same treatment. The aluminum tribal graphic looked killer without striping, so I left it with the masked edge.

22. Every model car project ends with transfers or stickers. This kit came with very nice headlights, taillights, a grill, and even some graphics and logos. I liked the headlights, grill, and taillights. Graphics and logos are a lot easier to cut and stick on than paint from scratch. I eighty-sixed them anyhow.

Here ya go: one RC crowd pleaser truck body ready to be mounted and destroyed in a race. Sorry, had to say it. While I enjoy working on these projects, I rarely spend too much time on them, knowing they'll get seriously used. Every now and then I'll go all out on a display model. Yet I also enjoy working on paint jobs that will see the track as well as the shows.

This paint job was a little of both worlds. While I did spend time on the external pinstriping and extensive graphics, it was still a viable race body that not only looked great but was durable enough to withstand quite a few races, and even a couple of wrecks. Besides being fun, the nice thing about the RC industry is that it's a constant source of revenue—not so much because new people get into the hobby every day but because those already in it go through a heck of a lot of bodies when racing.

If you'd like to find out more about this cool hobby—how you can get into it, or at least into painting in it—visit your local hobby store. Most today are no longer merely places to buy yarn and a few tired snap-together models. They are performance shops for this new hi-tech sport. While not specializing in actual RC vehicles, Dave Monnig's Coast Airbrush is one of the best stocked supply houses for RC kustom painting needs. Not only does Dave sell just about every hobby paint and tool for RC work, but the guy is a serious RC hobbyist himself from way back. Be it planes, cars, boats, helicopters, or blimps, Dave has owned them, raced them, and wrecked them. (Hence, he knows a lot about repainting them.) I'd also recommend contacting Racers Haven in Bakersfield, California, www.racers-haven.com. Ask for Frank or Kent; they can hook you up with any of the cars or tools you've seen in this chapter.

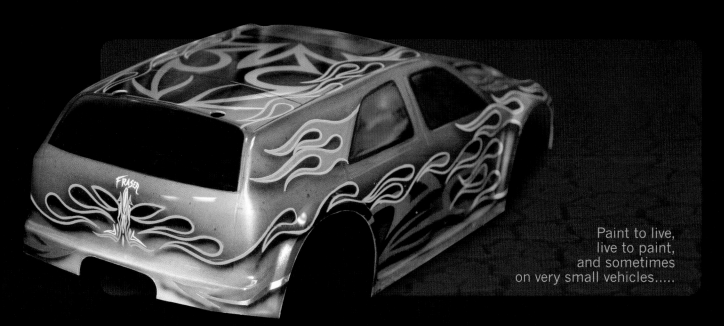

Paint to live,
live to paint,
and sometimes
on very small vehicles.....

DRAGON DRUMS

Kustom Painting A Set Of Drums For Sonor, And The NAMM Show

While painting guitars is fun, there's nothing quite as challenging as painting a drum kit. Aside from the fact that the surface area to be painted is larger than you would think (in many situations, more square footage than a small car!), the visible area is small and often confusing. By the way, there's also hardware to be mounted all over the shells, so whatever design you choose, plan on it being covered by metal every six to eight inches or so. Now, if that isn't enough, you have no idea what angle or rotation many of these drums will have once they're assembled. Unlike a car, bike, or guitar, with a drum kit, your own paintwork can get in the way of your paintwork depending on the angle at which it is viewed. So basically, you're looking for a design that's recognizable from a distance, yet looks good up close, with obstructions, and at varied angles. No problem, just another day at our shop...heheheh.

For this chapter, I chose a drum set that I kustom painted for Sonor Drums and the musician Mark Hernández. Mark had an image of a classic Japanese dragon in a hand-painted style. He also handed me a collection of different rice papers. He wanted the finished drum set to look like it was wrapped in rice paper with the dragons hand painted on it. Each drum had to have a dragon and his "M H" logo within a fireball.

The trick was going to be the bass drum. He wanted there to be identical dragons on each side, starting from the bottom and meeting at the top, with his logo between them. As I mentioned in the previous paragraph, drums are difficult because only half of each drum is visible to the audience from one particular viewpoint. I wanted the dragon's head to be the most visible to the audience, but I still needed to balance out the entire shell and fill the other areas with the body of the dragon. I decided that coiling the body of the dragon was the best way to fill the space. The base canvas for this artwork was a set of plain white shells—nothing better to start with.

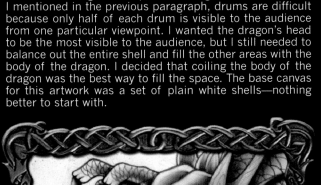

1. The one thing I like to do with my clients is to make sure we're on the same page. For this design, I created a test pane by airbrushing the rice paper effect and the dragon, and then e-mailed a pic for approval. With the drummer happy with the design, Dion and Lambie sanded the shells with damp 600-grit sandpaper. (Never use wet sandpaper with wood instruments. Although dry sandpaper loads up, wet paper causes splitting.)

2. To create the rice paper effect, I incorporated marbleizing in the first stage. Using a custom mix of transparent marblizer with Gold Rush pearl, I textured the entire surface using plastic wrap. I combined spraying the surface and the plastic wrap with an Iwata TH-3 trigger airbrush to achieve a unique effect. The more layers, the better the texture. The trick is to remember how many layers so that all of the shells match.

3. I needed a stippled texture to match the grain and impurities that were in the rice paper samples, so I mixed a batch of HoK Solar Gold and violet pearl basecoat. Using the edge of a squeegee, I stippled the shells using the TH-3 airbrush. I started with the smallest drum to get the effect I liked, then I kept that drum on the table as a reference for the rest of the shells.

4. To match the same yellow tint as the rice paper, I mixed KK-12 Pagan gold kandy and SG-100. I used a random spray pattern over the shells to give an uneven aged look to the surface.

5. With the rice paper effect finished, I sprayed on a protective coat of SG-100 so that I could start sketching the artwork. Using a blue Stabilo pencil, I drew the initial sketch of the dragon. I did this real lightly so that I could wipe it off once I started airbrushing. Nice thing is, if I make a mistake, rubbing alcohol will take it right off.

6. Using the Kustom Micron C airbrush, I added Rootbeer, Oriental Blue, and Violet Kandy to SG-100. This gave me a dark Sepia kandy to render the dragon. It worked well for the shading, and by layering it, I got the dark line work. For the outline work, I added a few drops of black to my Sepia mix for coverage. The rest of the Sepia was saved for the shading.

7. With the line work done, I wiped the drum down with HOK KC-20 water-based precleaner. This removed the Stabilo marks but didn't damage the artwork. It's important to do this step before shading. The shading and shadowing would actually lock in the Stabilo, and you would never get it up. For any areas that were difficult to remove, I used a little alcohol on the rag. Too much could pull the line work. Any damaged lines are easily cleaned up in the next step.

8. With the Micron Kustom C airbrush, I sprayed the pure Sepia kandy I made earlier with no black in it. I wanted the final artwork to resemble a Japanese wood block print but also have the subtle shading of a tattoo. The airbrush was a perfect tool for this.

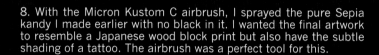

9. The most tedious part of the mural was the multiple scales of the dragon. They took forever to line out and get the right shade, so I jumped around a lot on the design to prevent monotony. It's also a good idea to keep an eye on your reference shell to prevent overworking one of the drums more than the others. Here you can see how the coiled and bending body filled up the rest of the drum shell. Keeping the design in the center is important so that the artwork is not lost in the hardware.

10. Here are all the shells waiting for their last coat of clear. Actually, waiting for me to sand them—then Dion would put on the last coat of clear. (You see, Dion and Lambie sanded them the first time, so I got to sand them the last time. Wheeee!) Again, we used 600-grit damp sandpaper. Then Dion cleared them with his trusty LPH-400 gun and some UFC-35 clear. Another bout of sanding (yep, me again) with 1500-grit sandpaper, and the shells were buffed out and ready to be shipped to Mark Hernández for final assembly.

Well, here are the finished pics—quite a bit different once they're assembled. With all the hardware on them, you can see how the design is balanced, free-form, yet completely visible around the chrome. This was not luck. I made reference marks before the drums were disassembled and made sure that I was aware of the visible areas. Whenever you paint a set of drums, or a guitar, you need to know your canvas. Luck will get you a pickguard covering your guitar mural or a drum ring cutting off your dragon's head! Mark was happy, and the manufacturer, Sonor, liked them so much that they decided to use them as their featured kit in the Sonor booth at the National Association of Music Manufacturers (NAMM).

As you can tell from this article, there's a lot more work in painting a drum kit than you might think. But it's well worth it. An airbrushed guitar is definitely cool, but it's not always seen from a distance, and it may only be one of many guitars that the musician will have onstage for a concert. The best thing about a drum kit is that everybody can see it, and that sucker is usually onstage for the duration. You just have to hope your favorite drummer does not go Keith Moon on you! (Those of you from my era know exactly what I'm talking about!) Next time you want to get a look at some killer drum paintwork, check out the NAMM show. It's basically the SEMA show but for musicians. Lots of eye kandy, and thanks to kustom paint work on instruments, the shows are not just for musicians anymore! Keep on drumming!

Craig Fraser and Mark Hernández

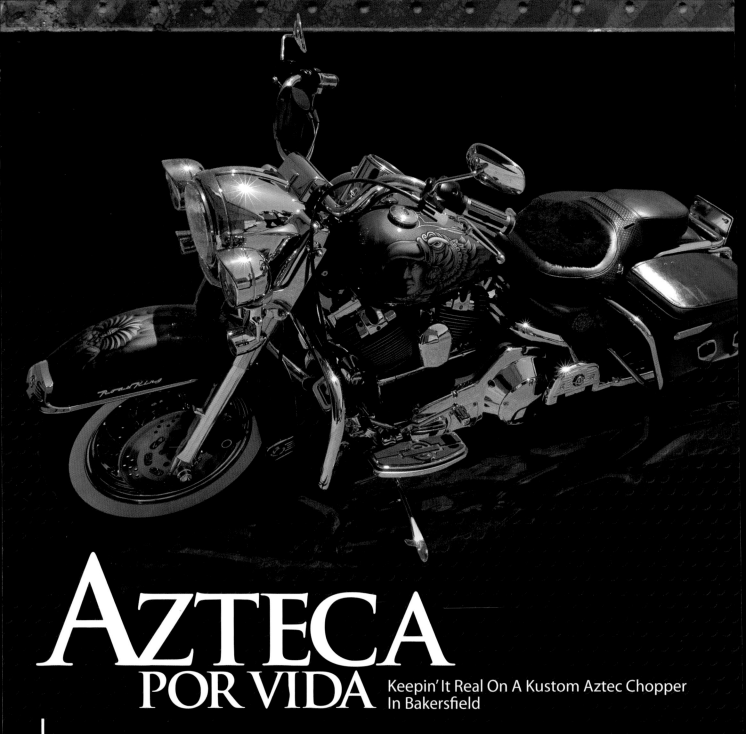

AZTECA
POR VIDA

Keepin' It Real On A Kustom Aztec Chopper
In Bakersfield

I know what you're thinking: "Why is a white boy from Bakersfield kustom-painting Aztec murals?" Well, why not? Who ever said murals should be segregated? Growing up in Bakersfield, California, I was surrounded by the lowrider community and the art that went with it. In fact, my first influences in automotive mural work were all Hispanic—Joe Montano, Mr. Cartoon, Tramp, et al. And, as an honorary member of the Latin Airbrush Association, I even have the credentials to prove it. Granted, I may be the token "güero" (the Spanish equivalent of "whitey"), but I've never had a complaint. It's all about the art, after all.

For this mural, my client had a killer old-school-style Harley-Davidson bagger that just needed a bit of a face-lift. He had painted the bike himself with an Oriental Blue kandy over a heavy metallic base. All that was missing was some mural

work. He originally just wanted a profile of an Aztec king on each side tank and a little pinstriping to tie in the other pieces of tin. I recommended a bit of airbrushing throughout the bike—tanks, fenders, side covers—using realistic fire and pinstriping to tie them together. He also wanted a Harley-Davidson tie-in, but one that didn't use the actual name. I decided that an Aztec calendar with a single HD wing coming off the circle would mimic an old HD logo, yet also have the correct Aztec styling. As for color, he wanted all the artwork in silver, with only blue as coloring. I suggested we use a black/violet kandy to airbrush the details over the silver base and incorporate violet and blue for added depth. When everything was decided and he had a concept sketch in his hand, I took his deposit and got started.

1. In preparation for the artwork, I sanded the fresh paint with 3M's 600-grit sandpaper, using plenty of water to keep scratches to a minimum. Masking off half the tank with Automask, I started the fun by sketching the design with a #2 pencil. That way if I made a mistake, I could correct it with a gum eraser. Using some of the client's photo references—and my imagination—I sketched a traditional Aztec warrior with full headdress.

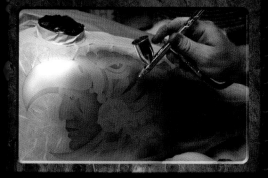

2. I know you've seen this step before; I do love sequential masking! I pulled off piece after piece with an X-Acto knife and sequentially airbrushed the underlying base coat and design sketch for airbrushing later. For the other tank, I would later transfer the design—using Automask and Saral paper—from a trace of the sketch.

Are you wondering what I did for the other tank? At this point, nothing. I had already traced my final sketch, which I would later transfer onto the Automask with Saral paper. Simple.

3. Piece by piece I airbrushed silver directly over the sanded blue kandy base. Which silver? Ah, that's the trick! I wanted a silver that was very sparkly, yet covered well without a big edge, so I mixed a blend of BC-02 Orion Silver, Platinum Diamond Pearl, and MC-01 Kosmic Krome Aluminum in a ratio of 2:2:1, before reduction. Kosmic Krome gives killer coverage, and unlike the competition's aluminum micro-pigment, will mix with any of the HoK base coats.

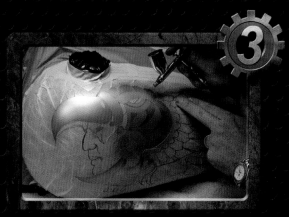

4. With all the cut masking removed, I freehand-airbrushed the same silver to clean up any edges that were too harsh. This step also knocks back the blue in case it creeps in on you. At this point I turned my attention to the other tank. Once you've established the value of the silver on one, match it immediately on the other. Matching might be impossible later on.

5. With everything unmasked, it was time to add the realistic fire. Using my favorite flame stencil (regardless of your stencil preference, the effect is the important part), I created realistic fire using only the kustom silver. This could never be done with plain Orion Silver because the overspray would kill the design, and it would take forever to get the base color up. You still need to be careful about overspray, however. Have a rag and precleaner handy for wipe-downs.

6. Time for the fun part: the detailing! I don't have a favorite area I like to start in; I just go with whatever catches my eye. However, be sure to mimic your starting point on the other tank as well—believe it or not, it makes a difference in the end result. The color I used was a mix of BC-25 black, KK-17, KK-21 Majestic Blue (this color has since been discontinued), and SG-100—just enough color to show up, and just enough black for killer coverage. My airbrush of choice for detail work is the Micron Kustom C+.

7. The small circles in the detailed trim were done by blowout. Here you can really see the violet coming through in this black kandy, which is by far my favorite detail color. I use it on just about everything. Even though lines and edges may not be perfect with freehand airbrushing, I believe it gives a better result than masking because it lends itself to a more realistic look, and it's a heck of a lot faster than all that mask cutting.

8. After finishing the details on the warrior's profile, note how the design has come together. The best part about using this black kandy mix is that I never have to switch guns or colors. It's the same color throughout. Don't be shy about using it for the drop shadow as well. Heck, I used it for everything, including the opposing color for the realistic fire.

9. What Aztec mural would be complete without the famous image of the warrior carrying the dead princess? I didn't know the complete story, so I asked the owner, but he didn't know it either.

10. I figured I might as well crank out the rest of the pieces at the same time, since I had already finished the hardest part on the tanks. I couldn't include all the details in the calendar, but I really didn't need to. By creating a stylized image, I got the point across and kept the scale of detail the same throughout the bike. You never want one part of your paint job to be more detailed than the others. Keep the continuity clean by scaling the detail and balancing the design.

11. You can see the rough sketch of my character through the silver. At this point it was time to bring out the flame stencil again. This stencil is made of the same material used on the bottom of snowboards. No, you don't need to get some; I just happened to have a lot lying around because I do snowboard designs. Use whatever material you have—stencils are temporary anyway.

12. The Aztec logo did not get any fire, but detail work made up for it. I added a little drop shadow, and we were good to go! Want to know how I made both pieces the same? I finished one, then copied. Keep it simple. Painting on both sides of a single tank? Put a mirror against the back of your table. Works killer!

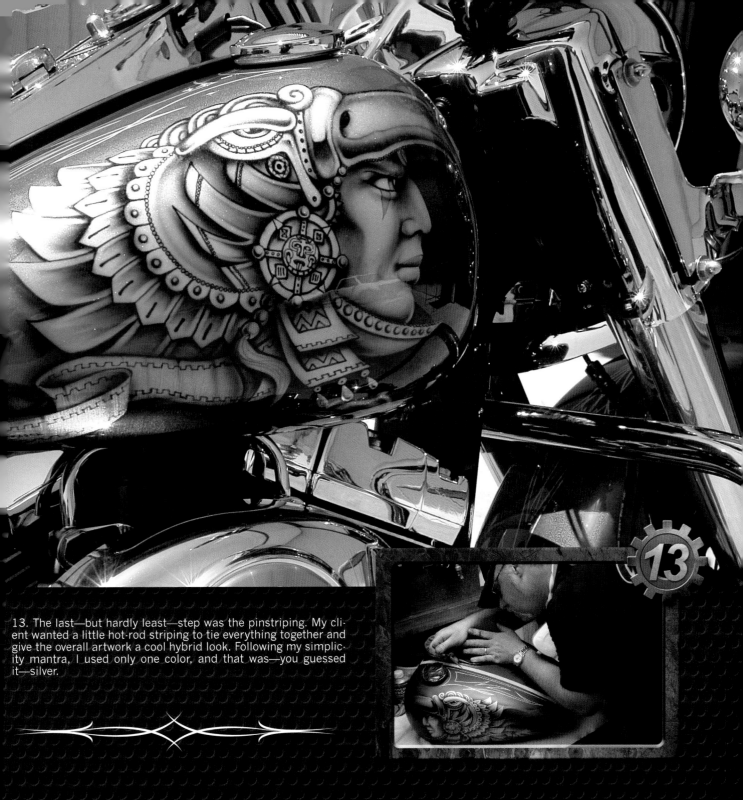

13. The last—but hardly least—step was the pinstriping. My client wanted a little hot-rod striping to tie everything together and give the overall artwork a cool hybrid look. Following my simplicity mantra, I used only one color, and that was—you guessed it—silver.

No clear-coat step here. This is the only chapter in the book in which the final piece was not cleared, simply because the client didn't want it. That's not bad as long as you inform the client of the risks and explain that you're not responsible for any of the multitude of problems that may occur. Nonetheless, I did give the artwork a protective coating of SG-100 intercoat clear. Although intercoat clear won't completely protect the job, it will help.

The client returned to the shop a few weeks later with the finished bike. He was very happy, and even amazed, at how many people responded to the bike. I strongly believe that paint is the first thing people see and the last thing they remember. Anyone who argues that paint doesn't make the bike just doesn't get it.

Not only was I happy about the paint job surviving the buffing and assembly, I was actually surprised to see the bike again at all. All of you kustom painters know what I'm talking about. Our portfolios are filled with dozens of paint jobs that are never photographed when completed because we never hear from the client again. If you want to make sure you'll never see a bike again, just make the client promise to bring it by for a photo!

Latin Airbrush Association Por Vida!!

SCORPION

A BREAKDOWN OF A HYBRID PAINT SCHEME

The reason I refer to this type of a graphic job as a composite is because of the multiple techniques and styles incorporated into one paint job. I have specialized in composite design since day one working with Dion at Kal Koncepts. While many artists tend to lean toward being purists and focusing on individual styles of painting, I find that hybrids are much more interesting. A hybrid is something that you get when you combine more than one style or technique. If done properly, you end up with a design that is more than the sum of its parts—in other words, badass.

Our clients for this particular job were ZZapp Motorsports/Focus Central. They had built up a tricked-out street racer Focus that was to be the centerpiece of the ZZapp booth at the 2004 SEMA show. They wanted a paint job that would appeal to the racer boys, but it had to have their ZZapp name on all four sides, as well as their new scorpion logo. We decided to make the scorpion more of a mechanical version, almost in an anime styling. Due to the size restriction of the car, we decided to make the scorpions the

main element of the paint job, with a little realistic fire flying off the tail sections. The only linear graphics on this bad boy were the extended "lightning bolt" tails from the "Z" on the logo. Knowing they were going to be plastering some "racerboy" sponsor stickers on it, we left the kit alone. It was the first time they were pulling a booth at SEMA, and the company really needed a paint job that would catch the attendees' attention and reel 'em in. Well they came to the right place!

So getting back to our composite concept, let's do a shopping list of what we're going to incorporate in this American-made rice burner: a sequentially masked mural of the robo-scorpion (itself a composite of masking, cutting, and freehand airbrush work); lettering, striping, and a little realistic fire thrown in for good measure. Not too much to order, especially for SEMA. Did I mention we had one week to do it? The SEMA curse it's called, but we're used to it. 'Nuff said, time to paint.

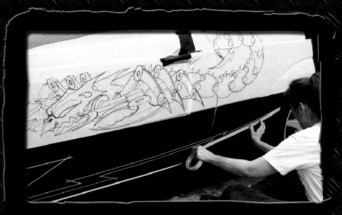

1. After getting our modified scorpions approved by the boys at Focus Central, I sketched them out on Automask transfer tape and mocked them up on the sides for placement. Deborah used the proportions of the scorpions to get the graphic Z laid out for the ZZapp logo and masked it off in preparation to spray. Because of time constraints, we worked on both the logo and lettering simultaneously, flip-flopping the masking paper around as we sprayed.

2. With Deb masking off the logos on the side, I set to cutting out the main scorpion on the hood. Remember when I referred to sequential masking? Well, this is it. The trick to sequential masking is actually in the unmasking. By sequentially removing cut sections of your design as you spray, you can get a very tight monochromatic version of your artwork to leave alone or color later. It gives you a killer mural that looks like you spent forever on it in a fraction of the time.

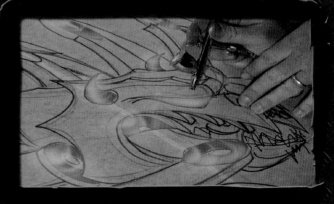

3. Using House of Kolor BC-26 white, I began rendering the individual details with the Eclipse CS airbrush. Even with the basecoat white being opaque, you can get a killer rendition of the overall design just by your airbrushing. Plus, it gives you hardly any edge. This is a big advantage when you have little time for extra leveling clearcoats.

4 Fast-forwarding ahead, you can see how killer the monochromatic beginning of the mural was—almost nice enough to render without color. Hard to believe, but this section of cutting, unmasking, and airbrushing with white took only about an hour. You might have noticed in some of the other chapters how I like to use this technique in my layouts. Hey, if something works...

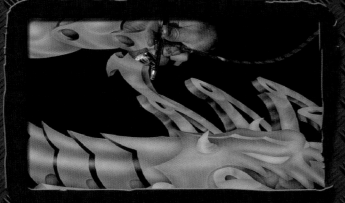

5. One of the best parts of sequential masking is that if you're using kandies to color in your total design, and you're working over black, you can most likely get away without any additional back-masking since the overspray from the kandies is hardly noticeable over base black. The kandy I sprayed in at this point is KK-04 Oriental Blue—very subtle. Just enough to give the look of polished machined metal.

6. I mixed a combination of SG-100, KK-11 Apple Red, and Blue Blood red. This gave me a killer semi-opaque red that not only covered like an opaque but had the low-overspray characteristics of a transparent color. Just wanted a touch of the color so it would match the lettering and striping later on. Did I mention we also had logo colors that we had to stick to? Always restrictions, but the creativity is how you work with them!

7. Amazing what you can do with an airbrush and a little black HoK basecoat. The body looked a bit different in shade, because I added just a few drops of KK-17 violet to my BC-25 black base—just enough to have the legs and claws contrast the body. One of my favorite things about airbrushing with an Eclipse top-feed airbrush is that you can always add a few drops of paint to the top, pop the cap back on, give it a shake, and spray! Very cool.

8. I used the pure black to render in shadows to emphasize depth, and to blend in the background. This was also a good opportunity to kill any stray overspray that may have bled onto our background and to clean up any masking blems. I try to incorporate repairs into the actual rendering of the design. If you find yourself stopping, repairing, etc., you waste a lot of time. Plus, remember the famous mantra: "Kustom painters don't make mistakes, we just change our minds!" Heheheh.

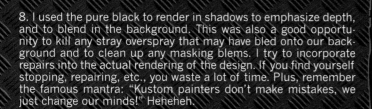

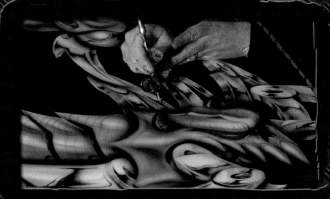

9. I kept the other two side logos up to speed at every step. This is the best way to keep continuity throughout the designs. If you do one at a time, you'll be able to map which one you did first, which one you got good at, and which one you were bored with. It's that simple.

10. With the "Z" sprayed with silver, I sketched in the rest of the logo, as well as a little realistic fire to add something special to the overall design. The low edge of the design would come in seriously handy now, with the fire being airbrushed right over it.

11. Switching back to my original basecoat white, I laid in the fire and logo. The blending of freehand with hard-edge masked graphics softened the edge and is the ultimate example of a composite technique. To get something that fell between freehand and masked, I broke out the *FH-01* Artool *Curve* template. This allowed me to truly sculpt the realistic fire.

12. Returning with the black basecoat and template, I was able to eliminate the overspray from the freehand work and blend the more subtle flames with the background black color. I used multiple Eclipse airbrushes to save on cleaning guns when switching back and forth from white to black. You'd be surprised at the time saved just from this.

13. With the white finished, I colored the flames and lettering with some KK-12 Pagan gold kandy mixed with SG-100 intercoat clear. Though I've mentioned it before, I'll mention it again: Never add more than 20% KK to the intercoat before reducing or you will have some bleed issues. Please don't be one of those artists who just uses pure KK, and if you do, please don't e-mail me to cry about it...heheheh.

14. Up close, you can see how I didn't completely cover the white with the Pagan gold. Just a little goes a long way. Plus, the extra white showing at the base, gave an added sense of realism and heat. You can see this minimalism of paint use throughout the majority of my artwork. Mies van der Rohe said it best; "Less is more." Unless you're talking margaritas, of course, and then more tequila is better (sorry, Mies).

15. Amazing what a little KK-08 Tangerine and a little KK-11 Apple Red can do to some airbrushed flames. You want the sequencing of color to be subtle, yet the colors themselves to come across strong. Airbrushing is the only way at this scale.

16. Just a thin line of HoK Roman Red striping urethane is all it took to seriously pop the silver Z. While I did the stripe with a Mack #10 000 striping brush, the lettering was done with my trusty Jensen Swirley Q lettering quill. By the way, note the cool fade with the letters. I airbrushed this at the same time as the fire, and also the rest of the fire on the rest of the vehicle. Remember, continuity!

17. One of the few times that I'll come back with an opaque is when rendering fire. The SG-101 Lemon Yellow really pops on the fire, while a kandy transparent would blend in too much. Yes, I did use the same stencil on the fire that I used earlier. Just be careful—that lemon yellow does love to overspray over all your detail work!!

18. If you do accidentally wash out your fire with overspray, you can always revive it by spraying a little Pagan Gold or Lime Gold over it. For the final touch, I like bringin' in a little of the white for the most subtle of highlights. When this thing is cleared, the fire is gonna jump right out at you!

19. With the white still in my airbrush, I added any stray highlights needed to really finish off the piece. White first, white last—that's the name of the game. One big full circle. Definitely something Zen about it...heheheh.

With all the artwork done, it was time for the clearcoating. Because we performed the majority of graphics and murals with the airbrush, and we kept the edges fairly low, Dion was able to bury everything in one session. Now, I don't mean one coat. One of Dion's sessions of clear consists of a tack coat, two medium coats, and a gloss coat, so there's more than a single coat of clear on the job. With the low edges, the pinstripes were buried with this single session, and the whole Focus was easily color-sanded and buffed the next day. We actually had enough time that week to crank out two aluminum sign panels with the same logos, and scorpions airbrushed directly over the grinded aluminum. Always go above and beyond, and you'll have a client for life! Job done. Happy client. Killer booth for SEMA. This Ford was definitely a big Focus in the building, no pun intended!

THE KANDY-KOLORED TANGERINE-FLAKED STREAMLINE BABY

Tricking Out The Paint On Gregg DesJardines Café Racer, *Hellion*

I know the title has been used before, but it fit this chapter—right down to the color. When Gregg called and asked us to paint another of his creations, I knew it was going to be over the top. I also knew I had to put this one in the book.

A little history first. Gregg Desjardines is the owner of and head builder for Gregg's Customs. He specializes in limited-production and kustom one-off motorcycle parts and accessories. Now and then, he also builds an incredible bike. This particular café racer was going to debut at Indy and, like his previous bikes, gain serious media attention. Gregg wanted the paint job to be conservative yet radical, bright yet subdued, classy but badass. (We're used to these requests). Instead of going with a modern-day tribal or murals, he wanted the high-tech look of the bike to contrast with a retro paint job. So we settled on scallops, probably the oldest graphic design in automotive kustomizing history.

Another thing we're used to is bare metal. Bare metal tins usually need everything from bodywork to primer to final paint. At Kal Koncepts we consider ourselves a one-stop shop for very good reason. With fabricators and builders like Lambie and Dion, the bike builders we deal with feel no need to shop for additional talent or expertise; they're confident that all by ourselves, we can make their creations look as good as possible. So, with notes taken from Gregg and a deadline less than two weeks away, we got to it.

1. Lambie grabbed the grinder to smooth out the welds and rough up the surface for bodywork. This tank, entirely hand-built by Gregg, was literally bulletproof. Even so, we had to be careful about grinding around the welds and seams. Using Rollock grinding pads, we were able to prep the metal without endangering the welds.

2. Lambie does love his body filler. It might look as though he was covering the entire tank; but in reality, most of the polyester filler wound up as sanding dust on the shop floor. Filler lets us smooth the weld transitions and fill the low spots. With the rough bodywork completed, we applied a coat of House of Kolor KD2000 (Direct To Metal) catalyzed primer/sealer. We would be doing the final bodywork and blocking over the primer.

3. Next we sanded the primer smooth with 600-grit sandpaper and let it sit for a day. (That allowed everything to cure, had there been any shrinking.) We then base-coated the tanks, fenders, and headlight body with an equal mix of FBC07 Gamma Gold, KBC08 Tangerine Kandy Basecoat, and MBC01 Pale Gold Diamonds, which gave a killer foundation for the flake to play off of.

4. To apply the flake we used the MF01 Gold Mini-flake. When mixing the flake coat he always adds just enough flake to coat the mixing stick yet pour off without clotting. If it clots, you have too much flake. Before Dion started to flake the tanks, he gave the base coat a coat of pure clear, without flake. The clear was then allowed to tack up, acting as the glue coat for the flake. When spraying a flake, stop between coats to spray the surface with air from the gun. That forces the standing flakes to lie flat against the glue coat, making for a smoother final finish. It also saves lots of clear and sanding.

5. After the flake, Dion gave the entire job a flow coat of UFC-35 clear. It may take a few sessions to get the clear smooth. (I'm not going to describe these extra clear steps; they're pretty self explanatory.) Next, we sanded the tins with 600-grit sandpaper and began laying out the graphics with 1/8" crepe tape. No computers here. Sometimes the old-school method is best.

6. Because of the tank's compound curves, I used the rip-and-tear technique with 1/4" tape for the main masking. While that may take longer than with transfer tape, you won't be cutting nearly as much, which is always a good thing. Just make sure to press all the wrinkles out, or you'll be fixing bleeds. Luckily the bleeds will be on clear coat, where they're easier to fix.

7. To keep the edge low, I decided to spray the graphic with my TH-3 Kustom Fan Head airbrush. Greg wanted an unusual color scheme with a retro look; I could think of nothing better than Kandy Tangerine Metalflake and sky blue. I created the sky blue by mixing BC-26 Basecoat White and PBC-36 Trublu. Three or four light coats gave me enough coverage without a huge edge that would peek through the pinstripe paint.

8. To give depth and color to the scallops, I mixed a batch of KK-04 Kandy Oriental Blue and SG-100, which I used just along the edges and tips. With the airbrushed fades finished, I sprayed a light coat of SG-100 Intercoat mixed with turquoise ice pearl over the whole thing. That made the scallops really pop when the sun hit them.

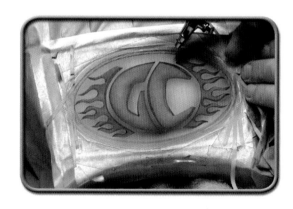

9. The scallops having been masked off, it was time to put Gregg's logo on the tins. With so much aluminum on the bike, I thought it would be a natural to use the Kosmic Krome Aluminum effect. A little burnishing with Scotch-Brite and the logo took on a cool brushed aluminum look. Be sure to spray SG-100 over the aluminum before masking on it. That locks down the effect and prevents tape tracking.

10. I could have done the logo work on my computer; but with only one logo to do, it was faster just to draw and cut it out of transfer tape. After the logo had been cut and removed, I hit the unmasked area lightly with transparent black. I wanted just a little shadow, not too much black.

11. Here, with the transfer tape removed, you can see the subtle difference between the raw aluminum and the black-shaded part of the logo. Now I needed to decide whether to outline the logo or leave it with a ghosted masked edge. I make many such design decisions along the way, allowing the paint job to dictate its own terms.

12. I decided to stick with the masked edge. To knock back the design a bit more, I sprayed the entire logo lightly with another coat of MC-01 Kosmic Aluminum. A bit more Scotch-Brite work and the final effect was an acid-etched finish very similar to the stampings on a metallicized trading card.

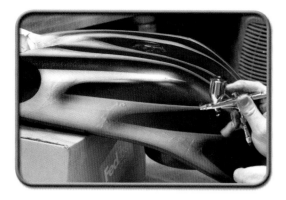

13. It may seem redundant to have remasked all of the graphics, but that was the only way to achieve a truly clean drop shadow for the scallops, especially when working with a color as light as the Trublu. I even blended a little tangerine kandy in under the scallops for added depth.

14. With drop shadows and airbrush touchups completed, I began striping the scallops with HoK Rich Gold. Normally I would have cleared, sanded, and then striped, but the edge was so low, and we had so much material on these poor tins, I decided just to have at it. Plus, I knew that for some reason, metallic pinstripe paints actually pull better over base coat than over clear. Might just be me...

15. After the outlining, I breathed a sigh of relief and had fun adding decorative striping around and between the scallops. The striping color may appear to be the same gold, but it actually had a bit of Copper added to give a subtle shift from the Rich Gold outline. I did all of this striping with a Mack series #10 size 000 sword striping brush, pound for pound the best striper out there.

16. With the majority of the chapters in this book showing Dion doing clear-coating, I thought it safe to leave that to your imagination here. I do show Dion and Lambie buffing out the tins. This is definitely a two-person job. Even so, you have to be careful not to fling these suckers across the room. The more oddly shaped the tank, the harder it is to buff out.

17. There you have it: one set of tanks and tins kustom painted and ready to be assembled on Gregg's bike. Normally we like to have the actual rolling chassis at the shop to be sure the parts of our paint job line up. Because of time constrictions and work being done on the bike four hours away, this wasn't possible. We improvised with photos of the raw bike assembled. With these I was able to get the graphics to point at the same angle and tie in together. When there's a wish, there's a way.

As you can see, the tins fit on the bike perfectly and looked pretty killer. The subtle colors matched the understated hues, yet the bright kandy and flake also contrasted well with what is, after all, a basically monochromatic bike. After seeing the completed bike in person, I was glad I'd added the extra Kandy Oriental Blue to the scallops, since they appear almost white by comparison with the basic color and other values of the bike. I would love to take credit for knowing that ahead of time, but I think we should chalk this up to a combination of me liking to add airbrushing and kandy to everything, and just plain luck!

If you ever see one of Gregg Desjardines's customs in person at a show, check it out closely. His workmanship is so incredible that I would have to say his are among the few vehicles on which a paint job of ours truly is an accessory and not the main attraction. (Ahem!)

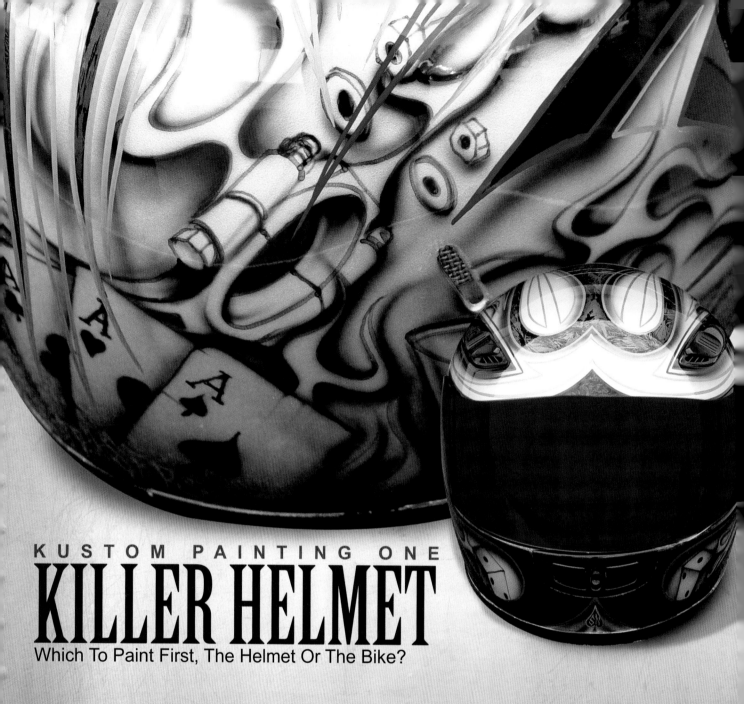

KUSTOM PAINTING ONE
KILLER HELMET
Which To Paint First, The Helmet Or The Bike?

How could there be a kustom paint technique book without a chapter on helmet painting? I've decided to give you one with a bit of everything. When I bought my Yamaha R1 back in 2002, I couldn't decide what to paint on it. I wanted something different, but also something I'd like longer than a few weeks. I really dug the stock silver and black plastics that came on the R1—so much so that, after de-stickering the bike, I left it plain for two years.

What I decided to do at last was paint my helmet with the design I wanted for the bike. If I liked the helmet for more than a year, the bike would get the same treatment. Sounds weird, but it worked for me. Turns out I did like the design, and the bike was finished in time to be showcased at the 2004 SEMA show and then featured in a step-by-step article for the now defunct *Autographics* magazine and a photo essay in *2Wheel Tuner*. Not

bad for a paint job that sat on my helmet for over a year! I had been so paranoid about someone copying the design for their bike before I painted mine that I never published an article on the helmet. That is, until now.

I rarely get the chance to use a silver/black combo because my customers are always going for crazy color schemes. Those who do want to stick with simple monochromatics rarely want off-the-wall artwork. What better way to scratch that itch than do my own helmet? I knew I wanted the design to combine freehand airbrushing, flames, and Von Dutch-style pinstriping. Though I favored monochromatics, I also recognized the importance of color to kick the design up a notch. So, with all of that spinning through my head, here's what I came up with. Hope you like it!

1. Now, before you start to criticize, let me be clear that I chose this helmet for its safety and fit, not its shape or artwork. At any rate, before I could paint it, I had to disassemble it, which is where many artists mess up. Carefully remove everything you can; mask off what you can't. When dismantling, be sure to keep all the parts together and notice whether there's anything unexpected or unusual about the way the helmet comes apart. If there is, jot it down on paper. If you don't, by the time you reassemble the helmet you'll have forgotten the key and you'll be completely baffled. And that sucks.

2. Biggest problem with today's helmets is that while the graphics have improved, they're more of a pain to remove. I always recommend buying a plain white helmet, but sometimes you don't have a choice. Try to peel off what stickers you can; those underneath the clear have to be sanded off. In this case, I used 220-grit sandpaper with a dual-action sander. I masked any areas I didn't want paint getting to, like the top vents, interior, and bottom rubber trim. With the helmet masked off, I used a red Scotch-Brite pad to clean areas the sander couldn't reach. Make sure every surface to be primed is at least scuffed up. Even the best primer/sealer needs a mechanical tooth in the fiberglass to grab onto for adhesion. Remember, the best paint job in the world is worth nothing over a bad prep job.

3. With the prepping complete, Dion primed the helmet and a couple of fiberglass fish with catalyzed polyester primer. This primer is easily sanded, very durable, and fills in any scratches or nicks your helmet might have encountered in its previous life.

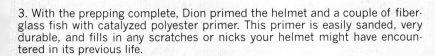

4. Having given the primer the better part of a day to cure, Nino started color-sanding in preparation for the application of... well, color. A good quality wet/dry sandpaper is recommended. We like 3M and Meguiar's for fine work. In this case, 600-grit sandpaper soaked in water for 15 minutes was just the ticket. Always presoak wet/dry sandpaper to prevent loading and scratching.

5. Now the helmet was ready for Dion to shoot with a base coat of Orion Silver. Currently, House of Kolor has a silver primer/sealer that replaces the need for following the primer with a base coat. But remember, this helmet was painted more than four years ago, when the new primer/sealer wasn't available. Perfect example of how HoK always has new products coming out to make our jobs easier.

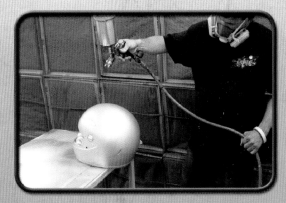

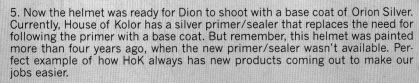

6. After giving the silver time to cure, I began laying out the design with blue 3M 1/8" fineline tape. Normally I'd use a crepe tape for something like this, but I would be spraying a kandy, and the vinyl fineline cuts through kandies much better than paper tape. Working from a centerline, I kept the flame and graphics symmetrical; being off by as little as 1/8" shows on something this small.

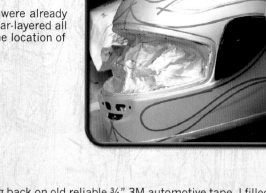

7. I didn't need to paint the side covers or the vents, since they were already black, and they never operate as well once you've painted and clear-layered all over them. Note how I designed the black graphics to flow with the location of the side cover and vent.

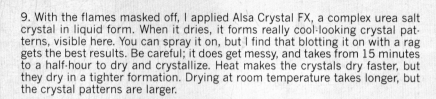

8. Falling back on old reliable ¾" 3M automotive tape, I filled in the areas that wouldn't be painted. With all the newfangled masking systems out there, I still use good old tan tape the most. Take your time on this step; fixing bleed-throughs can take much longer than masking correctly in the first place.

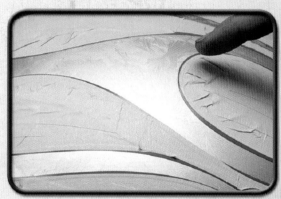

9. With the flames masked off, I applied Alsa Crystal FX, a complex urea salt crystal in liquid form. When it dries, it forms really cool-looking crystal patterns, visible here. You can spray it on, but I find that blotting it on with a rag gets the best results. Be careful; it does get messy, and takes from 15 minutes to a half-hour to dry and crystallize. Heat makes the crystals dry faster, but they dry in a tighter formation. Drying at room temperature takes longer, but the crystal patterns are larger.

10. With the crystals dry, I lightly airbrushed the helmet with overreduced HoK BC-25 Basecoat Black. You want just enough for color coverage, but not enough to hide the crystal texture. Too much paint will lock in the crystals, and you won't be able to remove them for the effect (see the next step). Don't apply the paint too wet; slight, dry applications are best.

11. Give the base coat a few minutes to dry, then take a damp terrycloth towel with a little liquid soap and scrub off the crystals. What's left behind is the paint that found its way between the crystal patterns. The result is a killer stencil effect very similar to marbleizing, but much tighter—almost like shattered glass.

12. Since I still had base-coat black in my airbrush, I took the opportunity to spray the other graphics around the helmet. Only the flames got the crystal treatment. I planned something else for the black-based graphic shown here. I always like to combine different effects within a paint job—sort of like adding different spices when cooking.

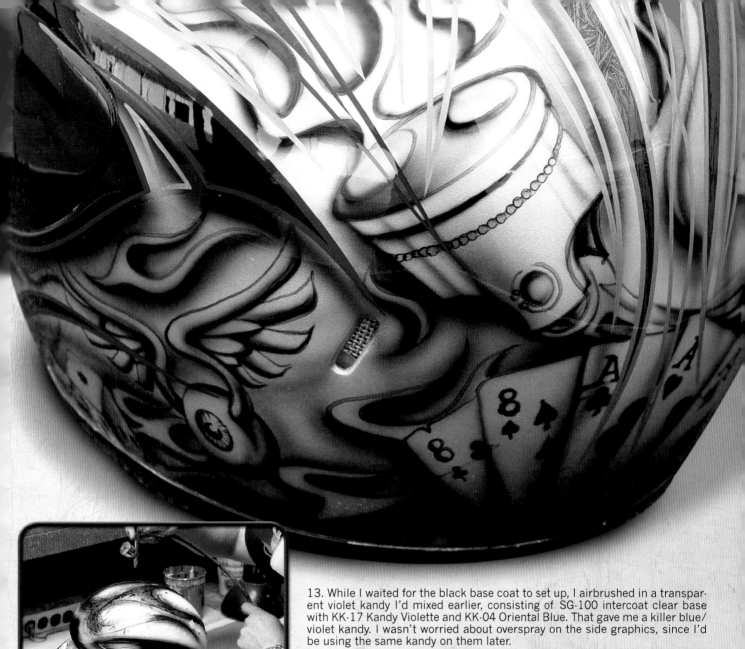

13. While I waited for the black base coat to set up, I airbrushed in a transparent violet kandy I'd mixed earlier, consisting of SG-100 intercoat clear base with KK-17 Kandy Violette and KK-04 Oriental Blue. That gave me a killer blue/violet kandy. I wasn't worried about overspray on the side graphics, since I'd be using the same kandy on them later.

14. With kandy layering done on the flame graphic—you'll need four or five layers to get the desired effect with a truly transparent kandy—it was time to play with the side graphics using HoK's MB-01 silver/white marbleizer. Instead of spraying marbleizer directly on the graphic, I sprayed it on wadded-up Saran Wrap and blotted. That resulted in an interesting texture and left some of the black base showing through.

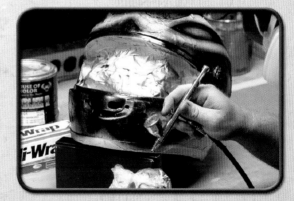

15. The marbleizer needed 15 to 20 minutes to fully cure, after which I layered on the same violet kandy. It had a darker look, since there was less silver showing than in the flames. Still, it flashed brighter at angles because the pearl in the marbleizer was brighter than the Orion Silver. Little touches like this make a big difference in the long run.

16. After unmasking everything, I gave the design a little drop-shadow love, just for depth's sake. Amazing what simple gradated fades can do for a paint job!

17. With white chalk, I sketched in the freehand airbrush designs. A few flying eyeballs here, a couple of pistons and some skulls there, and it was good to go. I wanted lots of icons in the airbrushed background—almost like the background art that came out of Roth Studios in the late 1960s. I wanted the helmet and bike to look like a leading-edge design at first glance, but to scream "retro!" when really looked at.

18. Switching from an Iwata Eclipse CS to an HP·CH Highline detail gun, I proceeded to airbrush/sketch in the background art. Because I used a simple overreduced base-coat black, I didn't need to remask the graphics. If I was really careful, what little overspray got on the graphics would blend in anyway. Cool, no?

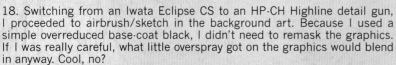

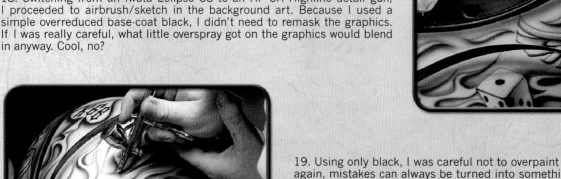

19. Using only black, I was careful not to overpaint or make mistakes. (Then again, mistakes can always be turned into something else. Heh, heh!) Since my design was monochromatic, I couldn't use white to repair or highlight. Couldn't use silver either, because the overspray would look whacked, and silver always looks different when sprayed with an airbrush instead of a gun. So if you want a highlight, you must think ahead and leave the silver there. It's called negative-space airbrushing.

20. With the airbrushing finished, it was time for everyone's favorite part, pinstriping. Besides all the other goodies I wanted on this brain bucket, Von Dutch-style striping had been a must from the get-go. I started by simply outlining the graphics before doing anything fancy. Keeping with the paint scheme, I used HoK's Lavender striping urethane and an Excaliber 000 Sword striper. No masking or roller stripers here; if you want the old-school look, you have to go with old-school techniques. Plus, it's a nice break from the airbrush. I highly encourage any airbrusher to give it a whirl.

21. Switching to a secondary color, I continued outlining and threw in a little artistic hot-rod stuff. The gold was a nice contrast with the silver and purple; it also matched a number of anodized accessories already on the bike. Pinstriping with a metallic is challenging, but it always looks so incredible after it's been cleared!

22. With the artwork done, it was time for clear-coating. To bury the pinstriping, Dion did two complete sessions of clear, using HoK UFC-19 and his favorite LPH-400 spray gun. Some good advice: unmask and remask the helmet between every paint or clear session. Otherwise you'll have nasty edges with permanently embedded tape.

After buffing lightly (even when there are no runs), a good color-sanding and buffing really bring out the shine in any clear—it was time to put the helmet together and enjoy my masterpiece.

Because the helmet came out so killer, I added even more goodies to the bike, as you can see in the photographs. (There's only so much you can do on a helmet!) The helmet was on display in the Iwata booth at SEMA 2003, and helmet and bike were shown together at SEMA 2004. Though such a pairing is not new to the kustom paint industry, it's amazing how many people still comment when they see a matching bike and helmet. In my case, the helmet wasn't a copy of the bike, nor was the bike a copy of the helmet. Though the designs matched, they did differ as well. Anyone can take an eight-inch section of a bike and throw it on a helmet, but to make something truly match without being a carbon copy is special. Whenever you, as an artist, take time to think through every step of a design, your work will be a testament to your talents, and your reward will be lasting public appreciation.

As a side note, and to show how long this book was in the making, the R1 and helmet are being repainted in Steampunk style for the Iwata booth at SEMA 2009. Who knows? That step-by-step might just turn up in the next book.

THE DONKEY FROG

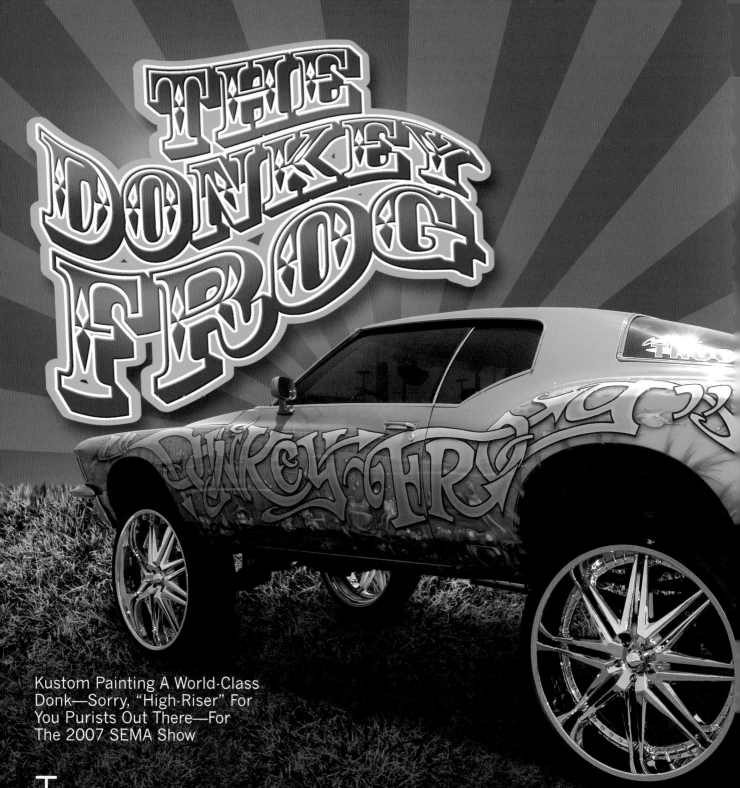

Kustom Painting A World-Class
Donk—Sorry, "High-Riser" For
You Purists Out There—For
The 2007 SEMA Show

The only constant in the automotive kustom industry is change. New trends pop up all the time. Some are merely flashes in the pan, instantly labeled fads that come and go as fast as the Macarena. Others stay for the duration, becoming staples of the industry, sometimes even classics. Pro Street, hot rods, rat rods, minitrucks, street trucks, lowriders, bombs: these established platforms for kustom painting have been around for years. Every now and then something new emerges that may have the legs to last. One of the newest goes by the name "donk."

"Donks," "boxes," "bubbles," and "high-risers" are names for vehicles having extraordinarily large wheels. We're not just talking 20" or 22". Those fit the category of "dubs." We're talking 26" to 30"-plus wheels. While this style isn't for everybody, one thing you can say about it is that it attracts attention, and it sure does showcase (and sell) wheels.

We were contacted by Deb and Marsha of California Truck Accessories, Bakersfield, California, concerning a build for the 2007 SEMA (Specialty Equipment Manufacturers Association) show in Las Vegas. This was not going to be a standard lowered or raised truck build, but a donk build. A 1971 boattail Buick Riviera had been acquired, and the folks at Cal Truck thought a donk version might be good publicity. At Kal Koncepts/Air Syndicate, we love a challenge. With the 12" lift and other modifications taking most of the build time, we were left with only about a week to prepare and execute the paintwork. Heck, who can say no to painting a donk? (Even if you don't know what one is.)

1. After receiving the Riviera, Lambie started molding the emblems and getting the car ready for kustom paint. He also found a trick way to section and move back the bottom edges of the fender wells so that the mongo-sized 30" wheels would clear with their 37" final tire radius.

2. Since the Rivi came to us with a decent white paint job, we decided to keep that as the base. After touching up and resealing the entire paint job with white Koseal, we sanded the surface and I started the layout process. Using Automask transfer tape, I laid out the "Donkey Frog" name in graffiti lettering with a pencil, and then with a Sharpie pen for the final lines to be cut.

3. With the side logos cut and unmasked, it was spraying time. Lambie loaded his LPH-400 spray gun with a mixture of BC-02 Orion Silver, MC-01 Aluminum Kosmic Krome, and MBC-02 Platinum Diamonds. This mix gives us a seriously killer metallic silver that shifted to black at certain angles. We named it Silverado, and it's truly amazing.

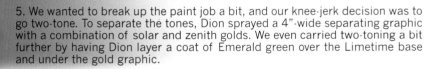

4. With the *Donkey Frog* logo sprayed and given a few hours to dry fully, we back-masked it and prepped the car for spraying the base color. The main color for the Rivi was to be PBC-38 Limetime Pearl. This color has an amazing lime-green pigment combined with a gold pearl. The result literally shimmers in the sun. Here, Dion used an LPH-400 to lay down a few good coats. PBCs cover well; he got full coverage over the white in three coats.

5. We wanted to break up the paint job a bit, and our knee-jerk decision was to go two-tone. To separate the tones, Dion sprayed a 4"-wide separating graphic with a combination of solar and zenith golds. We even carried two-toning a bit further by having Dion layer a coat of Emerald green over the Limetime base and under the gold graphic.

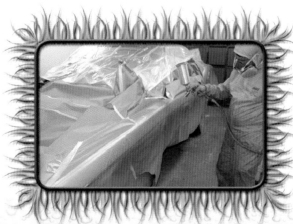

6. To break up the graphic a bit, I added stencil patterning. After cutting out an assortment of lily pads on one of my larger Artool stencils, I airbrushed the design using a mixture of KK-09 Organic Green and SG-100. The kandy green let the metallic gold show through—a cool look indeed.

7. Since we had only a week for the entire paint job, we had to layer the graphics and do all of the artwork on the raw base coat. (Extra clear coats would have taken time that we didn't have.) With the emerald-green metallic laid on the bottom half, I started on the murals. I roughed them out in chalk, then did the final sketch Basecoat White with a Kustom Eclipse CS airbrush. The murals were a freeform series of cartoon frogs that tied in with the theme.

8. With the white sketchwork done on the frogs, I used more of the emerald-green metallic and a mixture of kandy organic green and black for the details. I wanted to keep the murals simple and cartoony. It was the style the clients had approved in the early concept renderings, the frogs were fast to do, and they provided great filler effects for the background.

9. Finished with frogging, I unmasked everything but the *Donkey Frog* logo so I could create a floating drop-shadow effect without getting any of the kandy green/black mixture into the silver lettering. Strategic masking saves lots of time and materials in paintwork.

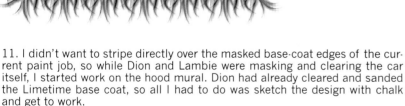

10. With the drop shadows finished, the lettering was finally unmasked. Using a mixture of KK-04 Kandy Oriental Blue and SG-100, I airbrushed in a centered fade to give the lettering more depth. Again, the kandy allowed the metallic in the silver to punch through. The lettering edge still looked rough at this stage but would be outlined later. Right now I just needed to take care of the airbrushing.

11. I didn't want to stripe directly over the masked base-coat edges of the current paint job, so while Dion and Lambie were masking and clearing the car itself, I started work on the hood mural. Dion had already cleared and sanded the Limetime base coat, so all I had to do was sketch the design with chalk and get to work.

12. For this mural, the client requested a pimped-out frog riding a donkey. The rest was pretty much up to me. The mural was fun because I rarely get to work on bizarrely hilarious murals. I wanted the mural to tie in with the theme of the donk, but I also wanted it to be very colorful and obnoxious. Before any of the colors were layered in, I laid out the mural and detailed it with BC-26 Basecoat White, again using a Kustom CS airbrush.

13. No self-respecting pimp frog would be caught dead without his pink pearl fur hat. Using HoK Hot Pink Pearl PBC, I rendered the hat with the same airbrush. It's important to be careful when airbrushing opaques and pearls, because the overspray can really mess with the surrounding paint job. With the background cleared, I could always sand off any overspray that got out of hand.

14. Working sequentially along the color wheel, I used violet next for his outfit. PBC-40 Violet Pearl worked great for that. Again, I used opaque PBCs here, so I had to go easy on the overspray. Small amounts of overspray can be removed with a water-damp rag. A little KC-10 precleaner added to the rag can help without damaging the underlying work.

15. For the gold, I grabbed some of the metallic mixture Dion had used on the beltline graphic. This stuff is very metallicky, but was worth the hassle since it gave the frog's glasses and other accessories a realistic sparkly gold appearance. Be sure to wipe down the mural after each color, no matter what type of paint you use—especially after pearls and metallics.

THE DONKEY FROG

16. The next color for the mural was transparent kandy oriental blue. I could blend this into the background green with little chance of negative overspray. As a matter of fact, all of the colors applied after the gold were kandies. They were used to color and blend in the surrounding opaques.

17. With the coloring all but completed, I outlined and added detail using a combination of BC-25 Black and kandy violet. The combination allowed the black to blend without killing the surrounding colors. Outlining and detailing in black are necessary for a true cartoon-style mural, but black in its pure form will dull colors.

18. As in all my mural work, the last airbrushed color is white.

19. While I was airbrushing the hood mural, Dion applied a leveling coat of clear and sanded the car smooth for the next step: pinstriping. Without a graphic edge, a stripe will not go on smoothly without peeking out of the final clear coat. After striping the separating gold graphic with lime green, I outlined the letters with HoK Lavender striping urethane.

20. Time for final clear-coating: Donning his space suit, Dion sprayed the entire vehicle with three wet coats of HoK UFC-35, using his trusty LPH-400 LV spray gun. The 1.5 mm tip, Dion's choice for final clears, gives him the perfect flow-out for these jobs.

Well, there you have it: one more chapter in the can and one more vehicle ready for the SEMA show. The *Donkey Frog* was more than just a success at SEMA—it was huge. Originally it had been sponsored by House of Kolor for a small outdoor spot; but after the car was seen, MHT Wheels, Inc., one of the largest companies of its kind in the world, wanted it indoors in their booth. Not only did they fully sponsor the wheels for the car, but it became the MHT feature vehicle for the show.

Even the magazine *Rides* featured the *Donkey Frog*, and *Donk* magazine had a few shots of it in their SEMA coverage. *The New York Times* ran seven photos, and the *Donkey Frog* was one of them. So, as I say, you may not like the style, but you cannot deny we made ya look!

DA KINE SURF-TIKI

CREATING A KUSTOM KULTURE TIKI-BOARD
FOR THE 2007 SEMA SHOW

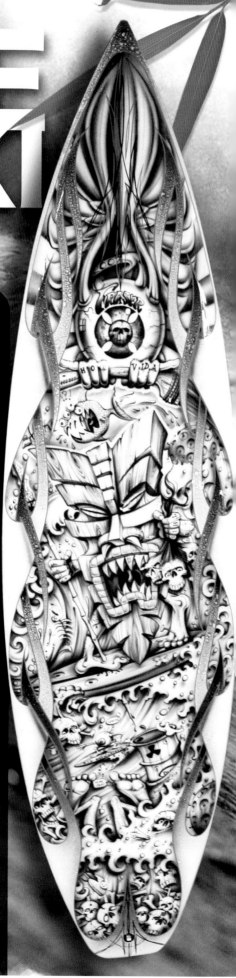

When I began working on this book several years ago, I wanted to include chapters about objects or canvases that are not automotive oriented, but that nonetheless embody the kustom kulture. What objects better symbolize the freedom of the kustom kulture than surfboards? In preparation for the 2007 SEMA show, Kal Koncepts/Air Syndicate Inc. cranked out quite a few painted goodies. The theme in the House of Kolor booth back then was "Surf's up." We painted a Ford Edge as a woodie-themed vehicle, with kustomized surfboards and motorized surf-racks. While that was the show's featured vehicle, the real showcases for art were the surfboards. House of Kolor commissioned Epic Surfboards to custom shape 11 boards for the HoK booth. These were then given to 11 artists to create mini-masterpieces on. The board they gave me is the subject of this chapter.

The painting of a surfboard may be approached in one of two ways. There is the traditional way that board builders have used for years; that is, apply the artwork to the raw, carved foam core before applying the glass. This is usually difficult, since you can't use materials that will react with the foam or run when the fiberglass resin is brushed or sprayed on. (This eliminates most urethanes, lacquers, and enamels, leaving you with tempura, water based acrylics, and some marker pens. Oh yeah, crayons are cool, too.) While this is definitely a challenge, it's not the best way to approach a subject for an art display piece. Hence, we used the second approach, basically treating the board like any other kustom paint job coming into the shop. We sanded it with 220-grit sandpaper, primed with HoK DTM, basecoated, cleared, sanded, and applied graphics. Now, you may wonder why I didn't just sand the glass with 600-grit sandpaper, add the artwork and graphics, and clear. Well, this could work, except for the many inclusions that tend to reside undetected in the original final glass coats of boards, especially the flat-finished ones. These inclusions may appear harmless when basecoating but can quickly turn into terminal fish eyes when the final urethane clearcoat is applied. A simple primer of basecoat white and clear will take a little more initial time but provide a much better foundation for your artwork. The catalyzed primer coat is also a lifesaver if you're kustom painting a used board. Any used board will have board wax, and you'll never get 100 percent of it out of the glass pores. Consequence? An infinite number of fish eyes. Better just to seal that sucker and start over with basecoat white and a nice sanded clearcoat.

Did we paint the entire board in this project? No, I chose to wrap my artwork around the rails and mask off the bottom of the board. Any small edge could be buffed out later and covered with a pinstripe. If a board is going to be seriously ridden, I will paint only the underside. Why? Deck wax usually covers all the artwork and makes it look like crap. Occasionally I will do rail designs or simple graphics, such as flames on the top, but detailed murals are lost on a working deck. The boards created for the HoK booth were for display only; and the way the board stands held them, the deck was the best location for the artwork. The underside retained the Epic logo, Tim Phares's signature, and a cool House of Kolor logo laminated under the glass by Tim. Enough introduction. Let's paint a surfboard!

1. After Dion prepped, primed, based, and cleared the board, all I had to do was sand with 600-grit sandpaper and lay out the graphics. The main graphic on my board was to be a rail design of tribal flames weaving all along the sides of the board. That left the center open for mural work. I laid out the flames using plain 1/8" tan 3M crepe tape.

2. Because both sides of the board can easily be seen at once, I wanted the designs to be perfectly symmetrical. That required a little tracing and pouncing. I used a single sheet of masking paper and construction crayon to trace the image I would duplicate in reverse on the other side. You've seen this old sign painting trick in other chapters as well.

3. With the design transferred, I added tribals to the pattern by free-handing the layouts with the 1/8" crepe line tape. I went back and forth with the additions until the design balanced out overall.

4. After I finished the left side of the rail pattern, I filled in the design with ¾" 3M crepe tape. In the process the design became a negative masked graphic. This means that while I painted the surrounding areas, the masked tribal flame remained white.

5. Time for the fun part, the mural work. Initially, I sketched out the freeform mural lightly with a pencil. You can see the original concept sketch on the paper hanging up. The design was not exact, but merely there to act as reference. Free-form mural designs are best when they don't restrict the actual layout too much.

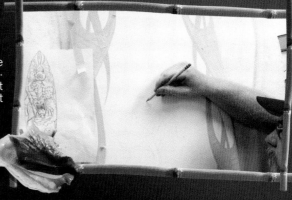

6. I then filled in the layout with BC-25 basecoat black, using an Iwata Kustom Eclipse airbrush. After the entire design had been sketched with the airbrush, I used a rag with a little pre-cleaner to wipe off the excess pencil marks. Subtle mistakes in the airbrushing can be removed with this cloth as well.

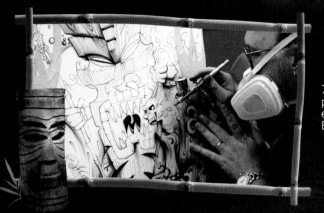

7. Notice how I started to shade and shadow with black. Unlike the pure BC-25 black I'd used for the linework sketch, this was a transparent black made up of BC-25, SG-100 intercoat clear, KK-04 Oriental Blue, and KK-15 Violet.

8. This photo shows the black's slight violet cast. To give the mural something of a tattoo quality, I separated the linework with the shading. When I give somebody a tattoo, I do the opposite, and make it look more like it's been airbrushed. (Just to be different.)

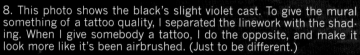

9. I unmasked the board before it was covered up again. It was important to fog transparent black along the taped edges early on, otherwise the negative flames would not show up as distinctly when unmasked.

10. After the board was unmasked, I checked it for any needed touchups, then back-masked the mural so that color could be sprayed on the flames. I wanted to take advantage of the white base, so I used glycerined water in a spray-bottle to create an acid-washed effect when the basecoat was sprayed.

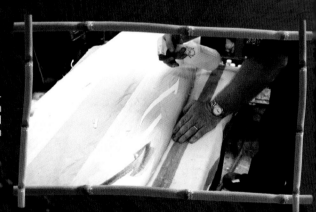

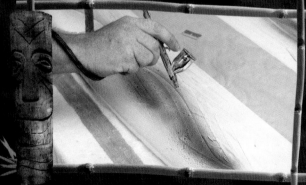

11. When I got the water beads on the surface just the right size—additional misting makes the beads larger—I carefully sprayed on PBC-40 Violet Pearl basecoat. It's important to keep the air pressure down; otherwise the water beads will run along the graphic and really mess up the effect. (This effect is actually pretty cool, in a freaked-out way).

12. The wipe shows the effect. Don't let the water and paint sit too long on the board, or it can give a rough look. Also, don't wipe too soon, or you might pull the still wet basecoat. Takes practice to get it right, but it's not too difficult once you've experimented on a few sample panels.

13. The effect came out killer, but I wanted something extra. To give more color to the board, I airbrushed the tribal tips with a combination of KK-04 Oriental Blue Kandy and SG-100. I even added a bit of Blue Ice Pearl to the mix to make the flame tips really pop after they were cleared.

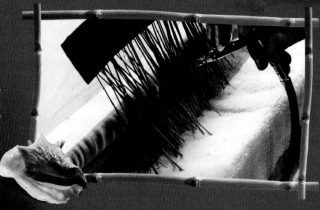

14. After finishing with the funky textures on the tribal flames, I airbrushed transparent black mixed with violet kandy and over-reduced BC-25. This color added depth to the tribals where they crossed over each other. Amazing what a little drop shadow can do for a paint job.

15. I wanted to add more textural effects on the board, so I used my old "whiskbroom" stencil along the rails. Basically, it's just a bunch of broom straws randomly taped together. Imparts a killer effect to any graphic, especially if you want a tie-dyed look.

16. Hey, it's pinstriping time. Just a little Lime Green and Lavender HoK striping urethane, applied with a Mac #10 striping brush, and we were in business. Not only did the Von Dutch touch finish off the flames, it tied all the murals in with the rest of the board.

17. After remasking the back of the board—so that the clear would wrap the original taped edge, this rounds the edge and makes it easy to stripe, and less likely to delaminate—Dion sprayed the entire board with four wet coats of UFC-35 HoK clear, using his trusty LPH-400 1.5 Anest Iwata spray gun.

There ya go: one kustom painted surfboard ready for the SEMA show. House of Kolor wanted the boards to reflect each artist's favorite style. I wanted mine to combine three distinct kustom styles: masked/airbrushed graphics, freehand mural work, and pinstriping—the hat trick of kustom painting. Perhaps you've noticed that most of my work for Kal Koncepts/Air Syndicate incorporates these three techniques, and I wanted my board to represent that.

I highly encourage any kustom painter to try painting a surfboard. Not only are they great attention-getters at car shows, but they look killer on your wall. (Definitely start with a new board. You don't even want to try and get all the old surf wax off a used one; it's not remotely fun!) Heck, if you can't find a good surfboard, paint up a few skateboards, or some of the longer sidewalk surf boards. All are a blast to paint and look great in your portfolio.

HEAVEN & HELL

Sometimes, just when I think I've seen every paint-job concept imaginable, I'm pleasantly surprised by new ones. I've painted my share of choppers with a hellish theme, and I've also done a number of heavenly paint jobs (though not as many). But, when I met the client who owned this chopper, I'd never kustom painted the ultimate definition of yin-yang on a bike: heaven and hell. I'm not talking about an angel on one side and a demon on the other; heck, I'd painted some good/evil pinups for Jesse James years before. I'm talking about taking into account the biblical definitions of heaven and hell and illustrating both on a bike, along with the Bible verses that support the theology.

This worked out well for the client and me. I was challenged by a paint job that would be both unique and thematic. The client got the benefit of my father being a minister—actually, Army Chaplain, Lt. Col., retired. So I had an excellent reference source for Bible verses and biblical interpretation. Theme paint jobs are especially fun because they challenge more than just your airbrush skills and technical ability. More than usual, they force you to think about what you're painting. I had to formulate a strategy for the theme: How much information to display? How much to hide or leave out? I've always hidden icons, messages, or characters in my murals—this makes for a more interesting design for myself, the client, and viewers of the paint job. So, after doing the research, writing out the Bible verses, and working up a couple of preliminary sketches for the client, it was time to paint.

1. I decided that an effective way to emphasize the separation of heaven and hell would be to have two different perspectives in the artwork. One sure way to get two perspectives is to use two artists. Deborah Mahan was employed at Air Syndicate at the time, so it was an easy matter to have her tackle the heaven side while I designed and painted the hell side. Here, she layed out the image with chalk using the approved reference sketch.

2. One chapter in the *Book of Revelations* has the Archangel Michael holding a spear and stepping on Satan. This was an image the client wanted depicted on the tank, half to be painted by Deb, the other half by me. Even though our styles are different, we kept the process similar so that the depictions tied in well together, not just thematically, but aesthetically. Deb began her mural by freehand sketching with chalk and airbrushing BC-26 white with a Kustom HP-CH airbrush.

3. While Deb was working on the top half of the gas tank, I started on the oil tank. Using the same chalk technique, I sketched a scene of lost souls in hell. To balance out the hellish scene on the tank, I added a crucifix with heavenly light emanating from it on the front. I used not only the Bible for reference, but also Dante's *Divine Comedy*. Much of what Christians and mankind in general think of as heaven, hell, and purgatory stems not from the Bible but from the descriptions in Dante's epic poem *The Divine Comedy*.

4. With both of us using the same process, I finished airbrush sketching the oil tank mural with BC-26 and a Kustom CS. Much of my design employed negative space, in this case the blue. Mists and ghostly arms reach up from the depths of hell. That allowed me to get as much mural work as possible into the painted space without wiping out the base color, which was an important aspect of this bike. While the bike balanced good and evil, it also balanced murals and Pearlescent Blue.

5. After Deb finished the archangel on the top of the tank, she rendered clouds and angels—some mounted on horseback, others flying—on the front. That signified the army of angels advancing to combat Satan and his army. The clouds here were important because they would be used to tie in various murals on the heaven side, the same way that fire and smoke tied in the murals on the hell side. Here, Deb used a torn piece of a business card to aid in creating the soft edge of a cloud.

6. The front of the bike was entirely heaven, the rear fender entirely hell. Deb used the same clouds and angels to define and amplify her aspect of the theme. The only colors in these areas were white and KK-04 Oriental Blue, covered with SG-100 intercoat clear. I didn't want black anywhere on this bike for fear it would kill the colors. We did all details with kandy mixtures. As shown here, Deb was able to get a killer balance of sharp detail and soft, cloud-like structures. The murals flow throughout the bike; they don't look as if they were just plopped down on it.

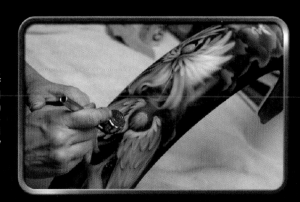

Text visible within the mural artwork:
...NY YEARS...
...M INTO THE BOTTOMLESS PIT... REV. 20:2
OF FIRE & BRIMSTONE...
...HEM, WAS CAST INTO THE LAKE
THE DEVIL, WH...

7. While Deb continued on to the front fender, I grabbed the tank to render Satan being stomped on by Michael. Deb was not yet done with her part of the tank; that work would be complete only after both sides had been rendered. In this way the murals would tie together even better, giving me the opportunity to work with what she had airbrushed, and her the opportunity to blend back into my work. This back-and-forth rendering resulted in not two but three styles: Deb's, mine, and a blending of our work.

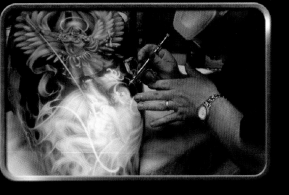

8. Using the same white and HP-CH Kustom, I rendered my part, wiping off the chalk sketch in the process. It's important to wipe down each step before proceeding to the next. That eliminates overspray and chalk buildup under the paint. Once the excess chalk had been wiped off, details could be filled in with white, which was also used to lightly sketch out the majority of the details. You've seen this in many of my murals, and it's an important step; that's why I always mention it. You'll also notice that Deb and I wore dual-cartridge active charcoal respirators when airbrushing. That's mandatory whether you use solvent-based or water-based paint. Make it a habit if you expect to keep your lungs.

9. To add color to the front fender, Deb mixed Spanish Gold, Pagan Gold, Kandy Violette, and Kandy Organic Green. The combination darkened certain details and shaded the images overall. Combined, these colors gave the illusion of black, though the end result was much softer. They also imparted warmth and tied in the heaven section better with the bike's "warmer" murals. It's tough to combine yellows and reds with blues and whites and not have greens in between. How did we do? You be the judge.

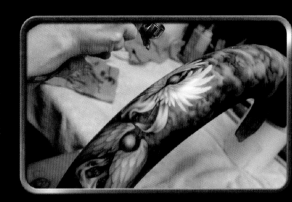

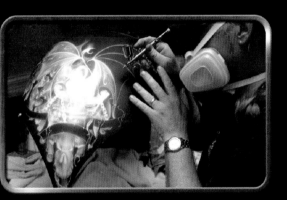

10. Continuing our tag-team mural work, I moved on to the rear hell fender while Deb finished off her Michael mural on the tank. In my white airbrushing, you can see the first signs of the scroll-like banner that would be a big tie-in for all parts of the bike. It would act as a unifying graphic, as well as an area in which to write Bible verses having to do with the individual murals. Because I was to be working with yellows and reds in the mural shown here, I had to employ negative space to actively break away from the surrounding blue. Tying these sections in with the rest of the bike was our biggest stylistic challenge.

11. Although the bike frame partly hides it, when assembled the front half of the rear fender still can be glimpsed through the structure. Therefore I needed to continue the mural work onto the front half, too. While I would not bring any of the primary murals into this space, I nonetheless continued the edge effect, airbrushing in hidden souls along the border, with surrounding smoke and ethereal flame. This created "hidden" features visible only when you're very close to the back of the bike. Show judges love this sort of thing. I've received more compliments for small details like this than for large murals that took much more time.

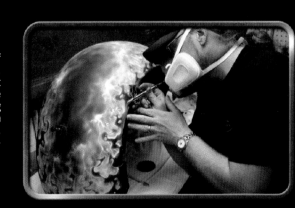

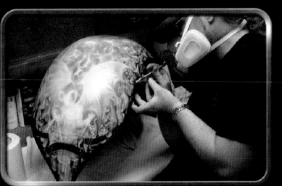

12. I tinted white areas of the mural with a mixture of Spanish Gold and Pagan Gold. That gave me the fiery base color for hell on the rear fender. I carefully avoided the blue areas; but even so, since I was working with kandies here, the effect on the blue was minor at worst. That's the great advantage of coloring with kandies: overspray is not only kept to a minimum, it becomes more of a constructive tool than a destructive presence.

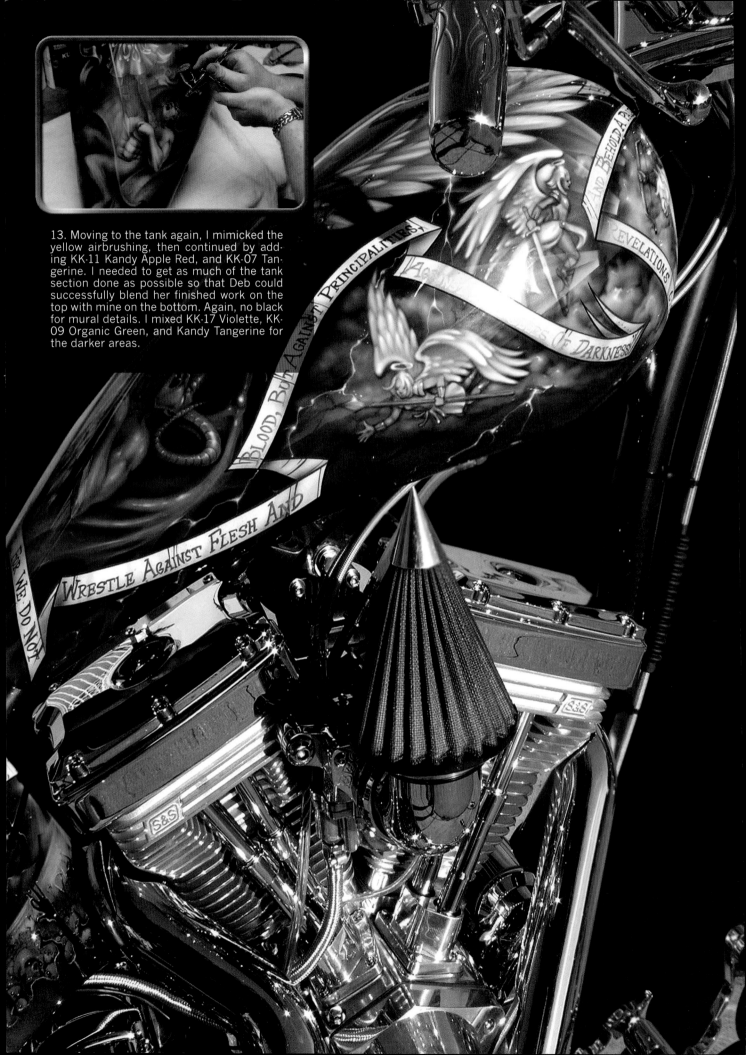

13. Moving to the tank again, I mimicked the yellow airbrushing, then continued by adding KK-11 Kandy Apple Red, and KK-07 Tangerine. I needed to get as much of the tank section done as possible so that Deb could successfully blend her finished work on the top with mine on the bottom. Again, no black for mural details. I mixed KK-17 Violette, KK-09 Organic Green, and Kandy Tangerine for the darker areas.

14. When I'd finished coloring my area, Deb added final details and highlights to Michael. Note especially the details in gold she added, and the fine white details throughout her section of the mural. Although our murals were diametrically opposed in many ways, they tied in perfectly visually and thematically.

15. As Deb finished her work on the tank and front fender, I caught up with my mural on the rear fender, being careful to use the same color mixtures and processes as on the rest of the bike. With back mural details completed, I added minute highlights to punch out the design. The rear fender depicts Satan chained in hell for all eternity.

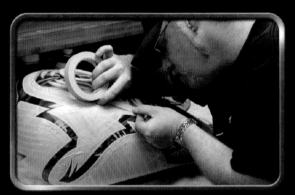

16. Because I was doing the scroll on a compound surface, I decided not to go for a cut transfer paper mask. 1/8" 3M masking tape, followed by 3/4" tape was perfect for this job. Approaching the scroll just as I would any graphic, I made sure it was exactly the same on both sides. Since it was going to look like a 3-D furling scroll, I needed to take cross-overs into account in the design. You may not see them at this point, but they will become apparent momentarily.

17. With the scroll masked off, I sprayed light layers of regularly reduced BC-26 White with a TH-3 fan-head airbrush until I got total coverage. Next, using a Kustom CS airbrush, I faded in streaks and fades using a mixture of Pagan Gold and Root Beer Kandy mixed 20 percent by volume with the SG-100. That gave the scroll a worn parchment look. A little KK-17 Violette Kandy added to the mix made for a good shadowing color.

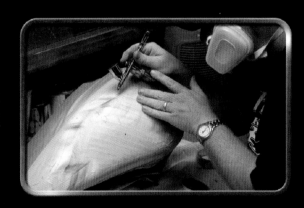

18. Unmasked, the scrollwork contrasted nicely with the rest of the mural. I also stippled a bit of that darkened color in the graphic to increase the aged effect. Since I wanted to stripe before we cleared it, I shaved down the graphic edge with a handy edge-shaver from Jon Kosmoski. This thing is a lifesaver for eliminating the peeking edge that can ruin a stripe job and require two coats of clear to bury. Shaves the edge right off, and doesn't damage the underlying paintwork.

19. With the edge shaved and the tank wiped down, I broke out the Steve Kafka-designed pinstriping brushes to outline and letter in the scroll. I did the border stripe with a mixture of maroon and Brindle Brown and the lettering with HoK Rich Gold metallic pinstripe paint. The Kafka long quills work great for small-line pulling on graphics and for lettering. I highly recommend giving them a try. I added a few drops of catalyst to the reducer, and the HoK striping urethane was locked in well enough not to pull, even if the clear got a run in it. I find that striping paint pulls better, too, if you add a bit of catalyst.

20. The last step was the addition of final highlights. These can be seen in the lightning, along the banner, and in any other area that screamed for attention. These white highlights were done with the Kustom Micron C using BC-26 reduced 200 percent to make it as thin and transparent as possible. When using white, be very careful or a wee bit of overspray may kill all that detail you spent so much time on.

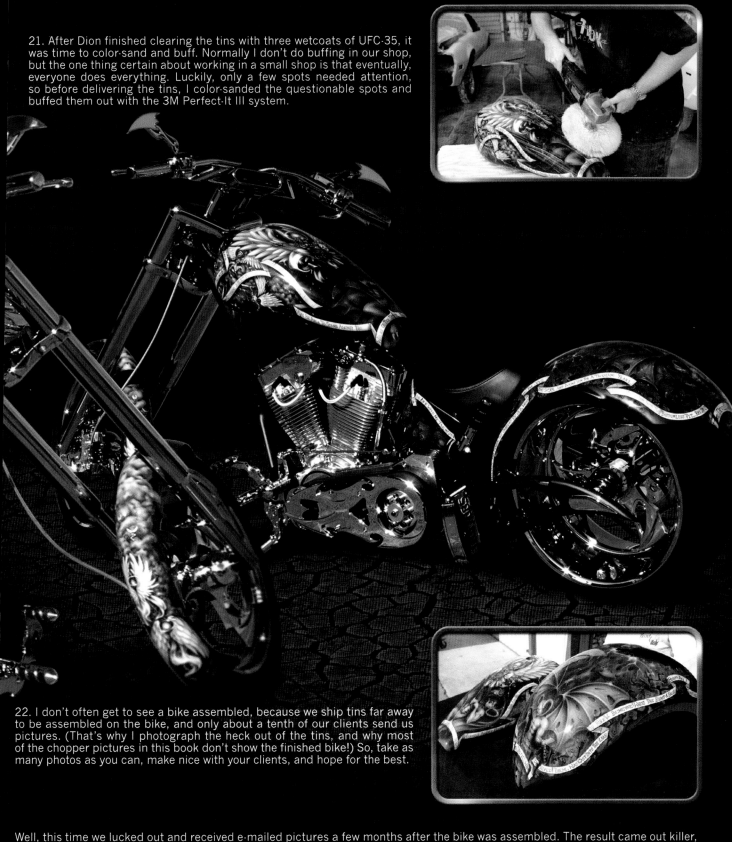

21. After Dion finished clearing the tins with three wetcoats of UFC-35, it was time to color-sand and buff. Normally I don't do buffing in our shop, but the one thing certain about working in a small shop is that eventually, everyone does everything. Luckily, only a few spots needed attention, so before delivering the tins, I color-sanded the questionable spots and buffed them out with the 3M Perfect-It III system.

22. I don't often get to see a bike assembled, because we ship tins far away to be assembled on the bike, and only about a tenth of our clients send us pictures. (That's why I photograph the heck out of the tins, and why most of the chopper pictures in this book don't show the finished bike!) So, take as many photos as you can, make nice with your clients, and hope for the best.

Well, this time we lucked out and received e-mailed pictures a few months after the bike was assembled. The result came out killer, and the client was very happy. Any time I can work on a thematic project with a client, I am more than usually enthusiastic. That's because I know that the paintwork will be more personalized and the job more interesting to me. Whenever you're especially motivated, your work will benefit. Indeed, if you consider yourself an artist, you'll always take your work personally. Your mood may not determine whether you show up for work, but it will determine the creative quality of your work.

It was also fun doing a paint job my dad actually approved of. (Amen!) He couldn't complain about this one, since he helped research the Bible verses. The paint job definitely had a message, but the message didn't overpower the design or the quality of the paintwork. That was the trick with this bike, and the challenge: giving the client exactly what he wanted, but more than he expected.

Green Dragon

A Study In Monochromatic Fantasy Muraling

You've probably surmised by now that I really dig monochromatic work. Well, shoot me! I dig painting skulls, too, and nobody complains. Probably the reason I like monochromatic is that it can be simple without being simplistic. I love the complexity in an Ansel Adams black-and-white photograph. In work like his, color just gets in the way. Now, don't get me wrong—I dig color; I just like to mess with it a bit. In this demonstration, for instance, the client wanted an all-green bike with dragons. Monochromatic? Not really. A true monochrome would be only one color, and in this design I used PBC-37 Limetime Shimrin, KK-09 Kandy Organic Green, SG-101 Lemon Yellow, KK-02 Lime Gold Kandy, and BC-26 White. Hmmm. Well, it looks like one color! And you know what they say: "Perception is reality." Point being, without contrasting colors to distract, all you have is the subject and the quality you rendered it in. Sort of like putting your ability under a microscope!

As I say, the client wanted an all-green bike with dragons. That literally was as far as the instructions went. We played with some color chips, but the artwork was left to me. (Regular customers get to trust you over time.) The first thing I consider when coming up with a design is what I don't want. First, I didn't want it to look like every other bike with a dragon. No offense to other artists; I just wanted mine to stand out. I also was very particular as to the type of dragon. I wanted the classic gothic kind seen in many fantasy books, so I chose to emulate some of my favorite fantasy artists. Probably my greatest fantasy-art influence has been Frank Frazetta. I wanted to use his style of movement and loose detail to give my dragons life. Other influences have been Michael Whelan, Luis Royo, and Gerald Brom for their different styles of dragon and the attention they pay to detail and anatomy. None of my dragons are copies of theirs, yet you can discover their styles in my work.

I also wanted the design to flow; I didn't want to be able to tell where the dragons ended and the bike began. I wanted it to be difficult to count the dragons—not because of their number but because of the intertwining design. My aim was to make every angle from which the bike could be viewed the best angle. Many painters make the mistake of having a showpiece angle, or sole focal point. I wanted this bike to have the same design throughout, and with killer detail that wasn't overly busy or crowded. Heck, I was harder on myself than my client was. Anyway, you decide if I accomplished my goal.

1. With the bike based in PBC-38 Limetime Shimrin, cleared, and sanded with 600-grit sandpaper, I laid out the design. By now you should be used to my fixation with plain white chalk for layouts. What can I say? It's easy, cheap, wipes off, and doesn't leave residue to haunt you later like pencils and Stabillos do. Try it. You'll like it. Keeping with the intertwining dragon thing, I basically went nuts over the whole tank—even on the tank's bottom, which would be visible on this high-raked chopper.

2. Using BC-26 HoK Basecoat White, I sketched the design, wiped off the excess chalk, and started filling in the dragons. Most of this bike was done freehand—not to show off or anything, but to maintain flow in the design. Whenever you start masking, then painting, then masking again, then cutting, and so on, you create stops and starts that your eye stops and starts at, too. Freehanding is like surfing—smooth-flowing from start to finish. Heck, even the "wipeouts" look cool sometimes.

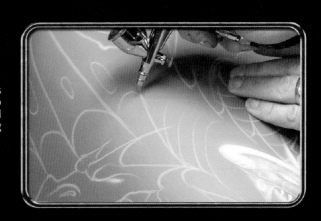

3. I used the same airbrush, the Iwata HP-CH, for the fine lines and for the shading of the white in the dragons. The ability to control the air at the gun and its fine-detail suitability allowed me to use one airbrush for all the artwork, without ever having to switch.

4. Even though I used only white base coat at this point, you can see much of the detail because of the way this airbrush layers color. Even the minutest differences between layers become visible. I worked with an opaque base coat, so imagine the differences in gradation possible with a transparent kandy!

5. To maintain continuity, I shifted to the rear fender and other parts before going to the next color. Note that the base color of the fender became the dark side of the moon in the background. Use of negative space is key to creating depth and details when working in monochrome.

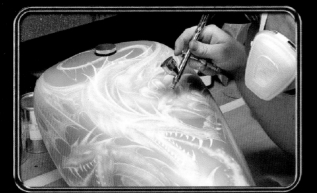

6. With the white artwork done, I layered in some Lime Gold Kandy. Because Lime Gold is a true transparent kandy, every detail of the white came through; and by varying the application of the kandy, I achieved even more depth and dimension of color. This kandy was a mixture of 20 percent Lime Gold KK-02 with SG-100 before reduction.

7. Now it was time to bring in the KK-09 Kandy Organic Green, which I also mixed 20 percent with SG-100 intercoat clear. I started in the darkest areas and left the lighter Lime Gold areas alone for the highlights. When freehanding, some overspray is bound to get on the highlighted areas. So instead of fighting it, I used it; this bike was supposed to be green anyway. Remember, one man's overspray is another man's gradated fade!

8. As I continued layering in the Kandy Organic Green, the tank got darker in color. Slowly adding layering like this will give incredible depth to the paint job overall, making the artwork appear to shift and come alive when light hits it. It's an effect that an opaque color can never duplicate.

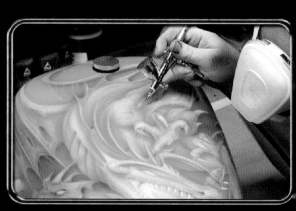

9. It might appear that in some of the darkest and finest of the details I'd added another color, possibly even black. Not so: it was all the same KK-09 Kandy. A true kandy, no matter how light in chroma, will always tend towards black when layered enough times. That's because the color in a kandy is like that in a stained-glass window—completely dependent on light to transmit the image. The more you airbrush, the darker it gets. Perfect for building details and shadows in a monochromatic design.

10. The only place I didn't freehand on this bike was the frame. There I used the *Dragon Skin* stencil from the *FX-II* series of templates I'd created with Artool. These flexible, solvent-proof templates are perfect because I can literally wrap them around the frame tubes to get the effect. This repeating stencil is so easy to use, anyone can do it; yet the result is professionally impressive. Just because a design or pattern looks difficult doesn't mean it's difficult to achieve. This stencil saved me easily a dozen hours on the frame.

11. I even carried the dragon motif to the backside of the rear fender. Although the transmission hides much of this dragon, added details like this earn best-of-show awards. You've heard me say it before: "The paint job is the first thing they see and the last thing they remember." Some painters have criticized me for artwork in places that few people see. But the number of compliments I've received from spectators, clients, and judges who did notice has made it well worth it.

12. SG-101 Lemon Yellow on the back fender made an excellent base for the fire effect and worked nicely as a secondary highlight for the dragon skin as well. Just be sure to reduce it substantially. Also, be careful when working with an opaque this late in a mural; the overspray can kill details. I had to come back later with more kandies to tone it down and eliminate the overspray.

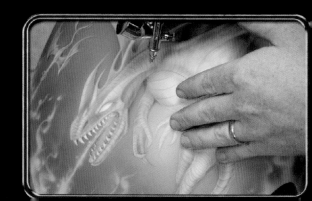

13. After relayering the Kandy Organic Green over the Lemon Yellow highlights, I added final highlights in white. So, coming full circle, I ended the paint job with the BC-26 White I'd begun with. Base-coat white can make or break your design. Just enough gives you highlights that literally jump out of the mural; too much, and it's a mess. Of course, you can always clean up the mess with kandy. Remember, you're only a color or two away from any repair when freehanding.

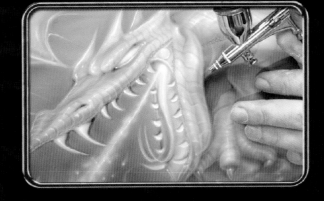

14. Perfect example: The white highlights I'd added to the fire were standing out a bit too much, so I layered in some Kandy Lime Gold from early on. That toned them down nicely, giving the fire a realistic glow. So now, at last, it was time for Dion to do his magic with UFC-35 clear.

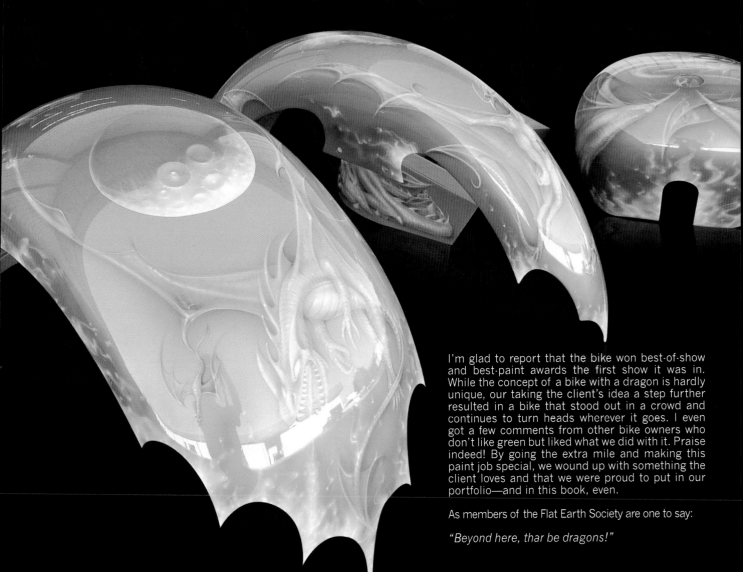

I'm glad to report that the bike won best-of-show and best-paint awards the first show it was in. While the concept of a bike with a dragon is hardly unique, our taking the client's idea a step further resulted in a bike that stood out in a crowd and continues to turn heads wherever it goes. I even got a few comments from other bike owners who don't like green but liked what we did with it. Praise indeed! By going the extra mile and making this paint job special, we wound up with something the client loves and that we were proud to put in our portfolio—and in this book, even.

As members of the Flat Earth Society are one to say:

"Beyond here, thar be dragons!"

PINKY

Kustomizing A Mini For One Of Our Own

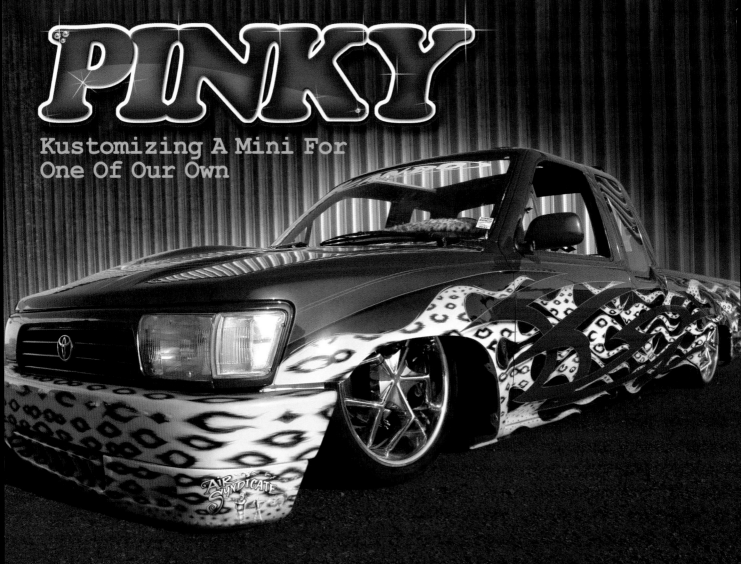

Long before SEMA 2006, Brandon Lambie—our body man, fabricator, and painter at Kal Koncepts—had been wanting to finish his Toyota mini. We'd been throwing around a few ideas, trying to come up with something unique, something that would be a tribute to the ol' school of graphics from the '90s that put mini trucks on the map. The only two things Lambie insisted on were a cheetah print incorporated into the paint job and pink as the main color.

Lambie's truck, which had already been seen at shows, was finished in House of Kolor Hot Pink Pearl. The paint job had seen better days, and he wanted to add a few accessories before painting. What better step-by-step chapter for the book, I figured, than something for one of our in-house guys? Mini-truckers seldom get to work on frame-off customs. The tune-up, or face-lift, kustom is far more frequent in our industry. In this instance, not only did the truck get a new look, but it magically changed from one club to another.

Alas! Such is the life of a mini-trucker.

1. Lambie's 1989 Toyota mini already had a four-inch body drop, monster notch, and 4-runner fenders, and just about everything had been shaved. The somewhat sleepy paint job was in dire need of a face-lift before the 2007 "Summer Madness" show in Bakersfield, California, not to mention the upcoming SEMA show.

2. Before painting, a little welding was needed. Lambie added a tail-gate skin and taillight covers from CanDo Specialties, Inc. After all, who needs a tailgate? A little MIG (metal inert gas) welding, and it was as if the truck had never had a tailgate at all. Let's skip all the body filler fun; after all, this *is* a paint book. (I'm sure there's a bodywork book in the automotive department of your nearby bookstore.)

3. After Lambie had bodyworked and smoothed out the entire back of the truck, it was time to make it pretty. With all of this bare metal exposed, it needed serious priming and sealing. House of Kolor's DTM (direct to metal catalyzed primer) was just the ticket, and Lambie liberally applied a few coats to the back before we got under way.

4. Here, Lambie had the back end all primed and ready to paint. Instead of repainting the pink base coat, we jumped ahead to the first set of graphics. The primary graphic was a border for the pink; we masked off that first so we could paint the background color. I know that seems backward, but stay with me. (By the way, if you crave a killer replacement for that rusted tonneau support, Lambie thinks he may be marketing them soon.) Hardcore mini-truckers seriously dig the bed treatment.

5. The background color for the graphics and two-tone was House of Kolor PBC-40 Violet, a pearlescent that goes well with pink. Lambie sprayed three even coats for coverage with an LPH-400 Anest Iwata spraygun. I know the color looks blue, but that's just the camera. Trust me, it's violet.

6. After giving the violet an hour to cure, I began laying out the flames with 1/8" 3M crepe tape. When one side was done, I transferred the design to the opposite side with a pounce pattern. Balance is important, since these flames wrapped all the way around and met in the middle of what had been the tailgate. You might not think this matters since you can't see both sides at the same time. But remember, with the doors open you see every little difference!

7. Of course, Lambie had all the fun of masking off the flames for painting. I believe it took about a dozen rolls of 3/4" tape. Lots of labor, but worth it in the long run. The best thing about the violet background is that any bleeds can easily be touched up. Think ahead. Things like that happen.

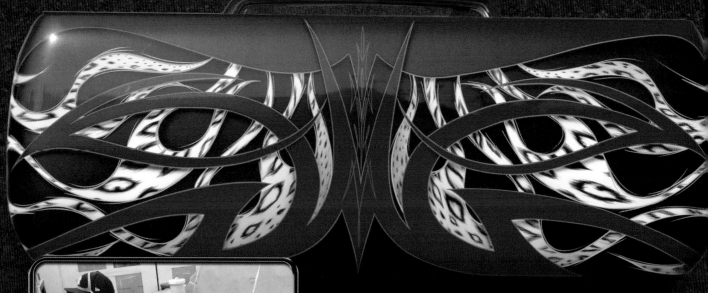

8. Now, this step may confuse the hell out of you. Where did the violet go? Remember, the violet was the background for the flames. For this paint job we had to think backward as well. Here, Lambie gave the flames a sunrise-to-tangelo fade from top to bottom, which would be the base for the cheetah print.

9. Before the flames were unmasked, I airbrushed a few freehand cheetah spots with a base-coat mix of Violet Pearl and Tangelo Pearl. They appear to be black, but actual black would have been too dominant, killing the surrounding colors. I did dagger strokes with the Iwata Eclipse to mimic cheetah fur. This freehand technique takes longer than using a stencil but looks better.

10. Now, this graphic was literally the negative of the first. With the graphics all sprayed, we masked them back off in preparation for laying on the Hot Pink. Luckily, this pearl base coat from HoK covers incredibly well, or we would have had to blend a transition color, such as Hot Pink mixed with base-coat white, over the primer spots.

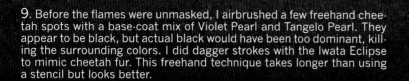

11. A coat of HoK Hot Pink Pearl on the rest of the truck took care of any imperfections in the original color and blended in the primer spots. If you were wondering why we did this last, it allowed us to butt all the graphics together against the background and main colors, leaving little or no paint edge. That saved an entire clear session and four-to five-mil of thickness in the final paint job. Cool, huh?

12. Before unmasking the graphics, I added a little stencil work. Lambie hankered for flying eyeballs, so I dug out the *Flyballz* stencil from Artool's Kustom Kulture series and airbrushed them using the same Violet Pearl. I also took the opportunity to drop-shadow the graphics since they were still masked.

13. With the graphics unmasked, it was time to clear-coat and then wet-sand with 600-grit sandpaper to level the graphics for striping. Complementary Lime Green and Bright Orange made the graphics really pop when they were finally striped. I couldn't stop myself with the slash stripe; the cheetah flames were screaming for it. Plus, Lambie asked.

14. Last but not least, Lambie threw on a few coats of HoK UFC-35 clear with the LPH-400 clear gun. I call it a "clear gun" because, while we may use the same model of gun for basing and clearing, we don't use the same gun. Even a little contamination can ruin an entire clear coat. After color-sanding and buffing, this truck was ready for the show.

As you can see, a few simple graphics can make quite a difference in your ride. While pink was still the primary-color, it no longer dominated. Combining minitruck two-tone tribals and old-school flames, we created a cool hybrid, all tied together with Von Dutch-style pinstriping. Watch for a future hood mural and more graphics on the tonneau. You know these mini-truckers—never done messing with their rides!

RODNEY'S CHOPPER

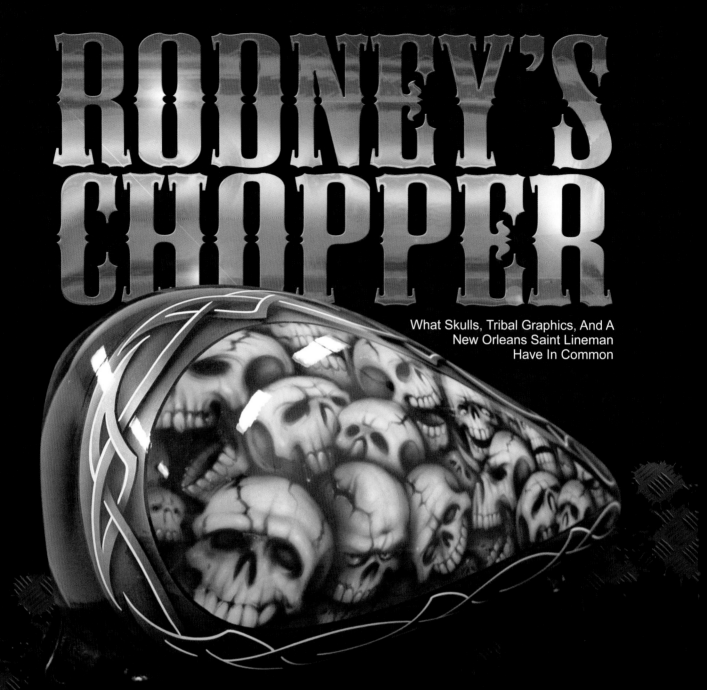

What Skulls, Tribal Graphics, And A
New Orleans Saint Lineman
Have In Common

At Kal Koncepts/Air Syndicate we try to treat all of our customers equally. But every now and then we work with someone special who merits something extra. Nothing wrong with that. In this case, Rodney Allen Leisle was an athlete Dion had coached in the shot put throughout high school. After a successful four years of football at UCLA, he was scouted and signed as a rookie lineman for the New Orleans Saints in 2004.

We painted his El Camino in high school, then fixed and re-striped it when he wrecked it in college, and were more than happy to paint the tins on the Harley he bought upon going with the Saints. He did get extra attention, but don't think we did it for free! I mean, he was a big shot now; he could afford it!

When Rodney shipped us the tank, helmets, and fenders what he wanted was simple. We needed to weld up and shave some holes and concoct a tricked-out paint job with matching helmets. The colors he wanted were silver and black, with yellow or gold airbrushing. He also wanted lots of skulls, with tribal banding or graphics tied in somehow.

He wanted the bike to be badass, imposing, and evil-looking. In short, appropriate for a lineman. No problem; we specialize in this type of work. Where we have trouble is with flowers and bunny murals. (Kidding, kidding.) ... Not really!

1. After Dion body-worked and single-staged the Harley's tins, Nino wet-sanded them with 600-grit sandpaper, and I layed out the panel. Using 1/8" 3M crepe tape, I mimicked the classic panel shape of the standard Harley Davidson Heritage paintjob. If you're wondering why Dion used single stage on the tanks instead of basecoat/clearcoat, it was for durability. Whenever we get the chance to use a catalyzed single stage over bodywork, we do it. It locks in the bodywork and adds protection against shrinkage and peroxide bleeding.

2. Making small marks an inch-and-a-half into the border, I laid in a second 1/8" of crepe tape, mimicking the outer panel. This area was to be the tribal band surrounding the inner panel of skulls. To get the panels just right I measured from the filler spouts down and eyeballed the design from the front and top. (Don't measure from the bottom, which is different on each side, especially because of the separate tanks.)

3. I wanted the tribal to have a brushed aluminum or bare-metal look; so before spraying, I massaged the masked band with a red Scotch-Brite pad. That put some really nasty linear scratches in the design. Then I sprayed the entire band with House of Kolor's MC-01 Kosmic Krome Aluminum effect, which found and amplified the scratches, giving the surface a truly bare-metal look. Typically, I spray Kosmic Krome paint with the Anest Iwata LPH-50, the smallest HVLP spray gun available.

4. To keep the aluminum from lifting after taping, I sprayed a light coat of SG-100. When this was dry, I laid in the tribal design with 1/4" 3M crepe tape. I had to figure out the pattern on paper first, then measure the lengths so the repeating order met up properly at the tail. Even so, I modified the tail pattern to end the design properly.

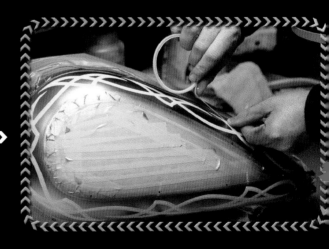

5. To give the tribal design a more etched look, I rubbed a red Scotch-Brite pad against the direction I'd taken earlier. I had to be careful not to damage the tape because more airbrushing was to follow.

6. With an over-reduced mixture of BC-25 basecoat black, I air-brushed lightly around the entire tribal design to punch it out. A little extra airbrushing underneath added a nice drop shadow and enhanced the 3-D effect. **>**

7. Carefully removing the tape from the tribal pattern, I wiped down the entire design with a damp towel and just a bit of pre-cleaner. Even crepe tape can leave glue residue behind if you're not careful. Employing the edge of a razor blade, I added drop shadows where needed to give the tribal an intertwining effect. A **<** very cool look when finished.

8. The tribal airbrushing completed, I back-masked the entire design to protect it from the SG-101 Lemon Yellow base. Instead of using a full-size spray gun, or even the mini LPH-50, I used Iwata's newest side-feed trigger airbrush. While it doesn't give the best coverage, it does move more material than the standard airbrush, leaving less edge at the tape. And that's what I was **>** concerned about.

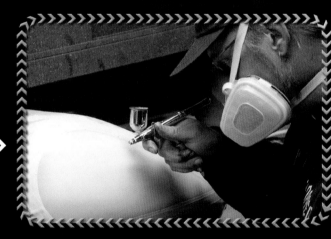

9. If I'd left the side panel yellow, I would have been more concerned about coverage. As it was, the stencil and airbrushed skulls would mask any possible mottling and still keep the overall edge low. The stencil I used here, with a mix of KK-08 Tangerine and SG-100 intercoat clear, was *Bones II* from the *Return of Skullmaster* series. You can use this stencil with *Bones I* to create an infinite **<** number of different skull patterns.

10. After dusting the stencil for reference, I went back over the skulls with an airbrush to hide stencil marks and gaps. This was the first step in eliminating tell-tale signs of stencil use. You want **>** these skulls to look freehand-airbrushed when you're done.

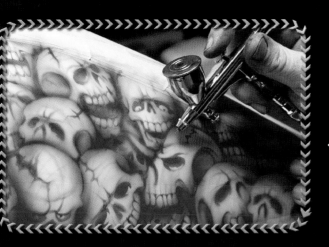

11. Sticking with tangerine, I continued building up the shading and shadowing for extra depth and realism. With an Iwata HP-CH airbrush (its adjustability and suitability for detail work make it perfect for shading, shadowing, and killer detail.)

12. As I continued to render the skulls and tighten the detail, I switched to KK-07 Rootbeer Kandy. To redo all the tangerine work would have been a waste; the Rootbeer was only for fine details and darkening the darkest areas. The more airbrushing I layered in, the more freehand the design looked.

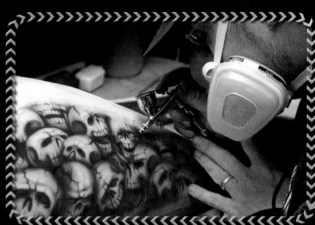

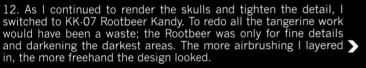

13. For the absolute darkest areas, such as the eye sockets and fine line work, I added a little KK-17 to the Rootbeer mix. The result looked as though I'd used black but had much more depth. Whenever you bring black into the mix, you risk killing colors and depth. I keep black as an ace in the hole in case I need something absolutely positively black.

14. Mixing up some over-reduced white, I added the subtlest of highlights to the edges of the skulls and teeth. The white was over-reduced to prevent spitting on and dulling the airbrush work. When I say "over-reduced," that's usually from 20 percent to double the amount of reducer recommended by HoK. Before you freak out, know that you can successfully over-reduce their basecoat systems 200 percent before getting into structural trouble. Just try that with the competition!

15. With everything lightly coated with SG-100 intercoat clear, I unmasked the design and started striping. Using an Excaliber 000 sword striper with HoK Lavender urethane striping paint, I outlined the entire panel.

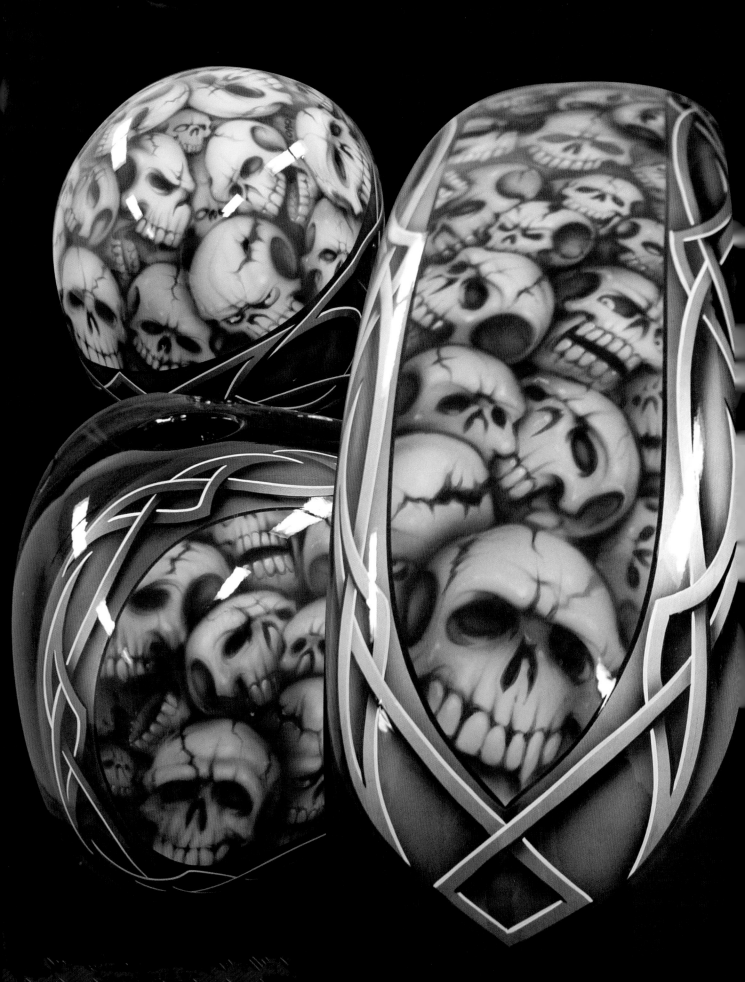

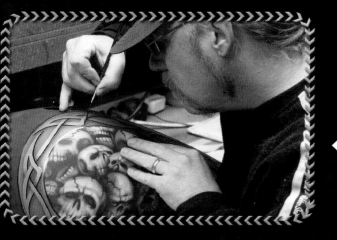

16. Originally I was going to leave the tribal designs unstriped, with that funky bare-metal look, but it wasn't working for me. Because all good painters must keep an open mind, I tried outlining the tribal with black—and liked it! So here we went: a little extra ❮ work with my Jenson liner quill.

17. Working around all parts of the bike, I continued to black-line the tribal. For even more of a 3-D look, I brushed white on the highlighted sides. That really snapped the tribal, giving me the look I ❯ was going for all along.

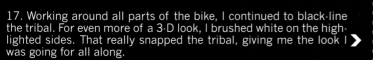

18. I designed the helmets to match the tank and fenders exactly. While working, I went from part to part and between helmets to maintain continuity. If you completely finish one piece at a time, ❮ you'll end up with parts that don't match in quality or in color.

With the artwork completed, Dion applied a full two sessions of clear to level all the designs and give us enough thickness to color-sand and buff. Since the set was to be shipped cross-country, we gave it an added few days to fully cure, then applied a wax/sealer to the buffed clear, and packed up the pieces. A packing tip: bubble wrap can save a lot of heartaches, but can also cause some. It leaves marks on even the most cured urethane clearcoats, probably because it has the same chemical properties as the clear. To prevent marking, wrap the tins in either pillow cases or foam sheeting available from packing stores. Pack the tins tightly and well-cushioned in the boxes you received them in, mark "fragile" on them, insure the hell out of them, and cross your fingers.

Besides the worry of shipping, the problem with long-distance paintwork is that you rarely get to see the assembled bike. Even when the owner is a friend, the photos are a long time coming. Yet, despite the hassles of shipping, painting at a distance is a great service to offer your clients, and one we enjoy quite a bit of business from. I'd guess we do as many choppers shipped to us as are ridden in, and two to three times the number of helmets. If you limit your work to local clients you ignore a large segment of your market, especially with today's Internet business.

Paint to ship, ship to paint!

RICE FINK

A Kustom Tribute To
Ed, "Big Daddy" Roth,
And The Crazy Cars He Built!

One of my biggest influences in the kustom industry is Ed "Big Daddy" Roth. Not only was Ed the creator of Rat Fink and numerous other kustom kulture cartoon characters, but he's also the builder of some of the most outlandish kustom cars in history. I had the pleasure of actually working with Ed on poster designs and airbrush work for CoProNason galleries during the early 1990s. I was also honored to present the *Airbrush Action* Vargas award for lifetime achievement to Ed in 1999. Dion and I had been talking about building a tribute vehicle for years, and it looked like this year would be it.

Twenty years earlier, Dion had traded a paint job out on a couple of old Subaru #360s. He sold the van but kept the microtruck. You've probably seen these vehicles used as greenskeeping trucks on golf courses, but in 1966 this was the sole production truck from Subaru worldwide. While not legal on highways, they were often used as delivery vehicles and utility trucks throughout cities in the United States. After two decades of vandalism and neglect behind two separate shops, all that was left of the truck was the cab. We literally had to hand-fabricate the frame, drivetrain, rear bed, interior, steering, electrical; did I leave anything out? All we needed to get started was a purpose, and the tribute to Ed Roth and Rat Fink was a perfect fit. Now all we needed was a name. Since the Subaru was originally a Japanese vehicle, we figured a play on words, "Rice Fink," was perfect.

Rice Fink rendering:

After talking about what we wanted on the micro-truck, I went home and sketched it out. Dion had decided to use the front and rear suspension from a dune buggy, and the motor out of a 1998 Yamaha 600 FZR. For practicality, we decided to use some older Kurtis flat-bottom-boat seats, and for fun, we opted for a full race wing on the back. Taking the shopping lists of what we wanted on the truck, I put together a sketch and brought it back to the shop in the morning for approval. With a few minor changes, you'll see that the end result was pretty close to our initial concept. So with a mere three months to SEMA, and only a cab to work with, it was time to get to work. As Jesse James is always so fond of saying: "Nothing left to do but everything!"

1. Yep, that's red spot putty on the cab. The last time this cab was worked on was more than 12 years ago. Lambie had his work cut out for him. Before the bodywork could even begin, there were some metal mods and repairs that needed to be taken care of. Here, Lambie demonstrates his "TV reality show" welding style (and, of course, his politically incorrect use of government warning signs as filler metal)!

2. This is the fun part—piecing together the kustom body. Here, Dion, Nino, and I fabricated the rear fenders for the bed. These were necessary for two reasons: They would look killer, and the rear end was about two inches wider then we planned! Hehehe. These fenders had been made by using a 1979 FLH Harley rear fender, a 1959 Impala wheel skirt, and some spare scrap metal. Ed would be so proud!

3. The downside with any patchwork fabrication is that it does require bodywork. Lucky for us, Lambie lives for body filler. After grinding the areas to be worked on down to bare metal with 80-grit sandpaper, Lambie used Evercoat filler to hide the welds and eliminate all the body waves.

4. With all of the bodywork done, Lambie sprayed all of the finished panels with HoK Direct to Metal catalyzed primer. After guide-coating and final sanding with 600-grit sandpaper, Dion sprayed the Rice Fink with a nice coat of HoK Orion Silver. After clearing and sanding again, it was time to start rendering the graphics.

5. To get the graphics to lie correctly, we preassembled the truck, and I started laying tape. While I normally would work on one set of graphics at a time, I combined these by laying out the top scallops at the same time as the flames. This gave the overall paint job that Ol' School patterned look. All of these designs were laid out using 1/8" 3M Crepe tape.

6. The first color that Dion sprayed was HoK Kandy Apple Red. This was the primary color that was seen on the "rising sun" flag pattern on the front and inside of the truck cab. The one thing that Dion wanted on the *Rice Fink* was for all of the graphics to be kandies. Not just Kandy basecoats, but true kandies layered over the Orion Silver base.

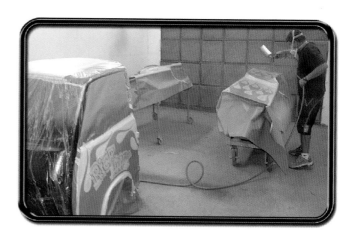

7. The trick to spraying multiple graphics at once is merely strategy. After spraying the six coats of Kandy Apple Red over the front of the vehicle, Dion gave the paint an hour to cure, then draped the front. The second color was the base for the flames. It was a Spanish Gold Kandy Koncentrate that was mixed 20% by volume to HoK's new USG-100. This created a killer catalyzed kandy that was not only sprayable but dried faster to the touch than the older UK system.

8. As Dion layered on the kandies, he progressed along the color spectrum. When the Spanish Gold was finished, he transitioned to Tangerine, then finished off the fade on the flames with some classic Kandy Apple Red. The best thing about the kandies for these graphics was that throughout all of the transitions, you could still see the metallic evenly through the graphics. As good as this looks indoors, it will be amazing when the sun hits it!

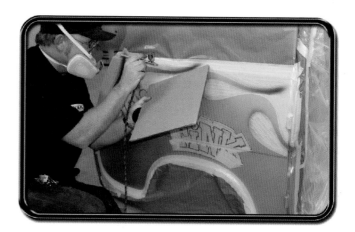

9. Loading my Kustom Eclipse CS with Kandy Apple Red (for airbrushing, I mix the Kandy Koncentrate 20% with SG-100, and then reduce), I proceeded to tip all of the flames. Notice my vintage masking system. When in need, a piece of cardboard will always work! Best to use the Ol' School techniques on the Ol' School paint job.

10. With the flames finished, we back-masked those areas and Dion laid the Oriental Blue kandy on the masked scallop patterns. When spraying kandies, Dion prefers to use the same brand LPH Anest Iwata that he clears with using a 1.5 nozzle. (Yes, Dion usually wears his "shoot suit," but I rarely like to be in the booth while he's spraying, so allow us some set-up shots!)

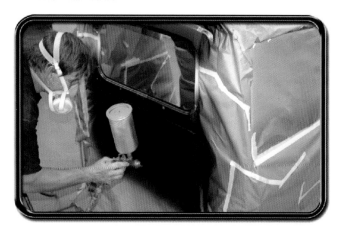

11. For the final graphic, Dion sprayed a Cobalt Blue rally stripe down the center of the cab, and even inside. We wanted to create a stable Cobalt Blue that would not bleed, so we created a mix of three parts KK-17 Violet Kandy, to one part KK-04 Oriental Blue. The color was almost an exact match to Cobalt Blue but incredibly stable—no bleeding or blotching. We even threw some extra ice pearls into it for punch. You can't see it in this pic, but the roof of the cab is not just silver based, it's actually metalflake. This thing is going to seriously sing in the sunlight.

12. After masking off the Rice Fink logo (in typical Rat Fink–style lettering), I decided to give the letters a very hip machine-turned look. Instead of the traditional gold leaf trick, I broke out the air-grinder with a red Scotchbrite pad glued to the Rollock grinder pad. These machine-turned marks in the clear will remain and show up when the Kosmic Krome Gold is sprayed on next.

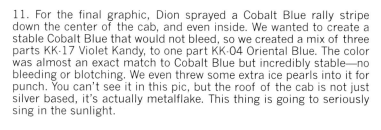

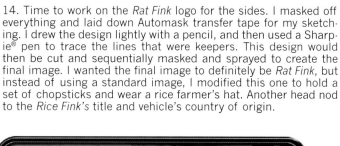

13. As you can see, the MC-04 Kosmic Krome Gold looks pretty decent over the machine turning. It mimicked the dull yet metallic glint of real gold leaf. The pigmented aluminum is so fine in grain that the particles find each sanding scratch and amplify it to the naked eye. This works incredibly with other brushed-metal techniques. When using any of the Kosmic Krome paints, remember the key rule of thumb: Less is more.

14. Time to work on the *Rat Fink* logo for the sides. I masked off everything and laid down Automask transfer tape for my sketching. I drew the design lightly with a pencil, and then used a Sharpie® pen to trace the lines that were keepers. This design would then be cut and sequentially masked and sprayed to create the final image. I wanted the final image to definitely be *Rat Fink*, but instead of using a standard image, I modified this one to hold a set of chopsticks and wear a rice farmer's hat. Another head nod to the *Rice Fink's* title and vehicle's country of origin.

15. As you've undoubtedly seen in other chapters, I systematically cut and remove bits of the design as I airbrush the white basecoat with the Kustom Eclipse. This gives me a subtle sketch in white that I can then layer with kandies, shade, and detail, and finally outline. The end result looks like a cross between Ed's fine art poster work and his pinstripe art.

16. The first color I used was a Pagan Gold kandy, followed by a mixture of Kandy Organic Green and Limetime pearl basecoat. The Limetime gave the Rat Fink a very cool pearlescent look when the light hits it just right. It's important to use this early in the rendering. Pearls have a tendency to overspray a lot when used in the later stages.

17. I chose the opaque Blue Blood Red from HoK for RF's shirt and tongue. I did this for a few reasons: One, it covers quite a bit faster than the kandy, and two, it's the perfect color for the shirt. As with the Limetime, you just have to be careful when spraying these opaques. I kept the air pressure at about 30-psi and worked very close to the surface. Any random spray can be blended and taken care of in the details and shadow work.

18. Here, I mixed a shading color of BC-25 black and violet/blue kandy, finished all the details and shadows, and then polished off the airbrush work on *Rat Fink* with a few choice hot spots. While I could have used my Micron airbrush for this, I prefer the Eclipse for its ease of use, the scale of detail is correct to the size of the image, and it's just a fast airbrush to work with.

19. With Finky and the airbrushing done, it was time for a little outlining and pinstriping. Using a Kafka liner brush, I gave the logo a bit of character with an outline of HoK striping black. The center line work in the lettering is another tribute to Ed, being that it's the same style lettering that *Rat Fink* has always had on his shirt.

20. Shifting over, I continued the same line work around Finky. This popped out the design, and gave him the traditional cartoon look he's well known for. While I don't actually need any catalyst in the HoK striping paint, I prefer to add a few drops into my dipping reducer. This locks in the color and prevents any pulling in case we get a clear run.

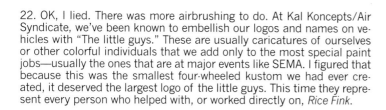

21. Switching to a Mac #10 000 sword striper paintbrush, I began pulling the lines on the flames and larger graphics. While the liner brushes are amazing for short strokes and details, the sword stripers are necessary for consistent long lines.

22. OK, I lied. There was more airbrushing to do. At Kal Koncepts/Air Syndicate, we've been known to embellish our logos and names on vehicles with "The little guys." These are usually caricatures of ourselves or other colorful individuals that we add only to the most special paint jobs—usually the ones that are at major events like SEMA. I figured that because this was the smallest four-wheeled kustom we had ever created, it deserved the largest logo of the little guys. This time they represent every person who helped with, or worked directly on, *Rice Fink*.

23. After a few necessary touchups, I finished the flames on the rear bed panels. Airbrushing the drop shadows was the first step, before finishing the necessary pinstriping. With the cab off, it's important to remember the exact position of the pinstripe. Whether you're to the top or bottom of a tape edge can make a difference of up to a ¼" in the long run. This is important for parts that need to match up after assembly.

24. While I drop-shadowed the flames for a 3-D effect, I left off the drop shadow for the top scalloped patterns. Those got simple pin-striping, Ol' School style. After these last bits of pinstriping, Dion took all of the panels into the booth and sprayed a couple of good coats of UFC-35 clear. If memory serves me correctly, we sanded and repeated the clear steps one final time to bury the striping and give us enough material to buff on.

There you have it. Delivered and staged at SEMA. One tribute to Ed "Big Daddy" Roth and his alter ego, Rat Fink. Of course in true Ed Roth style, there were plenty of mishaps along the way to the show. For starters, we burned out the clutch and seized the front steering box. My favorite was the trailer ride to Vegas. Evidently the power was left on the hydraulics, and when the trailer hit a bump, the switch box fell out of the seat and landed upside down on the floor. The *Rice Fink* had its own "low rider" hopping show in the back of the trailer, shearing the two A-Arms in half and sending the front hydraulic rams through the floor of the trailer. No problem. A furniture dolly and all of us pushing got it into the HoK booth just fine!. It just needs to look killer! Dennis and Daryl Roth, Ed's sons, gave us the thumbs-up on the tribute.

The *Rice Fink's* debut came out killer and was a big hit in the House of Kolor booth at SEMA 2008. As a matter of fact, *Popular Mechanics* named it one of the top 12 vehicles at SEMA. Not bad for a rusting cab shell that sat behind the shop for 20 years. Point being? A kustom vehicle does not need to be the most expensive, flawless, well-engineered vehicle to be cool. Actually, the majority of innovative kustoms out there are far from perfect. Innovation is all about experimentation. Perfection, (while unattainable by defi-nition) is something that is attempted quite a ways down the road from the initial creation. So for all you kustom builders out there, strive to build the best, but please never stop coming up with those head-turning, show-stopping innovations!

Rat Fink Por Vida!

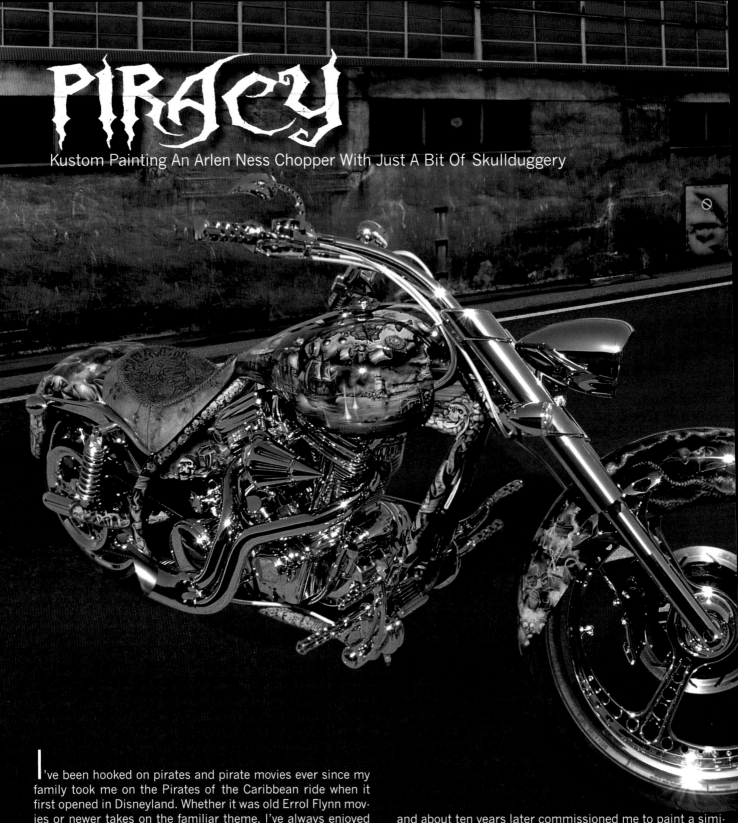

PIRACY

Kustom Painting An Arlen Ness Chopper With Just A Bit Of Skullduggery

I've been hooked on pirates and pirate movies ever since my family took me on the Pirates of the Caribbean ride when it first opened in Disneyland. Whether it was old Errol Flynn movies or newer takes on the familiar theme, I've always enjoyed the artwork and styles that surround the legends of the privateers of old. So you can imagine how happy I was when Disney finally created a proper dynasty of buccaneer films, known affectionately in the industry as Pirates.

Back in 1993, I painted the hood of a truck named "Point of Know Return." My mural, based loosely on Peter Lloyd's airbrushed cover for the Kansas album of the same name, showed a collection of pirate ships dueling in a classic maritime battle scene. To date it remains one of my favorites. The fact that it was in my first book testifies to that. A friend and client of mine, Kevin Overturf, never forgot that hood mural,

and about ten years later commissioned me to paint a similar theme on his bike.

It wasn't just any bike, but one of the new limited-production lowliner custom choppers from Arlen Ness. He was currently working for the production company owned by Jerry Bruckheimer and was interested in doing a bike with a *Pirates of the Caribbean* theme. I quickly suggested that we stick with the theme but stay away from making the bike look like a movie poster. I wanted to create my own imagery and not have to jump through the hoops associated with licensed products. He agreed, and I quickly got to sketching some concepts. Let me show you.

1. The bike required little bodywork, so Dion and Lambie prepped, base-coated black, and cleared the tins for my paintwork. After sanding with 600-grit sandpaper, I sketched with my traditional chalk. Pretty low-tech, I know, but no one has come up with anything better. I used photo references from several books for my ships, including scenes from the actual Disneyland ride. The only reference I used from the movie was the gold coin you see here. It featured a simplified Aztec calendar, so there were no trademark issues.

2. With the chalk work finished, I continued sketching with an HP-CH Kustom airbrush loaded with slightly overreduced BC-26 White. Because I use a white base for all design and detail work, I can easily make changes with just a bit of black. This push-pull form of rendering is the easiest and cleanest, and really punches out details.

3. I gave the same treatment to the rear fender. I rarely finish one piece of a vehicle before moving on to another, preferring to bring all the parts up to the same level of detail at roughly the same time. That gives them continuity and consistent quality.

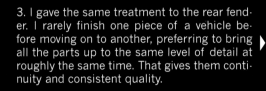

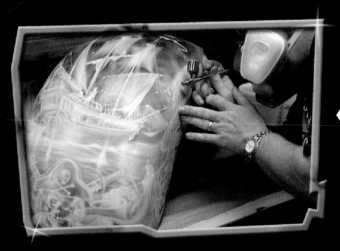

4. With white details rendered on all of the parts, it was time to add color. As you've probably figured out by now, I work along the spectrum from yellow to red to blue. For yellow, I often pick SG-101 Lemon Yellow, but I wanted these colors to be deeper and more muted. I opted for a mix of KK-12 Pagan Gold and SG-100 Intercoat Clear at 20 percent by volume of the KK to the SG before reduction.

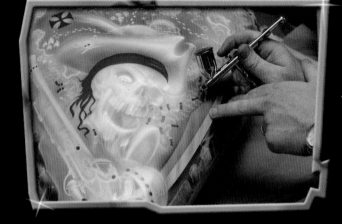

5. Here you see the extent of the Pagan Gold I applied to the design. Not all of this was to remain yellow; much would be an underlying color for something else. The red I applied next was the only non-kandy color in this design. It was HoK Blue Blood Red. I wanted its pure form, so I opted for an opaque base coat. I'd get the depth I wanted from the kandies to be layered over it later.

6. Following my spectrum rule of color progression, I turned to KK-04 Oriental Blue and SG-100. Keep this color away from the yellow if you don't want green. If you do, a little KK-04 layered over any yellow will give you such a killer green you won't want to buy green paint anymore. (Oh, well, maybe I wouldn't go that far!)

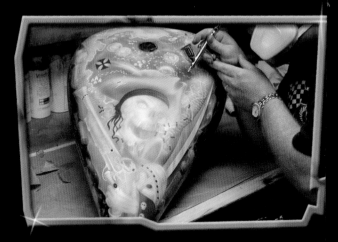

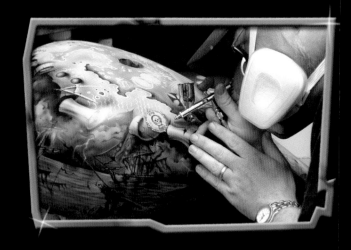

7. As I continued with my color progression, the details got tighter and tighter. For detail and coloring this fine I've created two different transparent blacks. One is a violet shade, the other a sepia. Funny thing is, neither contains black. The sepia is Kandy Apple Red, Kandy Organic Green, and Root Beer. The violet is Organic Green, Violette, and Oriental Blue.

8. By switching between these two detail blacks, I created the illusion of many more colors in this piece than there really are. Fogging the blacks lets the dominant colors really show through and function as great washes. By avoiding it, true black becomes my ace in the hole, should I need serious separation between two already dark areas.

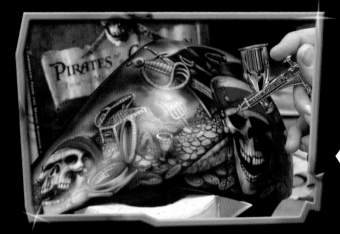

9. Although this step-by-step shows how the piece came together, success in process painting comes when the steps cannot be detected in the finished piece. The cool thing about working with transparents is that you can easily correct mistakes with base white, then layer in the kandies again. No opaque overspray to worry about.

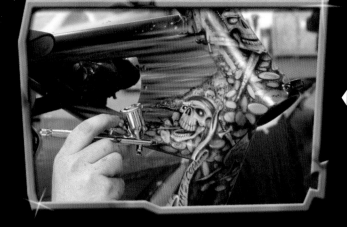

10. While I've shown the frame being muraled in this chapter, it wa actually done nine months later. That's something to consider wi each of your jobs. Don't overwhelm your client by insisting ever thing be done at once. When possible, pace a paint job so the clier can bring it back for you to elaborate on, to keep fresh and ne for upcoming shows. This bike looked killer at SEMA with the blac frame. Now it looks incredible with the muraled frame.

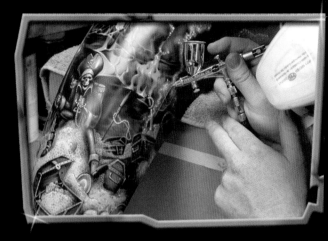

11. When rendering murals on bikes, pay attention to details on even the most obscure areas. In this case, the back of the front fender got as much detail, or more, than the front. The bubbles were done in stages: first, laying down white bubbles as blowouts; next, layering kandy; finally, adding more white bubbles.

12. All of the tins got their white highlights with my Micron C+ Kus tom airbrush in this step. Be sure to really reduce, and even strain BC-26 White. HoK puts more titanium pigment in its white than an other company. Because of this, HoK white is killer but will also spit Never use retarders or slow reducers; they can cause issues and ar unnecessary. Just add SG-100 and RU-311, then strain.

13. On a job this elaborate I plan a final step in which I go over every inch, troubleshooting areas that catch my eye. That's like proofreading an article you've just finished writing. Too bad there's no spell-check program for murals. It might be called "Screw-up Check." I could make a *fortune!*

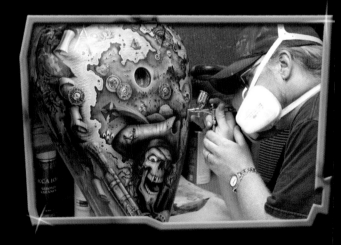

14. After clearing with UFC-35, the colors really come to life. Some-times a color will come more to life than you'd like, and blend and bleed. If that happens, or your highlights get washed out, just sand, touch up, and reclear. It won't happen on the second pass. For mu-rals, I always plan on two clear sessions, with touch-ups in between.

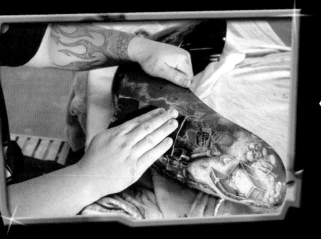

15. With the last coat of clear on the beauties and everything looking killer, it was time for buffing. Lambie started color-sanding before the buffing process began. When color-sanding, we like to start with 1500-grit Trizac from 3M and work our way to 3000. Looks killer, and no swirls—not even in black! Be sure to soak the sandpaper in water for at least 15 minutes beforehand. A few drops of liquid Ivory soap in the water will lubricate the sanding and prevent scratching.

16. When buffing, always have two people hold the parts you care about. That prevents airborne disasters. Dion likes to start the buffing with a wool pad and a medium cut 3M compound. He quickly moves to a foam pad for the final polish. We currently like the 3M Perfect-It III system for buffing. For the final wax we're suckers for Meguiar's Cleaner Wax. It's the only stuff we recommend to our clients.

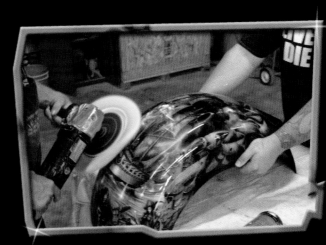

After a week's worth of bodywork, prep, paint, and more than 100 hours of airbrushing, we were done! The bike was a hit in the House of Kolor booth at 2006 SEMA. I'm proud to say that Kevin has taken Best Paint in every show he's entered to date, not to mention Best of Show awards. *Piracy* was recently shot for an *Easyriders* feature, and Kevin is already planning a second build. Needless to say, we have one happy client. Besides the added muraled frame that Kevin had me do in mid-season, he also wanted the seat redone. I remembered Billy Lane, the leather crafter, and insisted Kevin have him stitch it up. I sketched the design, which Adam Croft of Last Ride Leather did an incredible job executing.

Not only does the artwork match the bike's design, but the color of the leather is spot on with the bike's colors as well. Couldn't ask for anything better!

The *Piracy* bike is a good example of a job that comes around every now and then to establish a new level for your work. I find it amusing that two of the murals I'm best known for are based on pirate themes. I don't mind. I had a great time painting them and actually was bummed when I'd finished. Working on something you're really into makes up for all the jobs that are more work than fun. Painting a bike for a good friend like Kevin makes it all the more worthwhile.

Avast there, ye scurvy scoundrels! Look lively and paint!

El Diablo Blanco

Kustom Painting The Great White Road Yacht

Probably the toughest design I ever tackled was for my personal ride, a '64 Cadillac Coupe De Ville. For one thing, it was a family heirloom, so I had that constituency to deal with. Secondly, it had some pretty big tires to fill, succeeding as it did my kustom '61 Buick. I had never thought much about how challenging the Caddy was going to be until I started working on it. Then, after a few dozen painters asked me what I was planning to do with it, I started second-guessing myself.

I had always wanted an older Caddy, and had actually just sold my '60 Cadillac Crown Royal Superior Hearse Combo, which I had never finished kustomizing (I might have been intimidated by the length of the name). I knew I wanted to create a Larry Watson–style kustom with flake, flames, scallops, and pinstripes, but I didn't want it to look like a cookie-cutter car. In bucking the trend, I opted for a set of 20" Foose Nitrous wheels with Coker whites. I did not want a pure show car but a

daily drive that looked like one, much as my Buick had been. I drove that sucker every day for almost a decade, yet it still won awards and attracted attention wherever it went.

So, with enough ideas in my head for three Caddies and a vanishingly small budget (I'm better at spending other people's money than managing my own!), I set off to kustomize the road yacht. I decided to keep the Caddy's stock white base, since white is a very unusual color to work with and has a classy look. Plus, white makes the car appear even bigger than it is. My last kustom was named Devil or Angel, so I decided to follow the devil theme and name the car Diablo Blanco. I pushed the theme even further with "whiskey tango" references—trailer park icons, and other obscure imagery in the murals. Because I grew up in Bakersfield, which is saturated with localisms like Oil Junction, Weedpatch, and Pumpkin Center, the name seemed to fit somehow.

Diablo Blanco started out as a bone stock '64 Cadillac Coupe De Ville. My wife's grandfather, Bob Dodson, had purchased it secondhand back in the '60s. When Grandpa Bob turned 99, he felt too old to continue driving and sold it to my brother-in-law. Except for an immense amount of bodywork (he never did say how many times he had run into things), the car was in fairly decent shape.

1. I won't bore you with details of the bodywork. Needless to say, there was lots of it. After all the panels were straight again, I sprayed the entire car with Valspar Single-Stage White. Although this Caddy was going full kustom, I matched the factory white for old-school's sake. Here, Dion sprayed the roof with Orion Silver followed by a few heavy coats of F-15 Silver Metal Flake and Rainbow Splinter Flake.

2. After a few sessions of clearing and sanding to get the flake flat, Lambie and I laid out and masked the graphics on one side of the roof. Then I transferred the designs using a pounce pattern and pounce chalk. You can tell I enjoyed this part.

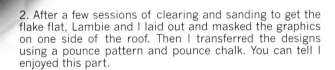

3. Following the chalk transfer line, I laid out the scallops and flames to match the other side. While it's possible to eyeball the balance on the hood and trunk, the roof is too high for a good perspective. That makes the transfer pattern very important.

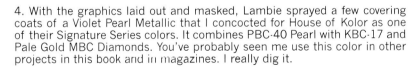

4. With the graphics laid out and masked, Lambie sprayed a few covering coats of a Violet Pearl Metallic that I concocted for House of Kolor as one of their Signature Series colors. It combines PBC-40 Pearl with KBC-17 and Pale Gold MBC Diamonds. You've probably seen me use this color in other projects in this book and in magazines. I really dig it.

5. After unmasking, we leveled the graphics with a few coats of clear and some sanding. Flake jobs always use lots of clear; graphics don't make it any easier. Without leveling, the graphics would peak the striping, and the job would look terrible.

6. I laid out the trunk design freehand, incorporating the scallops and flames in a balanced pattern. I planned a centralized mural, with Von Dutch striping for both hood and trunk. I did not use the pounce or chalk because blue chalk tends to leave traces behind in the white.

7. For the long lines pulled the length of the car, I used 1/4" tape because it doesn't sag as much as 1/8" tape and makes straighter lines. I also used green crepe tape for the layouts because it can be seen more easily than tan over the white and is stickier, minimizing tape bleeds.

8. Mixing a color similar to the roof's violet, I added more of a red violet into the batch with PBC-65 Passion Pearl. This, and the background white, gave the violet side graphics a different cast and added color to the paint job overall. Here, Lambie applied the new mix with an LPH-400 spray gun, keeping the edge to a minimum since coverage is easy over white.

9. We masked off both the silver graphics and the violet side graphics at the same time. After spraying the violet, Lambie backmasked it and sprayed the silver. The silver is another kustom kolor I created for HoK. Called Silverado, it combines BC-02 Orion Silver with MBC Platinum Metajuls and 10 percent Kosmic Krome Aluminum effect. Kosmic Krome gave the silver a killer value shift. Silverado also covers twice as fast as Orion alone.

10. With the silver graphics still masked off, I airbrushed the darkened tips and inside mouths of the flames. The black was not pure BC-25; it was a combination of BC-25 Black, SG-100 intercoat clear, and a mixture of KK-04 Oriental Blue and KK-17 Violet. This mixture countered the natural sepia of the black to give the shadow work a cool gray/violet tone.

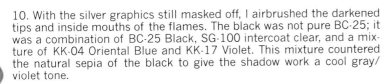

11. After finishing all the airbrushing, it was time to unmask and clear the entire car. Lambie did this, again with his LPH-400 spray gun and UFC-35 clear. This clear coat not only leveled the graphics but gave added protection to the underlying single-stage white. I mixed some base-coat white matched to it in case I needed to repair or touch up any unsatisfactory areas I missed before the paint job was cleared.

12. Finally, the part I looked most forward to—the muraling. For a different type of hood decoration I created a monochromatic "tattoo-style" mural that would be the underlying theme for the Von Dutch stylized pinstriping. The plan was for something a little different, yet familiar to kustom kulture. The mural started life as a simple light pencil sketch, then was airbrushed using my trusty Iwata Kustom Micron C.

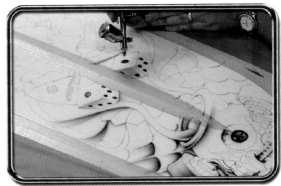

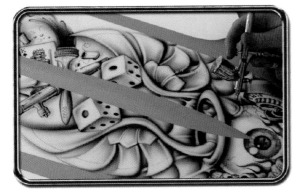

13. The black wasn't truly black; it was more like the violet-and-black mixture I had used on the silver earlier. Hyper-reduced with RU-311, it let me achieve killer details with the Micron airbrush, as well as a nice gradated fade. Before starting on the gradations and final details, I wiped the surface with KC-10 to get rid of the pencil marks.

14. The final step in the mural was the application of over-reduced BC-26 White. That helped pop out the details and fix any screw-ups left in the black. To keep a balance of design and style between hood and trunk, I went back and forth while completing the job, rather than finishing one and then doing the other. This is a trick I use to maintain continuity throughout large paint jobs. It works.

15. Using a combination of House of Kolor lavender striping urethane with various amounts of white added, I layed down long, straight stripes on the graphics. Probably my weakest ability in pinstriping is pulling long, straight lines, so instead I created a series of straight scallops down the length of this land yacht. Artist, know thyself.

16. I always save the fun stuff for last. Since I enjoy decorative, or Von Dutch–style striping, I waited until all the outlining had been done before giving myself the luxury of the final design work. Using a combination of pure white and lavender pinstripe urethanes, I created a complementary single-line pattern to frame the mural work and tie the trunk and hood designs together.

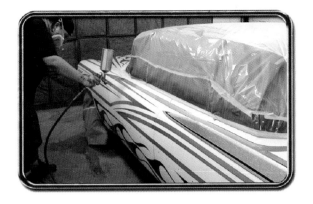

17. Clear-coating completed the paint puzzle. While I do know how to clear coat, and have had to prove it on many occasions, it was nice to work with somebody like Lambie to give myself a mental break. Plus, let's face it, he's a better clear-coater than I am.

18. After giving the clear a few days to cure, we sanded, starting with 1500-grit Trizac sandpaper and working down to 3000-grit. Then, we turned the polishing job over to our good friend Angel, of Angel's Detailing. In one day they buffed the Caddy to perfection. Looking at this car you understand that it's big, but only when sanding or buffing it do you realize it has the surface area of about three Hondas!

We did not complete Diablo Blanco until literally the eleventh hour before the SEMA (Specialty Equipment Market Association) show. At 3 A.M. the night before, we loaded it on the trailer for staging in Las Vegas. In fact, I added window stickers and final detailing even while we installed the car at the show. While this sounds horribly last-minute, it's actually par for the course. The only surprise at SEMA is if you complete a vehicle before the show opens!

Diablo Blanco has been a success on many fronts. Representing House of Kolor, it displays the breadth of finishes, from pinstriping to airbrushing, to flakes, pearls and metallics. As a representative of Iwata products, it shows all possible applications, from flake spraying to the finest detail work. On a personal note, Diablo Blanco more than fills the bill of replacing my kustom Buick, evincing the elegance of the classic Cadillac that I've always wanted to own, yet still standing out from the crowd of Caddies in its generation. As a rolling billboard, it represents the quality and style of airbrushing, graphics, and pinstriping that has become synonymous with Kal Koncepts/Air Syndicate Inc. Best of all, it's an automotive tribute to the artwork, artists, and style of the kustom kulture.

Did I mention that it's a blast to drive?
E pluribus kustom!

CONCLUSION

I hope all this information was helpful to you. After my first book, *Automotive Cheap Tricks & Special F/X*, I never really thought about writing a follow-up or a sequel. I just simply hoped people liked the first one. However, I grew really inspired by the success of the first one, and was determined to make the second one better. I knew if it didn't blow the original out of the water, it would be highly criticized. I never left anything unresolved in the first book, so you really can't consider this book to be a true sequel or continuation. It's merely another collection of effects, and me rambling away about what I think of the kustom paint industry. Unlike people that write about what they observe in an industry, I can only write about and describe what I've experienced. Every trick and technique in this book was done in our shop successfully multiple times. In fact, the majority of the chapters in F/X II were actual jobs completed in our shop.

Do we ever have failures at our shop? Sure. But I don't write about them (I'm not a masochist!) I figure you'll have plenty of your own failures, so you don't have to cringe reading about mine. Instead, I've given you proven success stories. So, now it's your turn to take the ball and run with it. And, never forget my favorite mantra: As Kustom Painters we never make mistakes, we just change our minds." For those of you who offered recommendations, complaints, suggestions, etc from the first book, please note that only about 75% of those letters fell on deaf ears (just kidding!), and the rest *were* actually included in this book. A number of the suggestions came in the form of call-ins, emails, and my online forum, www.kustomkulturelounge.com. I'd really like to thank you for the interest, and I hope that this book lives up to the expectations of the 6,000+ members of that forum. For those of you who have never dropped by, give it a try. Unlike many forums online, this one is free of charge, is not sponsored by any manufacturer, and is the only one that is committed to the simple mission of answering your kustom paint questions. If you can't get the answers from my books, DVD's, or magazine columns, give the forum a try!

If you find this book to be as entertaining and educating as the first, then I've succeeded. I wish for you tons of fun and good luck in your kustom painting adventures and endeavors. If not, well, there's always EBAY (hehehehh!) Ciao.

"Now get your butt off the couch, and start painting!!!!!"

Paint to live, live to paint

Craig Fraser
Air Syndicate Inc.
www.gotpaint.com

GLOSSARY OF TERMS

Basically, all of the fun terms used in this book, defined for those who have not inhaled too many paint fumes.

Acrylic urethane: A coating based on urethane chemistry, which also includes acrylic chemistry as part of the cross-linked polymer backbone. (See Urethane.)

Adhesion promoter: Any additive sprayed onto a surface to create adhesion for a subsequent layer of paint or clear. Most adhesion promoters are sprayed onto surfaces that either cannot be sanded or are prone to lifting.

Air changes: A term used to gauge how often the air in an area, such as a spray booth, is completely renewed.

AP-01/02: House of Kolor's adhesion promoter. AP-01 is for just about any questionable surface, from plastics to metal. AP-02 is for polyethylene. A light coat is all that's needed for proper adhesion.

Automask: A brand of transfer tape designed for the automotive market and available exclusively through Coast Airbrush, in Anaheim, California. Similar to Transferite transfer tape, Automask is a bit more difficult to cut but withstands urethanes and clearcoats better.

Basecoats: A two-stage paint system for automotive refinishing and kustom painting. The first stage is paint application; the second stage is the application of a clearcoat for protection and shine. All basecoat systems include a clearcoat, without which the paint is left dull and unprotected against ultraviolet light.

Big D.A. (see D.A. Sander): An 8-inch dual-action sander is useful for rough work with fillers. Often referred to as a "mud hog."

Binder: The part of the paint that forms the film, so called because the paint "binds" the pigment and any additives into a solid, durable film.

Blend area: The area beyond an actual repair, but within the panel, used for fading out a refinish color.

Blend: The practice of fading out a color into the existing color in order to minimize any visual difference.

Block sanding: Sanding with the paper wrapped around a block, or other rigid object, in order to achieve a straight, smooth surface.

Buffing: A polishing technique for removing sanding marks or surface imperfections.

Buffing compound: A soft paste containing fine abrasives in a neutral medium. Used for eliminating fine scratches and polishing the topcoat.

Burn-through: Unintentionally exposing a lower layer of clear when sanding, buffing, or polishing.

Carbon fiber: Carbon fiber, a reinforced polymer or carbon fiber reinforced plastic (CFRP or CRP), is a very strong, light, and expensive composite material or fiber reinforced polymer. Similar to fiberglass (glass reinforced polymer), the composite material is commonly referred to by the name of its reinforcing fibers (carbon fiber). The polymer is most often epoxy, but other polymers, such as polyester, vinyl ester or nylon, are also sometimes used. Some composites contain both carbon fiber and other fibers such as Kevlar, aluminum and fiberglass reinforcement. Carbon fiber has many applications in aerospace, automotive fields, in sailboats, and notably in modern bicycles and motorcycles, where its high strength to weight ratio is of importance. Improved manufacturing techniques are reducing the costs and time to manufacture making it increasingly common in small consumer goods such as laptops, tripods, fishing rods, paintball equipment, archery equipment, racquet frames, stringed instrument bodies, classical guitar strings, drum shells, golf clubs, and pool/billiards/snooker cues.

Catalyst: An additive that initiates or accelerates chemical changes in a paint or clear system. A catalyst triggers a chemical chain reaction, causing hardening of the paint or clear. In automotive paint systems, catalysts usually consist of isocyanates or dibutyl tins that react with urethane resins.

CFM or CFPM (cubic feet per minute): A term used to gauge the volume of air traveling through a given space or opening in an airbrush or spray gun. Cubic feet per minute is a unit of measurement of the flow of air, gas, or liquid that indicates how much volume in cubic feet pass by a stationary point in one minute. To calculate cubic feet per minute from air flow (cubic meter per hour) divide air flow by 1.699 to get cubic feet per minute. CFM is used with air compressors, pneumatic tools, fog machines, hydrology, industrial hygiene, ventilation engineering, and HVAC.

Chalking: When a painted surface deteriorates to the point where the structure actually breaks down and leaves dust or chalk-like deposits on the surface.

Cheater valve: A device that, by restricting the airflow, can adjust the air pressure in a compressed air system.

Chroma: Chroma represents the "purity" of a color, with lower chroma being less pure (more washed out, as in pastels). Note that there is no intrinsic upper limit to chroma. Different areas of the color space have different maximal chroma coordinates. For instance light yellow colors have considerably more potential chroma than light purples, due to the nature of the eye and the physics of color stimuli. This led to a wide range of possible chroma levels—up to the high 30s for some hue–value combinations (though it is difficult or impossible to make physical objects in colors of such high chromas, and they cannot be reproduced on current computer displays). Vivid soil colors are in the range of approximately 8.

Clearcoat: The protective urethane finish sprayed onto a completed automotive paint job. Clearcoats can be either a) "air-dry," which, when sprayed, combine with reducers, then dry by evaporation of the reducers, or b) "catalyzed," which require a catalyst and a reducer solvent to harden. All finish clears on automotive vehicles are of the catalyzed variety.

Color master: Panels used by car manufacturers in the production of automobiles.

Color sanding: The first step after applying the clearcoat (and letting it cure properly), color sanding involves smoothing out the clearcoat so when it's time to buff the paint, you get the most mirror-like finish possible. While color sanding isn't hard to do, it does require lots of time and patience.

Cracking: Splitting of the paint film due to the improper curing, over-application, or over-flexing of an otherwise rigid paint system.

Cross hatch: A special tool that makes a multiple grooved cut in the paint surface. Used twice, overlapped at 90 degrees, it's most often used to test a material's adhesion to the substrate.

Dagger stroke: The most important and difficult of all airbrush strokes, the dagger starts about three to six inches from the surface as a broad or thick line that swoops in as close to the surface as possible to perform a fine, tapered point at the finish. Many airbrush techniques require a variation of the dagger stroke.

D.A. sander: Random orbit sanders, also called dual-action or D.A. sanders (referring to the rotation of the disk and the head) are hand-held power sanders where the action is a random orbit. They were first introduced in the early 1990s and quickly became tremendously popular. Random orbit sanders combine almost the speed and aggressiveness of a belt sander, with the ability to produce a finer finish than that available from a standard, slow speed, orbital finishing sander. The random orbit is produced by simultaneously spinning the sanding disk and moving it in an ellipse, which ensures that no single part of the abrasive material travels the same path twice. Because of this unique random sanding action, the tool does not leave swirl marks, and it is not sensitive to the direction of the wood grain. This makes it work very well when sanding two pieces of wood that meet at right angles. Random orbit sanders use sandpaper disks and many come with dust collectors. Disks are attached using either pressure sensitive adhesives or a hook-and-loop system. On models equipped with dust collection, the sanding dust is sucked through holes in the paper and pad, feeding it to a bag or canister.

Delamination: When two layers become separated from each other.

D.O.I (distinctness of image): A measurement of the accuracy of a reflection in a paint film.

Donk: Cultural nickname for an automotive style of kustomizing that originated in the southern United States. Donks may be any two-door car with oversized wheels, from 28 inches to 30-plus inches. A typical example is a late-model Chevy with oversized wheels.

DOT: Department of Transportation.

Drifting: A driving technique and a motorsport in which the driver intentionally skids the rear tires through turns, preserving vehicle control and a high exit speed off the skid. The driver is judged on style and technique rather than speed. As a motorsport, drifting was originated by Kousuke "Mad K" Kida, in Osaka, Japan, in the 1970s and has since become a worldwide, multibillion-dollar industry.

Drop shadows: An airbrushed shadow beneath a graphic that gives the graphic a 3-D or floating illusion. Often used in lettering.

E-coat: Slang for a variety of coatings applied through a process of electrodeposition. Most often used on replacement body parts and identified as a black primer.

Elasticity: The ability of a coating to stretch and return without damage to the structure.

EPA: The Environmental Protection Agency, a federal office charged with regulating, among other things, the use of chemicals in automotive manufacturing and refinishing. Its regulations and authority may supersede those of the various state agencies charged with protecting the environment.

Evaporation rate: The rate at which a solvent dries up. Knowledge of the evaporation rate of certain solvents and solvent blends helps a painter adapt to changes in any application environment.

F/X or Effects: Term used to describe the airbrushed or custom-painted pattern or texture on a graphic or mural.

FA-01: House of Kolor flattening agent. It's combined in a 1:1 ratio with RU-311 reducer, and then mixed with either UFC or UC-35 clear in a ratio of two parts clear and one part KU-150 catalyst. Flat clear functions as a final application, not as a leveling system. It goes over normal clear, giving a retro flat appearance.

Fade: An intentional gradation of two colors for an artistic effect.

Fading: The loss of color, usually due to UV rays deteriorating the pigment within a paint.

Fan: The spray pattern unique to a full-size spray gun. It's achieved by introducing air, from the side, into the stream of paint to form a tan or oblong pattern.

Faux: French for "imitation" or "artificial." Pronounced "foe," it commonly refers to the artistic rendering of wood, stone, or metal in paint, an illusion realistic enough to "fool the eye." The French term for such pleasing fakery is trompe l'oeil [pronounced TROMP LOY].

Fiberglass: A compound where glass fibers are laminated within a resin structure. This is usually done with a polyester resin. The glass fibers can be in the form of a woven cloth or a more random arrangement called "matt."

Film thickness gauge: A tool used to determine the thickness of a given film. Usually magnetic, the gauge will read in microns or mils.

Finish: Any coating, treatment, or effect used to personalize or identify an object.

Fish eyes: A surface depression or crater in the wet paint film. Fish eyes are caused by repulsion of the wet paint by a surface contaminant, such as oil or silicone. The depression may or may not reveal the surface under the paint.

Fixation: The ability of a material to hold a metallic, pearl, or other iridescent effect with a paint film.

Flake: A pigment consisting of flat reflective particles, usually aluminum or metallic, that impart special color effects to the final paint job.

Flex block: Similar to a long board and designed to flex for the even sanding of curved surfaces.

Flexibility: The ability of a substrate to flex while the paint system remains intact.

Flight loss: The evaporation of solvent from a paint mixture as the material flies through the air.

Galvanize: A process of bonding zinc to a surface in order to increase corrosion resistance.

Gravelometer (Chip Resistance of Coatings): The Gravelometer is a machine designed to evaluate the resistance of surface coatings (paint, clear coats, metallic plating, etc.) to chipping caused by the impacts of gravel or other flying objects. The primary usage of this test is to simulate the effects of the impact of gravel or other debris on automotive parts. The test sample is mounted in the back of the Gravelometer, and air pressure is used to project one pint (approximately 300 pieces) of gravel at the sample. The test sample is then removed and gently wiped off with a clean cloth, and tape is applied to the entire tested surface. Removal of the tape pulls off any loose fragments of the coating. The appearance of the tested sample is then compared to standard transparencies supplied by SAE to determine the chipping ratings. Visual examination can also be used to describe where in the coating/substrate system that the failure has been induced.

Galvaneal: A form of galvanized metal, galvaneal steel is different from conventional galvanized coatings. The galvaneal process creates a zinc-iron layer, instead of the usual zinc layer created during hot-dip or electrogalvanizing.

Gold leaf: Pounded gold sheets, or a substitute composite material manufactured to look like gold. The material is extremely thin and delicate, allowing it to conform to curved surfaces and be laminated onto vehicles as lettering, striping, or mural details. Gold leaf, normally sold in books, can be purchased through most hobby stores or automotive paint/sign suppliers.

Gradation: The gradual transition from one color to another.

HMIS: Hazardous Material Information System.

Hologram pearl: Often referred to as six- or eight-sided pearls, these are actually very finely ground hologram foils that shift through the color spectrum in up to eight different shades of color. Available in liquid form only, hologram pearls are costly, usually starting at about $450 for a sprayable quart. House of Kolor's line is known as Kameleon Kolors.

House of Kolor: Founded by renowned custom painter Jon Kosmoski in 1956, and, since 1997, part of the Valspar Automotive Coatings Division, in Picayune, Mississippi, House of Kolor is the world's largest manufacturer of kustom paints. Find them on the web at www.houseofkolor.com.

HoK: Acronym for House of Kolor.

Hue: Hue is one of the main properties of a color described with names such as red, yellow, etc. The two other main properties of light are saturation and lightness. Usually, colors with the same hue are distinguished with adjectives referring to their lightness and/or chroma; for example, light blue, pastel blue, vivid blue. Exceptions include brown, which is a dark orange, and pink, a light red with reduced chroma. In painting color theory, a hue refers to a pure color—one without tint or shade (added white or black pigment, respectively). A hue is an element of the color wheel.

HVLP (High Volume Low Pressure): Acronym for a type of automotive spray gun. HVLP spray guns apply a high percentage (about 90 percent) of paint material to a surface with minimum overspray, making them more economical and environmentally friendly than older types. (Older spray guns applied only 30 to 60 percent of the paint to the surface; the rest atomized and floated into the air as overspray.) All licensed automotive body/paint shops in the United States are required by law to use HVLP spray guns. A spray gun's HVLP status is determined by the weight-per-gallon-of-paint of the nonexempt volatile organic compound (V.O.C.) that serves as a carrier for the paint being sprayed.

Ice Pearls: A dry pearl compound made up of micro glass beads. The colors of the beads are determined by sending them through a titanium deoxidizer coating process. Although dry pearls are manufactured by a number of companies, House of Kolor owns the name "Ice Pearl" and pioneered the industry.

Intercoat Clear (SG100): An air-dry clear used between painting stages or basecoats as a protective barrier. HOK also describes SG100 as a protective clear for artwork tape-outs on SHIMRIN® Base Coats. May be used to blend SHIMRIN® Pearl and Metallic Base Coats, to mix Pearl and Kandy Koncentrates, and to cut the SHIMRIN, base for touchups and blends. NOTE: Use only when top coating with urethane enamel

Interference pearl: Either a mica or foil substrate that has the characteristics of a standard pearl but casts two colors (e.g., blue/green, violet/blue) instead of one. Interference pearls create a shifting effect in the color of the vehicle as you move around it. They are often referred to as "Flip-Flop" pearls.

Isocyanate: A hardening agent used with acrylic urethane and other two-component reaction-type paints. It reacts with acrylic polymer, etc., to form a very durable coating.

Isopropyl alcohol: An inexpensive, fast-evaporating solvent, co-solvent, or dilutant. Also called rubbing alcohol.

Jewelling: The act of spinning the surface to create a machine-turned effect. This can be done with a die grinder fitted with a velvet spool-on leaf, or with a Scotch-Brite pad. The technique is used for preparing an underlying surface for a coating of Kosmic Krome.

Jitterbug sander: A square sander that orbits the paper in a circular motion.

KK (Kandy Koncentrate): Kandy Koncentrates are used to richen any of the Kosmic Kolor® Urethane Enamel Kandys or Kustom Kolor® Acrylic Lacquer Kandys. Kandy Koncentrates may be added to SG100 Intercoat Clear (for urethane enamel topcoats) or SC01 Sunscreen Clear (for acrylic lacquer topcoats), for multi-colored Kandy tape-outs with minimal build. KK dries fast, so many colors may be applied in one day, and they have a long shelf life. Note: KK Kandy Koncentrates are additives and cannot be applied as packaged. They must be intermixed with either HOK sealers, bases, UK Kandys, or clears. For best results, House of Kolor recommends that you use only House of Kolor® products when mixing. Also, the following KK's have a tendency to bleed through artwork applied over them: KK03, KK05, KK06, KK10, and KK13 (KK18 Kandy Koncentrate Pink has limited light-fastness and should only be used on products that have limited exposure to sunlight. Use with discretion. KK18 is recommended for show vehicles. Do individual testing. See House of Kolor's tech sheet for mixing and application instructions.

Kandy: The term for the family of transparent colors used in automobile painting and customizing. The term "kandy" derives from the hard candy look that early lacquers gave when layered multiple times. Today's kandies are predominantly urethane-based but show that same look when sprayed. These highly transparent paints are perfect for color-process airbrushing and color layering in murals.

Kandy Koncentrates: A term coined by House of Kolor to name its line of Kandy Intensifier pigments. KKs are used either to intensify an existing basecoat system or in combination with intercoat clear for airbrushing. They are highly effective for airbrushing because of their very finely ground pigments.

Kevlar fiber: Similar to carbon fiber but lighter and stronger. Usually used only in racing, ballistics, or other extremely high-demand projects, Kevlar is the registered trademark for a light, strong para-aramid synthetic fiber, related to other aramids such as Nomex and Technora. Developed at DuPont in 1965, it was first commercially used in the early 1970s as a replacement for steel in racing tires. Typically, it is spun into ropes or fabric sheets that can be used as such or as an ingredient in composite material components. Currently, Kevlar has many applications, ranging from bicycle tires and racing sails to body armor because of its high strength-to-weight ratio—famously: *"...5 times stronger than steel on an equal weight basis..."*

Klown: A derogatory term for people who consider themselves custom painters yet lack the ethics, ability, creativity, or talent to be such; basically, people who are in it for the money and couldn't care less about the integrity of the art.

Kosmic Krome: House of Kolor's line of 6061 aluminum micropigmented paints that mimic metallic effects. Designated MC, these paints come in Mirror, Aluminum, Gold, Bronze, and Copper. Unlike its competition, they're not alcohol-based and therefore may be mixed with other HoK products.

Kustom: Anything that is modified from the original factory specification to produce a hot rod or the look of one. Custom with a "K" refers to any art form or vehicle from the hot rod genre.

Kustom Kulture: A term coined by the artist and cartoonist Ed "Big Daddy" Roth and painter Robert Williams, his some-time associate, for the automotive kustom industry. The term refers not just to the cars but to the music, iconography, art, clothing, and lifestyle—the whole cultural range—of the industry's people.

Lacquers: Paints that dry by evaporative loss of solvent. However, the film remains susceptible to attack by the same or similar solvents. Lacquers can be based on nitrocellulose or acrylic resins. For automotive applications, these paints are illegal, according to V.O.C. (volatile organic compound) regulations, in almost every state.

Latex: An emulsion, usually a dispersion of a polymer in water, often used in gloves or protective material. Also used as a liquid application masking system.

Lead: A metal commonly used in the manufacture of driers and pigments. Highly toxic, lead has been eliminated from most automotive spray products.

Lettering quill: A long-handled, short-quilled brush for lettering and touch-ups.

Lifting: When a material expands to a point where the forces of the expansion exceed its adhesive properties. When this happens, the coating will lift from the surface, often in a wrinkling pattern.

Liner: A long-handled, long-quilled lettering brush for outlining letters and some striping applications.

Long board: A long, flat, and often narrow sanding board. Most often used dry and for preliminary bodywork, fillers, and surfacers.

Macabre: Anything that has to do with dark, gothic imagery, usually something involving skulls or other symbols that emanate from dark fantasies. Often confused with the occult, macabre images are the opposite of anything that is light, pastel, or airy (i.e., "lame").

Mandrel bending: A method of determining a coating's flexibility by bending it over a rounded object or shaft. Measurements vary from about 4 mm to about 22 mm. This test can be specified at any temperature.

Masking: Any material used to prevent another material from being applied to a certain area. Paper, tape, and plastic sheeting are all types of masking.

Melt in: The action as a new application is absorbed into the previously sprayed areas.

Metajuls: Manufactured by House of Kolor, this pearlescent/metallic effect was originally entitled "Diamonds." Available in Black, Platinum, and Gold topcoats, they can give a color the illusion of being metalflaked, yet without all the work and millimeter thickness. In many cases, Metajuls can appear quite a bit brighter than flakework.

Metallic paint: Paint that contains metallic pigment, usually in the form of tiny flakes. Generally, these are aluminum or mica and are used to enhance visual appeal.

Mil: A unit of length equal to 0.001 inch (a "milli-inch", one thousandth of an inch). It is sometimes used in engineering and in the specification of the thickness of items such as paint coatings, paper, film, foil, wires, latex gloves, plastic sheeting, and fibers. In the United States, as the metric system became more common, thou began to replace mil among technical users due to the possible confusion with millimeters. However, the mil is still in common use in the United States for the thickness of plastic sheeting or bags.

Mottling: When a metallic, pearl, or other iridescent effect is uneven and not oriented properly.

NACE: International Autobody Congress & Exposition. One of the largest collections of buyers, manufacturers, and distributors of collision repair and automotive repainting accessories in the world. This show is held annually in Las Vegas, usually in December.

Negative space: Literally, the opposite of positive space. The area surrounding a graphic is known as the negative space. If you mask off the original base color in the shape of flames on a vehicle and then paint or shadow the area surrounding the mask, you have created negative flames. The original masked-off color becomes the flames—hence "negative," since you painted everything but the actual flame design.

Non-sanding: Similar to a wet-on-wet, however with no recoat window, a non-sanding option is more common in fleet and industrial painting.

Ol' school: In kustom painting, this term refers to any older method or technique, e.g., the "ol' school" method of painting.

Orange peel: An irregularity in the surface of a paint film, resulting from the inability of the wet film to level out after being applied. Characteristically, orange peel appears uneven or even dimpled to the eye but usually feels smooth to the touch.

Orientation: The act of even distribution of a metallic, pearl, or other iridescent effect within a paint film.

OSHA: Occupational Safety and Health Administration. Inquiries may be directed to OSHA, U.S. Department of Labor, Public Affairs Office, 200 Constitution Ave., Washington, DC 20210, (202) 693-1999. On the web, go to www.osha.gov.

Overall: A term used to describe the painting of a complete object, car, or motorcycle.

Overspray: As the paint film dries, it reaches a point when it will no longer melt in the new spray. The material left on the surface will stay as a dusty, low-gloss texture.

Oxidation: A process involving the chemical combination of oxygen and the carrier of a paint that allows it to dry. Alternatively, the destructive combination of oxygen with a dry paint film that leads to its degradation, or the destructive combination of oxygen with a metal (e.g., rust).

Pencil hardness: A test method where a coating's hardness is compared to, and rated against, different grades of actual pencils.

P-Tex: A brand of catalyzed polyester resin-based clear that's very hard and very transparent. Used on guitars because of its high luster and hard scratch-resistant surface. Very difficult to spray well, P-Tex will also take up to two weeks to fully harden before it can be buffed.

Pastels: An evil collection of colors that has done more damage to the automotive kustom industry than the world will ever know. Except in rare uses, such as with pink Cadillacs and occasional seafoam two-tones, these colors are truly lame and should be avoided at all costs.

Pearl: A mica substrate or any other substance used to add color or a metallic sheen to paint. Pearls come in a variety of colors and in dry, liquid, or paste consistencies. For airbrushing, the most popular form is the finely ground dry pearl. Pearls can be added directly to either the paint or the clearcoat. Their primary purpose is to create a secondary color cast to a paint job without diminishing the initial color.

Phosphate coatings: Used as a surface treatment, this coating will inhibit corrosion when used under a subsequent e-coat.

Pigment: Small particles added to paint to influence such properties as color, corrosion resistance, mechanical strength, etc. Pigments may be colored, semitransparent, black, white, or colorless. They must be incorporated into a paint system by a dispersion process.

Polish: A compound with a much lower abrasive than a buffing compound, it may contain additives for increased UV and environmental protection.

Polishing: The final step of buffing, used alone for minor surface restoration. Generally done with a softer pad or by hand.

Polymers: Very large molecules built up by the combination of many small molecules through a chemical process called "polymerization." Polymers often consist of thousands of atoms, usually in chains or networks of repeating units.

Polyurethane: Commonly abbreviated PU, polyurethane is any polymer consisting of a chain of organic units joined by urethane (carbamate) links. Polyurethane polymers are formed through step-growth polymerization by reacting a monomer containing at least two isocyanate functional groups with another monomer containing at least two hydroxyl (alcohol) groups in the presence of a catalyst. Polyurethane formulations cover an extremely wide range of stiffness, hardness, and densities. Polyurethane products are often called "urethanes". They should not be confused with the specific substance urethane, also known as ethyl carbamate. Polyurethanes are not produced from ethyl carbamate, nor do they contain it.

Positive space: The actual graphic you are painting. If there are flames on a car, and you painted the flames over the existing finish, then those flames are the positive space of your graphic. Positive space is balanced by its opposite, negative space (see above). The understanding of both is imperative for a well-designed paint job.

Pounce: Slang term for the chalk bag, the stencil, or the tool used to create perforations in a transfer sheet. To pounce something is to trace, perforate, and then transfer chalk through the perforations to another surface. Pouncing is used for replicating designs and for reverse-transferring graphics from one side of a vehicle to another.

Powder-coat: A system of painting metal in which a powdered material is sprayed on the surface and then baked at 350°-500°. The powder takes on the appearance of paint but is much stronger. Powder-coating is similar to ceramic glazing but performed at a lower temperature.

Powder-paint: A technology similar to powder-coating but performed at a lower temperature (140°). This is a more practical method because it can be used on plastics; it's not as durable as powder-coating, however.

PPG®: Pittsburgh Plate Glass Co., which is more currently referred to as "Pittsburgh Paint & Glass." PPG is one of the largest manufacturers of automotive paints and vehicle window glass.

Quick size: The recommended drying speed for the sizing glue used for leafing. Be sure not to apply the leaf until the sizing glue squeaks when you draw you finger down it.

Refinish: Repairing or otherwise duplicating an existing finish.

Regulator: A device that uses a diaphragm to automatically regulate the air pressure when compressed air is used for the spraying of paints.

Respirator: A device that positions a filter over a user's face in order to filter contamination from the ambient air.

Restification: The act of restoring or remanufacturing an object with updated performance or safety features while maintaining the original appearance.

Restoration: The act of restoring or remanufacturing an object so it matches its original condition.

RTS (ready to spray): Material that has had all hardeners, reducers, and any other additive already added is considered to be "ready to spray." This is useful in calculating the amount needed or the cost of any material needed for a project.

RU-311: A medium-temperature reducer from House of Kolor, the one I recommend most for airbrushing.

San Fernando Paint Job: A derogatory term for a graphic job where only the graphics are cleared and a pinstripe is used to hide the obvious edge, a procedure acceptable for fleet and work vehicles only. The term "San Fernando" is used whenever a job is botched or half-assed. It derives from slang references to the San Fernando Valley as the home of ditzy airheads.

Scotch-Brite®: Spun plastic scouring pad manufactured by 3M and used for scuffing or light sanding duty. Scotch-Brite is available in various grits identified by color. Red Scotch-Brite (3M #7447) is commonly used for prepping many surfaces.

SEMA: The Specialty Equipment & Manufacturing Association, the largest after-market automotive product show in the United States, held annually in Las Vegas in November.

Semi-gloss: Usually a clearcoat that has neither a fully glossed nor a matte finish. Often referred to as a "satin" finish.

Sheering: When a surface flexes, layers within the film with different elastic properties may sheer apart as they stress the adhesion of each layer.

Silver leaf: A pounded aluminum alloy that has many of the same characteristics as gold leaf, without the high cost.

Single-component material: A material that dries by the evaporation of the solvent contained in the liquid form. A single-component material is often "reversible," creating a specific recoating hazard.

Single-stage: Refers to a type of catalyzed or air-dry painting system that needs no clearcoat, hence a "single-stage" application. These paints tend to be slow drying, and those that contain catalysts are more toxic than the airbrush-friendly, two-stage basecoat systems.

Sizing: The glue that fastens gold or silver leaf to a surface. Though there are a number of water-based sizings, the original solvent-based sizing is still the best for automotive and exterior signage applications.

Sharpie® marker: A brand of felt pen, usually black, used for layouts on transfer tape, and for marking areas on bare metal to be fabricated. The ink is waterproof, and the pen will write under most conditions—excellent for use by a kustom builder and painter.

Solvent/reducer: A liquid that dissolves something, usually resins or other binder components; commonly an organic liquid. In automotive applications it refers to any type of petroleum-based liquid used to thin or clean solvent-based automotive paints or clears. Reducers are usually rated by the ambient temperatures in which they are to be used, or by their drying speed. The cleaning solvents are normally more caustic or evaporative.

Solvent popping: Bumps or small craters that form on the paint film, caused by trapped solvent.

Spot repair: The category of repair where only an area of an object is painted.

Squeegee: A rubber block used to wipe off wet-sanded areas and to apply filler, putty, or vinyl application tapes.

Standard formula: A refinish manufacturer's original, most commonly occurring, or most popular formulation for an OEM color formula.

Static charge: The electrical charge, from static electricity, that can attract dirt and even sparks to a plastic part.

Steampunk: A kustom kulture style based on neo-Victorian-era vintage technology. The era of the Industrial Revolution in which artisans felt the need to embellish technology with brass gears, intricate clockwork mechanisms, and rich, warm materials such as wood, leather, and hand-rubbed bronze. Visit www.doctorsteel.com.

Substrate: The surface to be painted. It may be bare metal or an old finish.

Supplied air system: A device that provides independent air flow to the user's face to avoid contamination from ambient air.

Sword striper: A type of short-handled, long-bristled brush for pinstriping. The name "sword" reflects the look of the brush head.

Tack coat: The first clearcoat medium spray application, allowed to flash only until it is quite sticky. Also, a protective coating to prevent reversion by the wet coat to the underlying surface.

Tail solvent: A slow-evaporating solvent that leaves the paint slowly, allowing the film to continue to flow and level. When trapped under layers of material from overapplication, tail solvents can cause solvent pop, or worse, delamination.

Thinner: Solvent added to a lacquer to reduce its viscosity to a sprayable consistency. (See Solvent/reducer.)

Tint: A pigment from a family of pigments used on a mixing machine to produce a color sympathetic to the color of the vehicle to be painted. Sometimes called "tinting base" or "base system."

Toner: A base pigment system. (See Pigment.)

Touch-up gun: Any small spray gun used to spray small areas, graphics, or door jambs in a vehicle. These tools are characterized by their small size and equally small spray pattern.

Tribal: Any graphic that has a tribal nature to it, whether it be Gaelic patterns, Celtic knotting, or Polynesian tribal tattoos. Usually used to describe any graphic that comes to multiple points and interweaves with itself or other graphic patterns. Currently somewhat overused in our industry, tribals tend to refer to anything that is not a flame or a scallop.

Trizac®: A 3M sanding system for use with a dual-action orbital, or jitterbug, sander. Trizac paper is used for the final wet sanding of a paint job before buffing. Close to 3000-grit, this system can easily eliminate, with only two sheets per car, all sanding scratches and swirls from even a black paint job. This stuff rocks!

Two-component material: A material consisting of two separate components that, when fully reacted, will form a third new compound. Two-component materials tend to be nonreversible, making them more stable choices for surfacers, clears, and products requiring substantial durability.

Two-stage: Any automotive paint system that requires a second stage of clearcoating to seal and gloss the finish. (See Basecoats.)

Urethane: A type of paint or polymer that results from the reaction of an isocyanate catalyst with a hydroxyl-containing component. Urethanes are noted for their toughness and abrasion resistance.

UV inhibitor: Any additive to a paint or clearcoat that blocks the sun's damaging UV (ultraviolet) rays from penetrating the clear and either fading or oxidizing the underlying basecoat color. UV inhibitors act in much the same way as sunscreens.

UV stabilizers: Chemicals added to paint to absorb the ultraviolet radiation present in sunlight. Ultraviolet radiation decomposes the polymer molecules in paint film, thus UV stabilizers prolong paint life.

Variant formula: A formula developed to compensate for field variations in an OEM formula.

Velocity: A measurement of a material's speed of travel.

V.O.C. (volatile organic compound) rating: A measure of the amount of material released into the atmosphere during paint spraying or product manufacturing. V.O.C. ratings relate to the level of a chemical's toxicity and its ability to diffuse or break down in the atmosphere within a given amount of time.

Water-based: Any paint or clear that consists primarily of water or uses water as a reducing element in its chemical makeup.

Waterborne: A type of paint that uses water as its primary carrier rather than other solvents. The term does not refer to a water-based system; in a waterborne system, the water serves as the carrier for a solvent-based, microencapsulated system.

Wet-on-wet: The term used to describe a material's ability to be applied directly onto a fresh, partially cured material. One can identify a wet-on-wet material by the presence of a "recoat window" that dictates the time in which the subsequent coating must be applied.

Wet edge: The leading edge applied by spraying is the wet edge. Maintaining a wet edge will assure that subsequent passes will flow into the wet film.

Wet sand: A technique for sanding a surface while it's being flushed with water. This permits the smoothing of surface defects before subsequent coats are applied.

X-Acto®: Brand name of a highly regarded handheld razor knife, especially with #10 or #11 blades.

Yertle the Turtle: A killer song by the Red Hot Chili Peppers; also a character in a book by Theodor Geisel (Dr. Seuss). An excellent way to fill up the worthless "Y" section of this glossary.

Zen: The unattainable level that everyone tries to achieve, or acceptance of the belief that the traveling of the road to perfection is the true goal. In automotive kustomizing it refers to the observance of and respect for what has come before, while still looking and moving ahead. (This is Craig Fraser's definition of Zen; any similarity to other definitions is completely coincidental and absolutely unintentional.) For other definitions, and to learn where Craig got it from, see *Zen and the Art of Motorcycle Maintenance*, a book by Robert M. Pirsig.

INDEX

FOR SERIOUS AIRHEADS.

AIR BRUSH·ACTION DVD's LEARN TIPS & TRICKS FROM THE PROS!

SPRAYGUN HANDLING TECHNIQUES
Everything you need to know about top pro spraygun handling techniques and methods for painting any and all surfaces with the esteemed Anest Iwata line of guns. 40 minutes. **$29.95**

INTRO TO AUTOMOTIVE AIRBRUSHING (FRASER)
The ultimate video guide for aspiring autmotive kustom painters. For beginners, this instruction includes airbrush drills, introduction to materials, paint, hardware, and much more! 90 minutes. **$39.95**

AUTOMOTIVE CHEAP TRICKS & SPECIAL F/X IV
Craig Fraser takes you step-by-step through a complex automotive graphic. This advanced video includes top pro airbrush techniques, pinstriping, layout, textures, and more! 75 minutes. **$39.95**

GHOST FLAMES
Flame master Vandemon demystifies one of the trendiest and profitable flame styles in an easy-to-follow instruction. Learn advanced techniques, and much more! 35 minutes. **$39.95**

KILLER KLOWN (JAVIER SOTO)
There's something for everyone in this instructional DVD, including how to employ brilliant color, how to render a variety of textures, use of kandies, realistic fire, highlighting, and much more. 59 minutes. **$39.95**

KUSTON CASH
Premier automotive custom painter, Charles Armstrong generously shares his advanced micro-airbrush and vinyl techniques for rendering paper currency and fire photorealistically onto any hard surface. 84 minutes. **$39.95**

MACK BRUSH REVIEW
World-class pinstriper Gary Jenson guides you through the array of Mack brushes from sword stripers to lettering quills to scroll brushes and more. A one-of-a-kind instructional DVD. Over 25 designs demonstrated! 45 minutes. **$29.95**

WIZARD'S PINSTRIPING BASICS
Become a master pinstriper with Wizard's revolutionary 10,000-stroke training method. The 10 basic strokes are broken down in complete detail. This is the most thorough video on the fundamentals of pinstriping! 76 minutes. **$39.95**

WIZARD'S DAGGER PINSTRIPING
Learn all the strokes necessary to make beautiful dagger style striping designs. This video includes palletting techniques, how to roll the brush, how to pinstripe a circle, painting without a grid, various designs, and tons more! 105 minutes. **$39.95**

WIZARD'S SCROLLBRUSH PINSTRIPING
Scroll style pinstriping is the fast track to big profits and Wizard reveals all about how to master this intricate art form. This highly detailed step-by-step course is geared toward beginning to advanced artists. 89 minutes. **$39.95**

ADVANCED PORTRAIT TECHNIQUES
Groundbreaking instruction from one of the world's top realistic portrait painters. For intermediate to professional artists seeking to take their work to the next level. 140 minutes. **$39.95**

HOW TO USE PLOTTERS & VECTORIZE IMAGES
Alan Pastrana unlocks the "mystery" of how plotters work and secrets for eliminating hours of tedious cutting with a knife. Perfect for all airbrush applications—automotive, T-shirt, hobby, fine art, body painting, and more. 50 minutes. **$29.95**

KUSTOM FLAME TRICKS & TECHNIQUES
Fraser, Giuliano, K-Daddy. Learn from the kustom masters how to create flames on all auto surfaces. Clearcoat prep, tribal flames, layout, troubleshooting, pinstriping techniques, and much more are included. 45 minutes. **$39.95**

KANDY PAINTING TRICKS & SPECIAL F/X
Kustom painters are often judged by their ability to spray Kandies. Kar Kustom masters Fraser and Giuliano demonstrate the top pro tricks of spraying Kandy urethanes on cars, trucks, helmets, motorcycle tanks, and more. 33 minutes. **$39.95**

AUTOMOTIVE AIRBRUSH CHEAP TRICKS & SPECIAL F/X (FRASER)
Learn all the top pro tricks to help you get the job done more quickly, easily, and effeciently, including pinstriping, surface preparation, masking, freehand techniques, and mixing. 115 minutes. **$39.95**

MORE AUTOMOTIVE CHEAP TRICKS & SPECIAL F/X
This is the hot sequel to Craig Fraser's original Automotive Cheap Tricks & Special F/X. In this video, Mr. Fraser demonstrates four top-selling designs in a clearly presented step-by-step format. 83 minutes. **$39.95**

AUTOMOTIVE CHEAP TRICKS & SPECIAL F/X 3
Craig Fraser shows you step-by-step how to create a complete hot-selling automotive kustom graphic using his top tricks & techniques. Cheap Tricks 3 is designed for intermediate and advanced airbrush users. 70 minutes. **$39.95**

CLEARCOATING CHEAP TRICKS & SPECIAL F/X
Clearcoating is one of the most misunderstood phases of kustom graphics. Craig Fraser & Dion Giuliano demonstrate the top pro tricks of clearcoating on flat and curved surfaces, pearls, ghost images, repairs, and much more! 41 minutes. **$39.95**

MASTERING SKULLMASTER
Fraser shares his top pro tricks using Artool's Skullmaster stencils. Developed for T-shirts, automotive work, tattoos, and more! Create topflight, professional designs with Skullmaster and this video! (Stencils not included) 58 minutes. **$39.95**

SKULLMASTER II (FRASER)
The art of the skull landscape, and to new heights in this continuing series about the best, most innovative stencil line available. This DVD guides you step-by-step through Skullmaster II's 5-stencil solvent-proof system. (Stencils not included) 75 minutes. **$39.95**

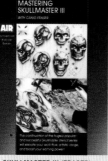

SKULLMASTER III (FRASER)
A continuation of Skullmaster I (the most successful stencil set ever) Stencils demonstrated include Return of Skullmaster, Frontal II, Screaming Skull II, Multiple II, and Lucky 13, a bonus stencil. (Stencils not included) 48 minutes. **$39.95**

REALISTIC FLAMES FOR AUTOMOTIVE PAINTING
In the first video of its kind, Vargas legend Craig Fraser reveals all on how to render killer regular and blue flames. For beginners to advanced artists. 30 minutes. **$39.95**

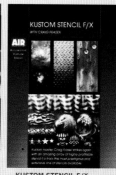

KUSTOM STENCIL F/X
Fraser strikes again! Learn an array of dazzling, highly-profitable stencil f/x from the most sought-after line of stencils, including Flamorama, F/X I, and Patriotica. 70 minutes. **$39.95**

PRO AIRBRUSH & PAINTBRUSH TECHNIQUES
In the first video of its kind, kustom sensation Cross-Eyed reveals how to produce an amazing photo-realistic image using pro airbrush, paintbrush, and ink pen techniques. 99 minutes. **$39.95**

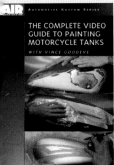

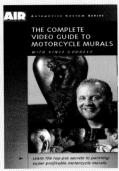

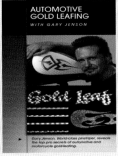

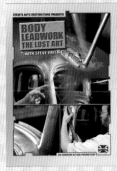

MASTER KUSTOM
PAINTING

THE WORLD'S BEST AIRBRUSH INSTRUCTIO

AIRBRUSH GETAWAY
WORKSHOPS

LAS VEGAS, NEVADA · ORLANDO, FLORIDA

AIRBRUSH MASTERY | AUTOMOTIVE GRAPHICS | POWER PORTRAITS | MURALS ON STEEL | PHOTOREALISM
PIN-UP ART | PINSTRIPING & LETTERING | T-SHIRT AIRBRUSHING | AND MORE

1.800.232.8998   w w w . a i r b r u s h a c t i o n . c o m